Essays, Civil, Moral, Literary and Political, Written ... by the Celebrated Marquis D'Argenson, ... Translated From his Valuable Manuscripts, and Never Before Made Public

ESSAYS,

CIVIL, MORAL, LITERARY AND POLITICAL,

WRITTEN

AFTER THE MANNER OF M DE MONTAGNE,

INTERSPERSED WITH

CHARACTERS, PORTRAITS, ANECDOTES, &c.

BY THE CELEBRATED

MARQUIS D'ARGENSON,

MANY YEARS PRIME MINISTER OF FRANCE;

AND WHO WAS HONOURED WITH THE PARTICULAR INTIMACY

OF THE LATE KING OF PRUSSIA.

TRANSLATED FROM HIS VALUABLE MANUSCRIPTS,

AND NEVER BEFORE MADE PUBLIC.

L O N D O N·

PRINTED AT THE Logographic Press,
AND SOLD BY J WALTER, No 169, OPPOSITE BOND STREET, PICCADILLY;
R BALDWIN, PATE NOSTER ROW, AND W. RICHARDSON,
ROYAL EXCHANGE.

M DCC,LXXXIX.

E S S A Y S, &c.

REFLECTIONS AND OBSERVATIONS

MADE FROM

READING AND EXPERIENCE.

CHARACTERS, PORTRAITS, ANECDOTES, &c.

E S S A Y I.

INTRODUCTION.

I Love *Montagne*, I read him with pleasure; not that I think always like him, but becaufe he gives me room to reflect, and to adopt a like or a contrary opinion to that of his own. Madame de *Sevigny* faid, when fhe read his Effays, fhe imagined fhe was walking with him in her garden, and that they were converfing together. I think fo likewife; and I find that *Montagne* appears frequently to advance propofitions in order to bring on a little difpute which animates converfation, and renders it more lively and interefting: this is affuredly a good method of engaging the attention of the

B   reader.

reader. I will ſtrive to follow it, in com-
poſing a book as irregular, as full of looſe
propoſitions, as problematical, and as full
of paradoxes, as that of *Montagne*. I will
treat of every thing which falls under my
pen, or comes into my mind ; ſpring from
branch to branch, exhauſt no ſubject, and
return at different times to the ſame. I
wiſh my book ſhould be read, as it was
compoſed, in moments of leiſure ; that it
ſhould be taken up and laid down at every
page, but that after being ſhut, each article
ſhould be reaſoned upon. I ſhall think myfelf happy, if, in the midſt of all this real
or apparent diſorder, there be found in me
ſome of thoſe advantages which *Montagne*
enjoyed. I do not envy him his greateſt
qualities, nor the ſtrokes of genius with
which his book is decorated, nor the energy
of his ſtyle ; but I dare aſſert, that I am
like himſelf, a zealous friend to truth, to
humanity, and to juſtice ; that I am frank
and honeſt in my words, writings, and
actions ; that I judge impartially the age in
which I live, my neighbour with mildneſs and
indulgence, and myſelf with ſome caution ;
for we ought not to be more ſevere with ourſelves, than with others.

E S S A Y II.

O N M O R A L I T Y.

MORALITY teaches us how we ought to live with men; what a number of difcourfes, fermons and books there are, which inftruct us in the firft principles of it! But there are few which teach us how to live with ourfelves, and for ourfelves alone: it is becaufe the mafter and the leffons are in our own hearts, and depend upon our characters. There are people who have lived fixty years without ever having known themfelves, becaufe they have never been at the trouble of ftudying their characters; for the moft trifling refearch, is fufficient to give us that knowledge to perfection. Let it not be imagined, that felf-love hinders us from judging truly of our own character; on the contrary, it informs us of our defects, and engages us to correct them, becaufe our happinefs is interefted therein: it only hinders us from confeffing them before others. Let us be fincere, we may be deceived about our defects, but we cannot totally conceal them.

B 2

ESSAY III.

ON IMAGINATION.

THE imagination is a quality of the foul, not only a brilliant but an happy one, for it is more frequently the caufe of our happinefs, than of our mifery; it prefents us with more pleafures than vexations, with more hopes than fears. Men of dull and heavy difpofitions, who are not affected by any thing, vegetate and pafs their lives in a kind of tranquillity, but without pleafure or delight; like animals which fee, feel and tafte nothing but that which is under their eyes, paws, or teeth; but the imagination, which is proper to man, tranfports us beyond ourfelves, and makes us tafte future and the moft diftant pleafures. Let us not be told, that it makes us alfo forefee evils, pains and accidents, which will perhaps never arrive: it is feldom that imagination carries us to thefe panic fears, unlefs it be deranged by phyfical caufes. The fick man fees dark phantoms, and has melancholy
ideas;

ideas; the man in health has no dreams but
fuch as are agreeable, and as we are more
frequently in a good, than a bad ftate of
health, our natural ftate is to defire, to hope,
and to enjoy.   It is true, that the imagination, which gives us fome agreeable moments, expofes us, when once we are un-
deceived, to others which are painful. There
is no perfon who does not wifh to preferve
his life, his health, and his property; but
the imagination reprefents to us our life, as
a thing which ought to be very long; our
health eftablifhed and unchangeable; and
our fortune inexhauftible: when the two
latter of thefe illufions ceafe before the
former, we are much to be pitied.

ESSAY

ESSAY IV.

ON COMPARISON.

WE cannot judge well but by compari-
son; and we cannot compare meta-
phyfical objects, (that is, thofe which
fall not under the fenfes) but by reflecting
upon ourfelves, and by comparing the fentiments of others with our own. From hence
it comes to pafs, that the firft fentiment of an
honeft man, inclines him to believe that men
in general are honeft; and that of a vicious
man, to believe that all the world is ill difpofed. Nothing but experience, knowledge
of the world, of men, and of things, can
bring us to a juft manner of thinking in
this refpect; and ftill the different conjunc-
tures, by which we may happen to be modified, confiderably bias our judgment therein. In general, the beft manner of judging
men, is according to their interefts; and the
beft method of perfuading them, is to let
them perceive how much it is their intereft
to do that which is propofed. It is not fo

eafy

eafy to deceive them as may be imagined; thofe who wifh to fucceed therein, muft give them no time for reflection.

I have read in the works of St. Evremond, a paffage which appeared to me, equally agreeable and natural: " I wifhed,
" faid he, to write characteriftic Tragedies
" and Comedies; but I have never been able
" to place my heroes in other fituations
" than thofe in which I was myfelf; nor to
" give them other characters than my own:
" it was in vain that I gave to my perfon-
" ages, Greek, Roman, Turkifh, or French
" dreffes, or that I called them by names
" taken from the hiftories of all thofe
" countries; when my piece was finifhed,
" I perceived always that I had reprefented
" nobody but St. Evremond."

B 4   ESSAY

E S S A Y   V.

ON THE PRACTICE OF MORALITY.

THE Chinefe are perfuaded that there is but one fcience which merits to be profoundly ftudied, and that it is neceffary to ftudy it one's whole life; it is morality: from this refults, fay our relations of them, that all the Chinefe are philofophers. I maintain, that thefe relations are not authentic; it is neither true nor poffible that they fhould be fo; and I fhould greatly pity a people, who paffed their whole lives in the ftudy of morality. The firft year of their ftudies, they would know every thing neceffary to be known; and when men obftinately purfue the ftudy of a thing, which they poffefs in the moft ample manner, they terminate in perplexity. What we ought to do during our lives, is not to ftudy morality, but to practife it; it may be very well practifed without being underftood, when we fuffer ourfelves to be conducted by thofe who know what it is; and much

much more fo, when we are penetrated by
its principles which are few in number, but
univerfally acknowledged, for fuch a length
of time paft, to be good, that there is nothing more folid. Afterwards, it is neceffary to apply them on every occafion ; and
to oppofe them to the fire of the paffions,
and to the trifling interefts, which incline
us to deviate from our duty. There are
profeffions in routine of which it may be
faid, in parodying a verfe of Boileau ; *The
practice is eafy, and the art is difficult.* It is
quite the contrary in morality ; the knowledge of its principles is fimple and eafy ;
but the practice is a difficulty which we experience every day.

It is not the vivacity only of our paffions,
of our character, and our age, which caufes
obftacles to the practice of morality, but
circumftances alfo, difficult to be forefeen.
However, *at all events the wife man is prepared.* It is particularly neceffary when we
are young, to reflect upon what we read and
fee ; to put ourfelves in the place of people
whom we hear fpeak, or whom we know
perfonally, and afk ourfelves, what would
we

we do were we in alike fituation? This is what
is called ftudying hiftorical books, and the
great book of the world to advantage. I
have for more than twenty years followed
this method, and I am of opinion, that I am
the better for it. Without ambition, or any
ardent defire of changing my prefent fituation, I like, notwithftanding, to build *caftles
in the air*: they amufe me and give me no
uneafinefs: they are agreeable dreams which
never make me ftart out of fleep, or give
me the night-mare. My friend the Abbé
de Saint Pierre, dreams continually that he
is reforming the ftate: I have a little more
right than he has to form fuch dreams. He
writes and publifhes what he dreams of; I
am tempted to do fo likewife; but I anfwer
for it, that my dr-ams fhall not be brought
to light during my exiftence; firft, becaufe
I do not believe the world difpofed to make
ufe of that which I think is for its advantage; fecondly, becaufe the example of
the Abbé de St. Pierre frightens me. With
the beft intentions, he has given much advice which would well deferve to be followed; but he has attacked in front, generally
received ideas; he has propofed impractic-
able

able means of arriving at happy ends; he has announced his ideas in an emphatical tone; and has believed that to be well expreffed, they have need of new words and an extraordinary orthography; all this has thrown a ridicule upon his writings, and perfon; and it was only by paffing for a fool and a dotard, that he avoided the hatred of thefe whofe intereft it was to maintain the abufes which he was willing to deftroy. It cannot be denied, that he merited, in feveral refpects, reproaches, and even derifion; but affuredly it was poffible to reap fome advantage from his ideas upon feveral objects, and to turn to a good account his idle fpeculations. A fine example for thofe who would ftill wifh to publifh projects of reform: but ought this to frighten a good citizen? No! at leaft, it will not hinder me from thinking, and even writing, were it but for myfelf, that which fhall appear to me beft to be done.

ESSAY

ESSAY VI.

ON IMAGINARY IDEAS.

THERE are chimeras which elevate the foul, and incline the mind to fortify itfelf with great and noble ideas; when a man believes himfelf deftined to do great things, he is never guilty of a mean action; he conceives no low projects, or any of which he is afhamed. A young officer, who afpires to the command of an army, ftrives to improve himfelf in tactics; he ftudies the great art of war, and if he does not become a general, he fucceeds at leaft fo far as to command a troop or a detachment. A young magiftrate, who thinks he has fenfe and abilities enough to attain the height of his profeffion, applies himfelf ferioufly to gain information, and ftrives at the fame time to render himfelf agreeable to protectors in power; if he arrives not entirely at the end he propofes, he reaps at leaft, a part of the fruit of his labour and hopes. The young clerk in a court of juftice, who has feen a

few

few celebrated advocates make great fortunes; the ftudent in anatomy, who has feen the fiift furgeon to the King die and leave upwards of an hundred thoufand pounds; the apprentice, who has feen the fhop of his mafter fo well accuftomed, that there was annually fold therein, merchandife to the amount of forty thoufand pounds; all thefe people are completely happy, if they have a hope, frequently chimerical of doing the fame thing. The defire of fucceeding, the conviction even that we fhall fucceed, the enthufiafm of our profeffion, or calling, aie powerful incentives, which ftimulate us to great actions. We muft not be difheartened; we muft indulge hope, give an inceffant application, and not ceafe to merit new recompenfes, till we have obtained all that we can defire. There are none but fools, who after having made trifling efforts, and given fome feeble proofs of their abilities, wait quietly by their fire-fide for honour and the price of their fervices, and complain of the injuries they have fuffered. Whoever has not the courage to fuffer many, does not merit to be in the end recompenfed by a brilliant fuccefs.

If

If we have not the noble emulation of rifing above our equals, we mult confine ourfelves to peaceful and focial virtues, and ufe with difcretion the fortune we have received from our fathers, if we be not willing to augment it ; we fhould make ourfelves loved in our families, efteemed in the neighbourhood, and enjoy the pleafures of a limited fociety.

ESSAY

ESSAY VII.

ON CHARACTERISTIC MODELS FOR IMITATION.

A Wife and juft man looks upon every difhoneft means of enriching himfelf as impoffible; and upon every projeƈt which he is unable to accomplifh, as a real folly; but even in the laft cafe he may carefs chimeras, and amufe himfelf with them, as we read a romance, without hoping to become the hero of it; or relations of voyages, without having the leaft inclination to go to fea, and leave our native country. It is in this manner that I put myfelf, fometimes in the place of thofe whofe hiftory I read; I figure to my mind the fituations they have been in, and afk myfelf if I fhould have got as happily out of them as they did? Were I a king, I fometimes fay, fhould fuch a prince be m model? Were I a general of an army, fhould I conduƈt myfelf like fuch or fuch a famous warrior? If I were a minifter or a magiftrate, fhould I adopt the princi-

I

ples

ples which certain perfons in thofe fituations
of my acquaintance appear to have followed? As I love to write what I think,
efpecially when I prefume that I can do it
with advantage, I have made an infinity of
notes from what I have read; and from converfations with people who were or are of
great confideration in the world, and with
whom I have been intimately connected; I
mean to make ufe of thefe notes in order to
fill up this volume.

I have frequently fought, among my acquaintance, fome perfon who might ferve
me for a model; but I have not yet found
one which is perfect, and to whom I could
wholly attach myfelf. The more particularly I have known the people I would fain
have imitated, the more I was convinced
that they were in many points far from that
degree of perfection to which I was ftudious
to arrive. Finally, I perceived that I
ought to imitate Praxiteles, who, wifhing
to make his Venus a real *chef d'œuvre*, did
not confine himfelf to a fingle beauty. Although there were charming girls in Athens,
and that he had Phryne before his eyes, he
chofe

chofe in a number, that which each of them had in the greateft perfection, and made of fo many united attractions, a ftatue, which has been judged to be the fineft piece of workmanfhip produced by the hands of man.

Befides, if even I found models capable of fatisfying me, and if I were abfolutely in their fituation, I fhould carefully avoid copying them fervilely: a copyift is in a fubaltern and abject ftate, however excellent may be the original. A free and noble imitation is alone worthy of a man, who feels elevated, and believes that he has fome genius.

E S S A Y   VIII.

ON THE UTILITY OF PLUTARCH's LIVES.

THE lives of Plutarch, if read attentively, are of all thofe of ancient authors,
the moſt capable of engaging young perſons
to make reflections ; and for which reaſon
they ſeldom fail to do it : they would wiſh
to be alternately Ariſtides, Lucullus, Scipio,
Alcibiades, or Socrates ; but independently
that ſuch ideas paſs very rapidly, theſe per-
ſonages lived in an age and a country ſo different from ours, that there are not many
applications to be made of our manner of
thinking and acting to theirs. The parallels
even that Plutarch ſtrove to make of the
Greeks and the Romans, are neither very
juſt nor uſeful ; becauſe there was already
too great a difference between the manners
of the two nations, and the ſituations of
their heroes. Nevertheleſs, we of the
eighteenth century may reap ſome benefit,
by conſidering theſe people dead, two thou-

ſand

fand years ago, at three thoufand five hundred leagues diftance from us.

If I had a model in antiquity to follow,
it fhould be *Julius Agricola*, father-in-law of
Tacitus. In fuppofing that his fon-in-law
has not over charged his portrait, this great
man has given the example of an individual, who, after having ferved his country
with honour, uprightnefs and difintereftednefs, in the higheft degree poffible, finding
himfelf obliged to 'renounce the fatisfaction
of being ufeful to the public, devoted himfelf to the exercife of focial virtues; made
his family and a fociety of chofen friends
happy, in the midft of which he was folely
concentred; and fighed in fecret, becaufe he
was perfuaded, that to cry aloud againft the
evils which he could not remedy, was to
encreafe them. My fon, to whom I have
communicated my manner of thinking with
refpect to Agricola, is of a different opinion;
he has found in ancient hiftory, other per-
fonages more worthy of being taken for
models, and I excufe him on account of his
youth and fituation. He is juft beginning
his career, and mine is perhaps already too

C 2   far

far advanced; before we think of going to
bed, it is neceffary at leaft to have dined.

I fhall never forget fome paffages of *Tacitus*
in the life of *Agricola* his father in-law . I
will tranfcribe them in my own language, for
I am of opinion, that they have not yet been
tranflated in fuch a manner as they deferve.

* " Agricola being young, was exceffive-
" ly fond of ftudy; perhaps more fo than
" a man deftined to a military life and
" public affairs ought to be : but his mo-
" ther regulated his foaring inclination by
" fciences and letters. Afterwards, age and
" reflection moderated his ardor, and gave
" him that juftnefs of tafte for philofophy,
" which is proper for a Statefman.

                                        The

---

* The reader will be pleafed to confider, that this paffage
from Tacitus comes into Englifh from the French of M. d'
Argenfon. M. d'Argenfon being of opinion, that no good
tranflation of it had ever been given, the tranflator chofe in
this cafe, rather to make M. d'Argenfon his original than
Tacitus.

" The people, whom he was charged to
" govern, did not remark in his conduct
" either humour, arrogance, or avarice:
" he was moderate and reasonable; and what
" is exceedingly rare, his goodnefs loft him
" none of the people's respect, nor his
" severity their affection. Although he was
" obliged to increafe the contrbututions,
" in order to provide for the subfiftance of
" his army, he made them suppoitable by
" an equitable division, and suppieffed vex-
" atious profecutions, which bear heavier
" upon the people than even impofitions.

" Being returned home, after having
" filled the moft honourable functions, he
" ftrove by the moft fimple and modeft ex-
" terior appearance, to make his great name
" and actions to be forgotten. He exercifed
" himfelf in the practice of private virtues,
" in the bofom of his family and among his
" fiends; many people on feeing *Agricola,*
" fought in him the great man, and few
" difcoveied him at firft fight.

" The affairs of the Empire becoming
" worfe, the public voice called *Agricola*

C 3   " to

" to his country's affiftance; thefe cries
" ftruck inceffantly the ears of the Emperor.
" Some perfons communicated them to him
" by way of advice ; others repeated them
" through malignity, and with a view of
" irritating the prince againft a man whom
" they had already unjuftly flandered. It
" was thus that the virtues of *Agricola* con-
" curred equally in loading him with ho-
" nour, and precipitating his ruin.

" *Agricola* was eafy about the fate which
" hung over him ; he did not brave the
" power of *Domitian,* and feared as little
" the evil he was capable of doing him ;
" he fighed for the fate of his country
" only, and this he did in fecret.   Let us
" learn by his example, that there is a kind
" of particular heroifm for thofe who live
" under the empire of tyrants. it confifts
" in not precipitating ourfelves foolifhly
" into ufelefs dangers, but in preparing our-
" felves to fupport every accident to which
" we are expofed under bad princes.

" If pofterity wifh to know fomething
" of the perfon of *Agricola,* he was rather

pro-

" proportionably formed than of a graceful
" figure; his phyfiognomy infpired con-
" fidence; his air was rather affable and
" polite than impofing; it was fufficient to
" look at him, to know that he was an
" honeft man; and people were not afto-
" nifhed when they difcovered that he was
" a great man. His career was not very
" long, if the ordinary courfe of life be
" confidered, as he died at the age of fifty
" years; but on examining the ufe he made
" of his time, he lived to a great age. Ho-
" noured with the confulate, and invefted
" with the triumphal robe, he had no other
" honour to defire; without being very
" rich, he was fufficiently fo to fupport his
" rank. He preferved till his death, his
" virtues, his reputation, the affections of
" his relations and friends, and the efteem
" of the public. finally it may be faid, that
" he gained happily a good port at the eve
" of ftorms and tempefts."

ESSAY

ESSAY IX.

CHARACTER OF AGRICOLA AND POMPONIUS ATTICUS

IF I was pleafed with the life of *Agricola*, and wifhed to take him for my model, my fon was as much fo with the life of *Pomponius Atticus*, which I made him read in *Cornelius Nepos*. He came to tell me, that the conduct of this wife Roman was that which he would imitate: my reply to him was as follows: " You do not yet, my fon, " perceive the difficulty there is in living " as happily as *Pomponius Atticus* did, in " fuch critical circumftances. You do not " conceive the danger there is in taking no " part in civil wars. Can a man flatter " himfelf with the idea of being equally " efteemed by both parties, to have friends " in one and the other, to render fervice to " all, and not to be fufpected by any? It is " almoft impoffible, when a perfon poffeffes

rank

" rank in life, and pretends to fome con-
" fideration, to act fuch a part. To
" meddle with nothing, is all that the ig-
" norant and obfcure can do, and in thanking
" heaven for their infignificance; but others
" are obliged to explain themfelves: I am
" firmly of opinion, that it is their duty to
" make known their manner of thinking,
" when they have employment which re-
" quire they fhould do it; and when they
" can contribute to fupport the lawful party
" and refift the unlawful one. I am per-
" fuaded that *Atticus* was blamed, that he
" was accufed of indifference and apathy:
" *Cornelius Nepos* fays fomething of it; it
" was afferted, and perhaps with truth,
" that he made his court to the tyrants;
" but that which faved *Atticus*, was the
" conftant equality of his philofophy; it
" did not change for a moment; and not
" the leaft word efcaped him, either againft
" *Sylla*, in favour of *Brutus*, or againft
" *Marc Antony.* He died at feventy-feven
" years of age, the friend of *Auguftus*; al-
" though he had calmly feen *Cæfar* affaffin-
" ated in a full fenate, he had no part in
" the

2

" the confpiracy, but on the other hand he
" took no means to revenge his death."

" Ah ! my fon, it is carrying indiffer-
" ence to a culpable degree ! Moreover, dare
" you flatter yourfelf with being like *Atticus*,
" fo amiable as to be equally fought after
" by both parties ? Either it is neceffary to
" be abfolutely innocent, or to have fuch
" fine qualities as are capable of making
" trifling errors to be forgotten. For my
" part, I avow that I do not believe I am
" capable of conducting myfelf like *Pom-*
" *ponius Atticus*. If I were unfortunate
" enough to live at a time when my country
" was divided into two parties, I think I
" could not do otherwife than declare my-
" felf in favour of the beft ; efpecially if I
" were powerful, rich, and young enough
" to be of fervice to it.

+ Pomponius Atticus did what was ftill worfe, Cicero,
his intimate friend, who wrote him fo many fine letters, whofe
brother was his fon in law, was profcribed and affaffinated by
order of Antony. Fulvia, wife of this Triumvir, caufed
the head of Cicero to be brought to her, tore out the tongue,
which had pronounced the Philippics, and by a refinement of
barbarity, pierced it feveral times with her needle. Pomponius Atticus was not only unconcerned at this, but fometime afterwards, Fulvia being embarraffed in her circumftances, having loft her hufband, he protected her, did her
effential fervices, and declared himfelf her fteadfaft friend.

ESSAY X.

COMPARISON OF LYCURGUS AND St. FRANCIS D'ASSISE.

IN reading the life of *Lycurgus*, in Plutarch, and the hiftory of Lacedemon, I could not but call to mind an odd comparifon, and without doubt ridiculous, which I have fomewhere read; it is a well drawn and very droll parallel, between *Lycurgus* and *Saint Francis D'Affife*. The principles of thefe two legiflators are, it is faid, the fame; the Lacedemonians made vows like the capuchin friars; namely 1ft, that of poverty, or at leaft *difappropriation*, fince they held all their property in common, lands, provifions, buildings and cloaths; gold and filver were forbidden them; if there were any at Lacedemon, they belonged to the State.—2d. With refpect to the vow of obedience, it was no where better obferved than in Sparta; the

the foldier was kept in the moft exact difcipline; the people had no part in the government; it was compofed of monarchy
and ariftocracy: the kings reprefented the
provincial and the guardian,† the ephori the
definitor. 3d. It is not fo eafy to piove,
that the Lacedemonians made a vow of
chaftity; for it is well known they had
ufages and cuftoms quite contrary: but the
principal object of the inftitutors of orders,
and by which they bound each member of
a religious fociety, and that of the Latin
church, (which fubjected in like manner all
its priefts) was to take away the right of
inheritance, and to concentre, or rather extend in general fociety, the intereft divided
otherwife among families.

Such was the fpirit of the laws of *Lycurgus*,
as well as that of *Saint Francis*: men forget
on entering into that order, their fathers
and mothers; they abjure the ties of con-
fanguinity; they are not even attached to
                                                      any

---

† Officers or infpectors belonging to the order of Saint
Francis.

any particular convent; they are cofmo-
polites as far as the world of *Saint Francis*
reaches. The fpirit of the inftitutions of
Lycurgus is loft, like that of the rules of the
Saint; every thing becomes corrupted, and
is in the end deftroyed, and generally by the
fame caufes.

The Lacedemonians found their manner
of living too auftere; they envied their
neighbours the agreeable life they enjoyed;
and thought that having conquered them,
they ought like them, to enjoy their riches.
In like manner, the Monks having made
themfelves refpected, admired, and efteemed, thought to take advantage of the confideration they had in the world, in order to
enrich, if not their perfons, at leaft their
monafteries. The mendicants even are become rich and proprietors. Philofophy,
fciences and arts, which produce eafe and
convenience, corrupted Athens, and ruined
Lacedemon; fo the Cordeliers have been
admitted into the Univerfity of Paris, and
have there canvaffed for the honours of
doctorfhip. no means are left of reconciling
thefe

thefe fine titles with the very aufterc life
they ought to lead, and thc extreme poverty
of which they have made profeffion. Different reforms have been in vain attempted
to reduce the monks to their firft inftitution.
Finally, having quite loft the virtues of
their order, it is eafy to forefee, that in a
little time there will be no more monks
than Spaitans.

ESSAY

ESSAY XI.

PORTRAITS OF ARISTIDES, AND ALCIBIADES.

I Have juſt read with the greateſt pleaſure, in Plutarch, the two lives and portraits of *Ariſtides*, and *Alcibiades* : theſe two illuſtrious Athenians form a perfect contraſt ; but their characters are equally worth ſtudying, and it is even uſeful to compare them, and to make of their different kinds of merit, application to the age in which we live.

The renown of arms was not that of *Ariſtides* :—he ſerved in the army, at firſt as a private ſoldier, or ſubaltern officer:—he conducted himſelf bravely, as every good citizen charged, as far as is in his power, with the defence of his country, ought to do ; but he was not ambitious of commanding, and ſerved his fellow citizens better with his head than with his arms. Always modeſt; contented to ſhew his talents when he was charged with the execution of any

paſti

particulai duty, or confulted upon any affair; he ceded the honour of rank to him who wifhed to poffefs it; neverthelefs, he could not fo far hide his merit as to prevent its being juftly admired. Efchylus having introduced into one of his tragedies the following Greek verfes,—" *He will not appear juft. but he will be fo.*" The people turned towards Ariftides, difcovered in him this character, and immediately gave their applaufe. The public efteem met him, if the expreffion may be allowed, and accompanied him, without his ever feeking for it. He had a violent enemy, and fo much the more dangerous, as he was a perfon of no mean confideration . this was *Themiftocles.* He made it a rule to contradict every thing which Ariftides propofed; and Ariftides took the refolution of getting others to propofe that which he thought advantageous to the Republic. Notwithftanding all his merit, we know that Ariftides could not fave himfelf from the rigour of the oftracifm; a fevere law, introduced into the Republic of Athens, with the view of maintaining equality. His great reputation of juftice and underftanding gave umbrage to his fellow

citizens :

citizens : he went into exile, praying that
Athens might never be in a fituation to regret his abfence.   His prayers were not
heard .—Ariftides was foon wanted, and recalled. Themiftocles, like a great politician,
went to meet him, and promifed him every
kind of deference and proofs of attachment.
Ariftides, more fincere in his profeffions,
anfwered : " Command me in war,—you
" are a great general,—I will obey you
" like a brave officer.   When we fhall be
" returned to Athens, let each of us take
" in the deliberations, that part which his
" ideas fhall fuggeft."   In fhort, the year
following, Themiftocles conceived a bold
and brilliant project, which might fucceed ;
yet it was not quite conformable to the rules
of juftice the people confulted Ariftides
upon it, he told them freely what he
thought ; and the Athenians rejected it.   So
true it is, that the people, when they have
time to reflect, and are temperate, conduct
themfelves in the moft juft and upright manner.   The virtue and reafon of Ariftides
made an epocha ; and when the morals of
Greece were become totally corrupted, *the
time of Ariftides* was quoted, in order to re-

D   fer

fer to the age of upright men.   During the reign of the Emperors at Rome, *the age of Cato* was likewife fpoken of, in referring to the time when this Cenfor defended the laws and ancient cuftoms of the Roman Republic ; but Cato was uncouth and auftere,—— Ariftides gentle and humane.   Another Athenian, endowed with more brilliant qualities than Ariftides, enjoyed during his life, and even a long time after his death, the greateft reputation ; this was *Alcibiades*, whofe character, &c. I will extract, as I have done that of Ariftides from Plutarch.

It does not appear that Ariftides either ftudied philofophy, or that he affociated with philofophers, the Academy
and the Lyceum, were not eftablifhed at the time in which
he lived ; philofophy was natural to him, and not acquired
his juftice was founded upon the virtue of his mind, and the
uprightnefs of his heart.

Since the death of Ariftides, there have, perhaps, been many
men, who, born with as much virtue, rectitude of mind and
heart as he was, have perverted thefe happy gifts, by ftudying
to reafon too profoundly upon the nature and extent of their
duties, and by comparing them with their interefts

ESSAY

ESSAY XII.

CHARACTER OF ALCIBIADES.

ALCIBIADES gave in his youth proofs
of what he was one day to become:
he was courageous, intrepid, ambitious,
haughty, and predominant; but knowing,
on great occasions, how to temper his paffions by policy;—witty, lively, full of grace
and agreeablenefs, but having an appearance
of being diffipated and imprudent. of a
charming figure. made to infpire love, which
in effect he did, appearing to return all the
fentiments he caufed in others; but he was
too much mafter of his paffions to be governed
by them He made his unreftrained ardour for pleafure fubfervient to his reputa-
tation, ambition and interefts. Fond of
wealth, although rich, and fometimes
thought extravagant. He cultivated the
arts, and gleaned from the belles lettres, juft
enough to make him amiable: he ftudied
philofophy. Socrates, the wifeft of men,
was his mafter, and fo well pleafed in giv-

D 2   ing

ing him leffons, that in another fenfe, Alcibiades was the mafter of Socrates. He was
married, and not very faithful to his wife
(Hippaiete;) fhe imitated thofe who had
upon Alcibiades lefs legal rights, and pardoned his inconftancy and errors on account
of his agreeable qualities. Every talent
was natural to him, as the virtues were to
Ariftides; therefore, he knew in cafe of
need, how to counterfeit all that Ariftides
really practifed. Particular circumftances
were the caufe of his going to Lacedemon:
and in that city, the rival of his country,
and whofe manners formed a perfect contraft
with thofe of the Athenians, he appeared
for fometime to become a perfect Spartan;
but he was only a fox cloathed in the fkin
of a lion. He had metamorphofed his exterior only · he feduced the wife of the good
King Agis; and fo far from the Spartans
converting him, it was he who corrupted
them. He went among the Perfians, and
appeared to be born to live in the court of a
defpotic King. A pliant courtier, he cling-
ed at the feet of him who was mafter: daring and haughty towards the Satraps, he
proved to them that he had as much or more
right

right than they had to favour, and to all the advantages which men acquire in a monarchy; after his return to his own country, he dazzled his fellow citizens with his magnificence ; but he delighted them with the tafte he introduced into the feafts which he gave them. The Athenians were capable of pardoning every thing in favour of the graces. nobody had this refource more at hand than Alcibiades. His end was tragical ; but he proved to his lateft moment that he was intrepid : befieged in his houfe by the Perfians, covered with their arrows, he expired ; and it was the beautiful Timandra who clofed his eyes, and took care of his interment.

After having read thefe portraits, and turning our eyes towards the age and country in which we live, we cannot but difcover that we have ftill fome fimilar to Alcibiades, but none to Ariftides. The 16th century produced a few of them, and they were acknowledged to be fuch ; becaufe in time of diforder and civil war, men who have as much firmnefs as virtue, who have principles, and who are obliged to defend them,

D 3 fhew

shew themselves without disguise ; but
when every thing seems calm and peaceful,
valour sleeps, and heroic virtue shines forth
no longer.   In countries where there are
neither lions nor dragons, who knows if
there be men that would be capable of tam-
ing them; but where no monsters are seen,
insects are in swarms ; which it is more
difficult to disperse, than to kill ferocious
animals.

Our age is capable of producing men like
Alcibiades.—Are there among us any perfect copies of this brilliant model? If I be
not deceived, I know one of them among
my cotemporaries . may my great grand
children admire and love him as I do !

ESSAY

ESSAY XIII.

THE ELOQUENCE AND CHARACTER OF DEMOSTHENES.

I READ the harangues of Demofthenes with all poffible pleafure, and his life with pain. I faw in him a man of the greateft abilities, and the fineft and moft lively eloquence; but I perceived that the qualities of his heart did not anfwer to thofe of his underftanding. The firft time he mounted the roftrum, it was to plead againft his guardians; he did not fucceed, becaufe he accumulated too many arguments one upon the other; overcharged his pleading with oratorical figures, and had a bad delivery. For my part, I think his caufe was not a good one: a young man like Demofthenes, ought to have found his judges difpofed to hearken to him, when he complained, that advantage had been taken of his weaknefs to deprive him of his property. It appears that, far from being difheartened by this bad fuccefs, Demofthenes

D 4 took

took infinite pains to become more able and
seducing. Sometime after, not having yet
obtained a good delivery, he compofed for
others ; and in a caufe wherein the Areopa-
gites were greatly embarraffed, becaufe the
pleading on both fides were of equal force,
it was difcovered, that Demofthenes had
drawn up both the one and the other : he
was thus an advocate for and againft. What
opinion can we have of the heart of fuch an
orator ! At length he found himfelf capable
of oppofing every thing which Phocion propofed, who wanted neither wit nor eloquence, and whofe opinions were more juft
and of greater advantage to the Athenians
Demofthenes had talents ftill greater than
thofe of Phocion ; he got the better of him,
and his fucceffes were the caufe of the lofs
of his country. Ought he not to reproach
himfelf with fuch a triumph ? When Demofthenes wanted argument and reafon, it
frequently happened, that he got rid of his
embarrafsment by pleafantry. This kind
of refource would appear lefs extraordinary
and difficult to the French to make ufe of,
than to other nations.

His

This advice was to go to war, although the Athenians were not in a situation to do it; it was however resolved upon. Obliged like others to join the army, he was the first who shrunk from his duty and ran away. He had harangued like a bad citizen, and he fought like a cowardly soldier. Nevertheless the Athenians recalled him to the rostrum, they wished to hear again this divine orator. Frivolous people! who admired nothing but the choice of words and turn of phrases, without giving themselves the least trouble about the object of the discourse. It was, however, the welfare of the republic which was in question. Philip being dead, Demosthenes maintained, that nothing was to be feared from the young Alexander; that he was only *a foolish boy*, (according to the expression of M. de Toureil.) The wits of Athens smiled, and gave their applause: it appeared by what followed, how far this judgment of Alexander was founded on truth. The King of Macedon destroyed Thebes, and forgave Athens, on account only of the arts,—of letters and philosophy; but he required that the orators who had insulted him should be given up. Demosthenes

thenes was the moft culpable; he was greatly afraid, and did what he could to fave himfelf the trouble of the journey: he invented,
and declaimed wonderfully, on the fable of
the fhepherds, whom the wolves prayed to
to give up their dogs. Demofthenes was by
no means a man precious to his republic; yet
he managed fo as to prevail upon his countrymen to pay a confiderable fum, rather
than abandon him to the refentment of the
King of Macedonia. Alexander took the
money from the Athenians, left them their
orator, and made a very good bargain.

The Conqueror having taken Sardes from
the King of Perfia, found proofs that Demofthenes was penfioned by the enemies of
his country.—in a word, a traitor. He made
this known to the Athenians, who only laughed at it: in fact, it did not hinder Demofthenes from being the beft fpeaker in Greece;
and the Athenians pronounced every thing in
favour of wit and courage.

He was one day to plead againft a certain
Harpalus, whom the Athenians wifhed to
banifh from their city, and who fully de-

ferved

ferved it : the culprit gave an elegant gold
cup to the orator. The next day, Demofthenes declared that he had a cold, and
could not plead · I believe it, faid Phocion,
thou haft got in thy throat the cup of Harpalus. This repartee was thought an excellent one ; but it was all that paffed upon
the fubject.

When we read Demofthenes, we are fo
delighted, that we do not think of weigh-
ing his reafons ; but, on reading hiftory,
their weaknefs is feen, in putting ourfelves
in the place of the Athenians. Phocion, on
the contrary, fpoke rationally, and always
to the purpofe. Hyperides faid to Phocion,
when wilt thou then think of going to war?
" When thofe in years, anfwered the fage
" Athenian, fhall know how to command,
" and the young how to obey : when the
" rich fhall be difpofed to contribute their
" property, and the poor their arms. When
" orators fhall no longer difplay their wit
" and talents at the expence of the repub-
" lic ! '" Thefe are fublime fentiments,
and which prefent at once, the evils and
their remedies.

Demof-

Demofthenes, on the contrary, began his harangues, by faying, " Athenians, the " Oracle of Delphi, has declared, that there " was one man in Athens, who was of a " different opinion from all the others ; are " you defirous to know this man ?—I am " he." This is certainly a fine rhetorical figure; but afterwards, Demofthenes was obliged to ufe great fubtility, to prove that he was right, in being of an opinion different from that of all his fellow citizens.— How could the Athenians have been fo far impofed upon, as to feize that which was falfe, and never that which was true ? It is certain, that Demofthenes deceived them.

I like Cicero much better; every thing in his pleadings breathes fentiment, equity, and a juftnefs of mind : his logic is clear, and at the fame time preffing. It feems by his manner, as if one honeft man was defending another ; and nothing proves to us that Cicero ftrove to deceive the Romans, nor that he fupported a bad caufe.

The Roman orator had great perfonal defects ; he was weak in council and in go-

vernment

vernment, and gave way to times and circumftances ; but he was not ftrenuous for
the bad party, and if he had not the couiage
to fave his country from falling, he did not
lead it to the brink of the precipice.   He
was vain, and believed that he had faved
Rome, by difcovering the confpiracy of
Catiline; but if he boafted too much of a
trifling fervice, he had nothing to reproach
himfelf with.   Something fhould be granted in favour of humanity, and feveral weakneffes ought to be excufed on its account.

ESSAY

ESSAY XIV.

CHARACTERS OF THE TWO CATOS, COMPARED

I Have read the lives of the two Catos with an intention of judging to which of them the expreffion, afterwards a proverb, *He is as wife as Cato,* was moft applicable : and I think Cato of Utica, ought to be preferred to his grandfather. In order to form a better judgment, let us compare their actions, confidering at the fame time, their refpective fituations. The Cenfor was more auftere, and lived at a time when it was lefs neceffary to be fo : confequently, his aufterity might be fufpected of proceeding from a particular turn of mind. He gained at firft, fome reputation as an orator ; but it was becaufe he was very violent in his pleadings againft the adverfe parties : fhewed an exceffive zeal for virtue and the laws, and criticifed feverely, thofe who acted contrary to either. He was named Queftor, in the army of Scipio Africanus ; and dif-

approved

approved of the moft trifling recompence, which that General wifhed to make to his foldiers. Scipio very juftly obferved, he thought himfelf more iefp nfible for the fuccefs of the great enterprizes with which he was charged, than the œconomy of the public treafure · Cato fell into a paffion, and abandoned both the Queftorfhip and the army. When he was Prætor, he was a judge of the moft perfect integrity; but his feverity was infupportable. Arrived at the honours of the Confulfhip, he was fent into Spain, where he foon found himfelf furrounded with enemies, which he owed, perhaps to the ftubbornnefs of his character. Perceiving that it was neceffary to relax from his feverity, he took out from the public treafure two hundred talents, with which he corrupted part of the Spaniards, and oppofing them to each other, conquered them all; razed the walls of their cities, and received in Rome triumphal honours. After having been ten years Conful, he folicited the Cenfo fhip, which he obtained: and never was that place filled with fo much intrepidity and vigour as by Cato. He paid no refpect to perfons, Senators, Knights, or

men

men of Confular dignity: he drove from
the fenate thofe whom he found culpable,
of whatever birth they were. He was
exact, fevere, incorruptible, inflexible and
refolute · he made himfelf dreaded by thofe
who infringed the laws; but he did not
render the execution of them eafy:—he took
no pains to make them efteemed, and never
thought of rewarding thofe who conformed
to what they prefcribed. He declared war
againft luxury, not by publifhing any fump-
tuary law, but by taxing the citizens according to their expences; without paying the
leaft attention to their real fortunes. At the
end of his Cenforfhip a ftatue was erected
to him, and he received the fur-name of
Cenfor, which he bore the remainder of his
life; and preferved the inclination of cenfur-
ing and criticifing his countrymen. He
made it a duty, and perhaps a pleafure, to
accufe them in open fenate. this was repaid
him,—he was accufed in his turn,—and it
happened, that he was more than once condemned to pay a fine. He was already advanced in age, when the Athenians came to
Rome, and made it the fafhion to ftudy the
literature and philofophy of Greece. Cato

chap-

difapproved of this ftudy,—he oppofed its
progrefs,—and cried loudly, that it was a
fpecies of mental luxury, which would ruin
the republic.   He went into Africa, and
lived at Carthage, between the fecond and
third punic wars.   He faw that this old
rival of Rome was full of flourifhing youth;
that the country was populous, rich and
commercial :—finally, that if Carthage was
left too long in repofe, it might again make
Rome tremble, as it had done in the time
of Hannibal.   From that moment, he gave .
it in the fenate as his opinion, that Carthage
fhould be deftroyed; and he was the caufe of
the third punic war, which was terminated
by the entire deftruction of that city.   Cato
died at the age of ninety, without having
ever been ill, or had recourfe to medicine.

Many things may be faid againft this
aufterc Cenfor of the vices and manners of
his country : he took up for his model,
Curtus Dentatus, a Roman in the beginning
of the republic; who was three times Conful, received twice triumphal honours, but
returned always after his victories to the
plough, and lived humbly in his farms.   It

E   was

was this Curius, who receiving from certain
ambaffadors confiderable offers of gold and
filver, fhewed them his kettle full of ra-
difhes and greens, faying, " judge if a man
" who is contented with fuch a repaft, has
" need of your riches."

Cato affected to lead as frugal a life; but
Curius, by living in this manner, only imitated his countrymen and cotemporaries,
Cincinnatus, Fabricius, Camillus, &c. inftead
of which, Cato made himfelf fingular, and
wifhed to be remarkable. We have fome
fragments of his writings; vanity, affectation of fingularity, exceffive œconomy
and even avarice, are manifefted in them.
He wrote upon a country life, and faid, that
nothing was fo agreeable as augmenting our
patrimony and becoming rich; that flaves
were the inftruments of labour, of cul-
ture, of œconomy and commerce; that
they ought to be made ufe of to improve
our fortune, and not to be confidered but
with this view. Plutarch, however indulgent he might be to thofe whofe life he
wrote, could not refrain from blaming this

manner

manner of thinking, which he looked upon to be inhuman and unjuft.

It is remaiked that Cato, who condemned fo many vices during the courfe of his fevere Cenforfhip, was favourable to thofe with which he was himfelf infected; fuch as ufury, which it is afferted, he practifed in the moft oppreffive manner. When he was reproached with it, he anfwered, that there was no law which forbade it exprefsly : it might be fo at that time, but did it become Cato to attach himfelf ftrictly to the letter of the law, and not to diftinguifh that which was juft and fitting, from what was not fo?— Cato the Cenfor, was, therefore, felf-inter-efted, avaricious, full of vanity, and per-haps, jealous of the great and powerful per-fonages whom he perfecuted openly. He was fevere to his equals, and inhuman to his inferiors : finally, his virtue was auftere and cruel ; which, as Montagne fays, with reafon, *is a trite and foolifh ornament for phi-lofophy.* What are called his *Diftichs,* are full of good fenfe and reafon ; but they are certainly not by Cato the Cenfor: let us fee if they do not better become his grandfon.

E 2 *Cato*

Cato of Utica, lived in times lefs happy
than thofe of his grandfather; and although
the age in which he lived had no particular
defe&t, he criticifed it, much more by being virtuous, than by declaiming furioufly
againft vices.   His wifdom was neither
cynical, jealous nor haughty.   He fought
not riches, but made ufe of thofe he had,
in being generous and liberal on proper occafions; equally incapable of a blind friendfhip, and an inveterate hatred: he loved
above all things, juftice and the Republic.
He was, when very young, under the tyranny of Sylla; and it is faid of him, that
he afked of every body he met, a fword to
plunge into the bofom of that oppreffor of
his country.   Forty years afterwards he
killed himfelf, rather than be obedient to
Cefar.   He faw, efpecially in a Republic,
that dignities were not vain honours, but
real charges; for the exercife of which,
men were anfwerable to their country.   He
was at firft Queftor, as his grandfather had
been, and he conducted himfelf in that
office like an honeft man, without being
more difficult than was neceffary, preferring
the good application of public money to
rigid

rigid œconomy.   A virtue which never ceafes for an inftant, cannot fail of being known ; for which reafon, he enjoyed the reputation he merited ; but the Republic was not very anxious to employ him a fecond time ; his way of thinking, far from being agreeable to his fellow citizens, infpired them with fear.   He was himfelf little defious of making a figure ; but feeing the people ready to elect for tribune an unworthy citizen, and fearing the evils which might be the confequence, he prefented himfelf with confidence, and was created. In fact, he found himfelf in a fituation to prevent, under the pretence of the confpiracy of Catiline, the recall of Pompey and his army to Rome, who was at war with Mithridates, and who had not yet conquered that fierce enemy of the Romans. If this propofition had fucceeded, on one hand, the great object of the Afiatic war would have been loft, for want of giving it the laft fuccours ; and on the other, Rome would have been overcome by Pompey, inftead of being difturbed by Catiline.— Cato deferred at leaft the ruin of his country, in preventing, for the moment, the re-

turn

turn of Pompey with all his troops to Rome. he was near being affaffinated on this occa- fion by thofe of the oppofite party, which included almoft all the Roman citizens, few of them forefeeing the confequences. The coolnefs and fteady refolution of Cato, at length opened their eyes, and they faved him from the hands of the other party. Pompey, informed of what had paffed, re- turned to Rome, and found that Cato was a man whom it was abfolutely nec ffary to manage: he fought his alliance, and afked his niece in marriage for his fon; Cato re- fufed him. I will not give, faid he, an hoftage to Pompey, againft his country: when his party fhall be the moft juft, it fhall be mine. he kept his word, as long as Pompey, Cæfar and Craffus, were united, for the Purpofe of tyrannifing over Rome; he was the enemy of them all. Pompey frequently got him reproached for it; he always replied, that in his actions he never confulted either friendfhip or perfonal en- mity, and that he had not, nor ever fhould have, any thing in view but the welfare of the Republic. All parties perceiving, equally, that it was impoffible to gain him over to
them,

them, they agreed to exclude him from the
Conf l'hip; and this man, fitter than any
other, to govern Rome, was never at the
head of affairs. I do not know if this was
a great evil to Rome; he would probably
have retarded the ruin of the republic but
for a very little time.—However this may
be, the name of the second Cato, to the
fhame of the Confular Calendars, is not
infcribed therein.

At length, the time which Cato the wife
had forefeen, came to pafs. The tyrants of
Rome were reduced to two, Cæfar and Pompey; the latter was conquered, and from that
moment Cato took his part, or rather, as
he fays himfelf, he followed not Pompey,
but attached himfelf to the remains of the
Republic. It was contrary to his advice that
Pompey gave battle at Pharfalia. Cato
could not wifh for a combat which was at
all events to give a mafter to Rome. However, the armies met, much againft his
will; Cæfar conquered, and was from that
moment the enemy of Cato. We know,
the latter retired to Utica, and feeing this
laft place of Africa obliged to fubmit, he

put

put himfelf to death, with a coolnefs and heroifm which have made his act of fuicide the model of all thofe paft, prefent, and to come.

What is principally to be confidered in the death of Cato, is to know if he did well in quitting life. A Chriftian cannot debate upon fuch a point; but Pagan authors have thought that Cato ought to have preferved himfelf for the Republic. For my part, putting myfelf in their place, I think naturally, that Cato of Utica took a good refolution. The liberty of his country was the object of all his defires and affections; which may, by fome, be deemed a foible, for every perfon has one. He faw the liberty of Rome deftroyed; in living a longer time he would have feen that, which he looked upon as a public misfortune, aggravated. Cæfar would have pardoned him, but he would have been under an obligation to Cæfar; and it is lefs painful to a man of fpirit to finifh his exiftence, than to kifs the hand of the tyrant who permits him to live.

It

It appears that Cato was a philosopher of the sect of the Stoics, whose principles have sometimes been carried to a ridiculous degree, but well understood, they are sublime and excellent. Those of the Epicureans, well conceived, tend likewise to make men wise and happy. Cato the Stoic, feared neither death nor pain,—such were the dogmas of the sect; but he still less fought for, than feared them : therefore, he did nothing in his life which tended to give him useless pain, chagrin, or contradiction. When they happened to him, he supported them courageously. He never meddled with state affairs, but when he thought himself called upon to do so : and as soon as he saw that he could no longer be of use to his country, and that he should be deprived of the enjoyments of a private life, because he had taken too great a part in public affairs, he put an end to his existence. If he was in some degree blameable in the effect, he was not so in the principle. The contrary happens in the greater number of suicides: men kill themselves for bad reasons, in general, or they take a wrong time to do it. This is a lesson for the English, and of which
they

they ftand in great need: they ought to be
put in mind, that there was formerly a law
in the republic of Marfeilles, which permitted the citizens to drink the *juice of hemlock* ;
but not till after they had given fufficient
reafons to the magiftrat s, and received their
approbation of them: by means of thefe
precautions it may be eafily imagined, that
nothing was fo rare in Marfeilles as a fuicide.

One laft reflection, which the lives of the
two Catos offer to me is, that their philofophical manner of thinking, had given them
both an unpardonable indifference for their
families. Odd circumftances of this kind,
which I will not repeat, are related of them .
I will only obferve, that thefe proceeded
from different motives. Cato the Cenfor,
given up entirely to avarice, vanity, and a
ridiculous attachment to the laws, confidered every thing in a civil order, and nothing
in a natural or domeftic one. His grandfon
was very differently affected; the welfare of
the Repu lic abforbed all his ideas :—however it may be, thefe two great men were
inexcufeable, in depriving themfelves of the

two

two greateft enjoyments of life, conjugal and paternal love.

The miftaken defire of i nitating the virtues of Curius Dentatus, authorifed the conduct of Cato the Cenfor. The example of Cato of Utica, appeared, to his nephew Brutus. a fufficient authority to aff ffinate Cæfar in full fenate: he committed this crime, or rather this cruel and ufelcfs vengeance, with as pure intentions as thofe of his uncle. He was, like him, the enemy of tyranny, without being that of the tyrant: the bafis of his action was juftice, and a zeal to maintain the eftablifhed laws of his country: but this principle was badly regulated and applied. Tyrants fhould be oppofed in the beginning, and even punifhed, if it be poffible; but there is but one method of treating confirmed and inevitable tyranny, which is that of foothing it fkilfully.

ESSAY

ESSAY XV.

CHARACTER OF LUCULLUS.

THOSE who know Roman hiftory but imperfectly, do not render fufficient juftice to *Lucullus*. We have heard fpeak of his magnificence and love of voluptuoufnefs; but we forget the fervices he did to his country, before he gave himfelf up to the amufements which fweetened and embelliſhed his retreat. He ftudied to advantage the Belles Lettres during his youth, became afterwards a ftatefman, a great general, and, towards the decline of his life, a philofopher. Being a friend to Sylla, he paffed over too lightly the cruelties of this dictator, but he was not his accomplice in them. He was executor to his will, and tutor to his fon, in preference to Pompey. After having held all the public employments, capable of forming great men, as well at home as abroad, he became at laft conful. After his confulfhip, the government of Cilicia becoming vacant, he had every right to demand

mand it; it was a delicate bufinefs, and he would have had much difficulty in fucceeding, had he not made *Cethegus*, tribune of the people, his friend. To obtain which, he found it neceffaiy to apply to *Precia* the courtefan; he feigned himfelf in love with hei, knowing that this means, employed with addrefs, was the moft fure one of fucceeding with women. He obtained what he wanted fiom the lover of his miftrefs, and little fcrupulous about the means he made ufe of to arrive at his propofed end, he turned all to advantage.

He went into Afia, and by his wife conduct pacified the troops which had rebelled and mutinied, led them on to battle againft Mithridates, and gieatly embarraffed this formidable enemy of the Romans. At the fame time he acquired the friendfhip of the inhabitants of the conquered piovinces; ftopped the depredations committed by the farmers of the revenue, who were for the moft part Roman knights, and forced them to eafe the people, or at leaft to regulate with equity the receipt of taxes. This act of juftice and moderation did him much

i honoui.

honour. Having glorioufly executed his firſt
commiſſion, he was fome time after fent
again towards Afia, and conducted himfelf
with the fame prudence and difintereſted-
nefs. He found that the true means of
conquering Mithridates, was to cut of the
proviſions from his army, which was immenfe; this fucceeded—he befieged Amifus,
which contained the chief riches of the
king. He conquered this capital, and the
Roman troops found in it a confiderable
booty. It did not depend upon the general
that the army was not as orderly in taking
poſſeſſion of thofe treafures, as the profit
arifing from them was great, but he never
could obtain this from his foldiers: they
were already greatly relaxed in their ancient
diſcipline: neverthelefs he thought of
puſhing ſtill farther his conqueſts. Mithridates had retired to the dominions of
Tigranes, king of Armenia, his fon in law;
it was there that *Lucullus* ought to have followed him.

Lucullus found means to difperfe the immenfe armies of Tigranes and his father in-
law, although his own was infinitely inferior.

By

By these means he gave the greatest proof of his knowledge in the art of war. He was enterprifing enough to form the fiege of Tigranoceita, capital of the kingdom of Armenia: its approaches were defended by an army of near three hundred thoufand men: the Roman general difperfed them and looked upon victory as certain the moment he had given a glance at their pofition. *We have them*, faid he: it was on one of thofe days which the Romans had marked in their calendar as unfortunate, becaufe it had formerly been memorable by defeats: *I will put it among the fortunate days*, added he; and he did fo accordingly. An hundred thoufand barbarians fell in the battle which followed, wherein it is faid, no more than five Romans were killed, and an hundred wounded.

The confequence of this victory was the taking of the capital. The conqueror marched towards Artaxata, the ancient capital of Armenia: he would have taken it, for Mithridates and Tigranes flew before him, making but vain efforts to fave it; but the cold being fevere, the Roman foldiers loaded

loaded with riches, declared openly they would not expofe themfelves to the rigours of a winter campaign, to gain a triumph lefs flattering to them than to their general. It was in vain that *Lucullus* fet them the example of braving fatigue as well as danger; his foldiers did not follow him, and he was forced to leave his army inactive, and to renounce the honour of terminating a war fo happily begun. During this time, intrigues were carried on at Rome againft him, and his fucceffor was named. When the feafon became favourable, Pompey took the command of the Roman army, eafily conquered Tigranes, and forced Mithridates to fuicide.

It was then that *Lucullus* ftrove to confole himfelf, by leading the moft eafy and voluptuous life, for the mortifications he had met with in his political and military career. He felt that he had a right to repofe, and that he could do nothing better than to make his reticat agreeable ; he had moreover, experienced fome domeftic vexations. He had fucceffively married two wives, whofe conduct had given him much pain, and from whom he had been obliged

to

to live feparate, although the fecond was
the fifter of the auftere Cato. He faw that
in Rome both fexes had violated the laws of
virtue, honour and decency : it feems as if
he had faid to himfelf, " I will think of
" my perfonal pleafures only, fince I can no
" longer hope to acquire glory : I will re-
" nounce the ambition of gaining the efteem
" of a people, who does not merit mine."

If *Lucullus*, loaded with the fpoils of Afia,
had ftill been ambitious of acting a great
part in Rome, he would have made himfelf
a party there, and have greatly embarraffed
Cæfar and Pompey; he would at leaft have
entered the triumvirate like Craffus, and
have had more weight in it, becaufe he had
more merit ; but he preferred the enjoyment
of his riches. He built himfelf magnificent and delightful habitations both in town
and country ; was profufe in the entertainments he gave to his friends, and to thofe
whom he thought worthy of being admitted into his fociety. He was noble and
generous to others, but without fuffering
himfelf to be importuned : he affifted them
with his purfe and credit, but did not ftrive

F

to

to make himfelf partifans, and required no kind of acknowledgment. He faw with indifference Rome agitated by different factions, took no part therein, and was not perfecuted by any of them. He had formed, as a man of tafte, collections of books, ftatues, and other cuiiofities,—cultivated letters and the fciences: finally, he denied himfelf no kind of fenfual pleafure, but declared that he was not a flave to his paffions. If *Lucullus* appeared to be an Egotift, and if he were actually fo, it was becaufe he had been a zealous citizen, a good officer, fufficiently ambitious, and even avaricious of glory. He had leaint, that, in certain countries, and in certain circumftances, when a man has paid to his country his contingency of zeal and fervices, it is fully permitted, and even wife, to think of nothing but himfelf.

ESSAY

ESSAY XVI.

CHARACTERS OF THE TWO GRACCHI.

THE life of the two *Gracchi*, cannot be read without concern, either in Plutarch, or in the hiftory of the confpiracy of the *Gracchi*, by the Abbé de Saint Real. Young men are naturally pleafed with the merit of thefe two young republicans ; they admire their audacity, and applaud their zeal for eftablifhing in their country good order and equality.   They foon think that if they were in their fituations, they would act as they did, and that if the execution were dangerous, at leaft the enterpiife would be glorious.

In maturer age, men judge of the *Gracchi* with more coolnefs and juftice, and do not over-rate their good qualities : for my part, I confefs that I think I fee in their conduct more ambition, impetuofity and rafhnefs, than true patriotic zeal. Grand children, by their mother, of the great Scipio, they

fignal-

fignalifed themfelves at firft in war. Tiberius, the elder of the two, gained ob-
fidional crowns, and did wonders in a battle
which the conful, under whom he ferved
in quality of queftor, loft by his imprudence. The young queftor was charged to
make peace with the conquering enemy:
he fucceeded in this with much addrefs,
confidering the difagreeable circumftances in
which the Roman army was; and if he did
not fave it, he fecured his own reputation.

This beginning warmed the ambition of
Tiberius; he wifhed to fly to glory and
riches, but found that the pretorial functions
would not afford him opportunities favourable enough; he thought that he fhould wait
too long before he arrived at the confulfhip
and the command of armies; the office of
tribune of the people, prefented to him new
and eafy means of fignalifing himfelf, by
fupporting the loweft clafs of citizens, againft
the rich and powerful: he therefore folicited and obtained the tribunefhip without
difficulty, perceiving the great advantages
which were attached to it. The tri-
bunes had equally the power, for the public

lic intereft, of oppofing new laws, and
foliciting the execution of old ones. He
attempted to renew the Agrarian law. This
law commanded that no citizen fhould poffefs more lands than he could cultivate himfelf, and that he fhould be obliged to give
the furplus to thofe of his fellow citizens,
whofe patrimony was lefs confideiable than
his own. It was excellent in its principles
for a rifing Republic; but it became no
longer of ufe when Rome had conquered fo
many kingdoms, and had carried her vic-
torious arms into the middle of Afia, and
efpecially to the coafts of Africa.

Yet the people, who confider lefs the
difficulty of deftroying certain abufes, than
the advantages which would arife from a
reform of them, approved of the propofition of *Gracchus*, who became immediately
their idol. The rich and great reprefented
to him in vain the embariaffments he was
going to throw them into ; he rejected their
reprefentations and followed his purpofe ;
and upon being afked if he meant to take
from thofe who appeared to be too rich,
the lands they poffeffed without making

F 3   them

them an equivalent, he declared that they
were to be paid for them out of the public
treasure, and this treasure was founded upon
their own wealth. Another tribune opposed
the passing of this law; but *Gracchus* carried things with so high a hand, that he had
much difficulty in saving his colleague from
the hands of the multitude who would
have torn him to pieces. *Gracchus* was
named Triumvir with his father in-law and
brother, in order to oblige all the rich
citizens to give their lands to the poor ones.
It may easily be conceived what disorder the
execution of this plan would have occasion-
ed, when, by good fortune, Attalus king
of Pergamus died, and made the Roman
people heirs to his kingdom and immense
treasures.

Gracchus claimed immediately, in the
name of the Roman people, this succession;
he pretended that the money ought to be
distributed among the new possessors of lands,
to enable them to cultivate them; and that
the kingdom of Pergamus ought to be governed in the name and for the advantage of
the Romans, without the Senate's taking

I   the

the leaft part therein.   This laft propofition, put the Senators out of all patience : they faw it was abfolutely neceffary to get rid of *Gracchus*, without which, he would deftroy the ariftocracy, and by the aid of the people and the democracy, foon become mafter of Rome. The deftruction of *Tiberius Gracchus,* was therefore determined, and he was put to death in a very fingular manner ; the Senate in a body was his executioner.   The Senators fet out from the capitol, and crof-fed the city, went to the affembly of the people, followed by their clients armed, having themfelves cuiraffes, and fwords under their robes.   The people were at that time giving their fuffrages for the continua-tion of *Gracchus* in the office of tribune, or rather they were to give them; and although almoft all the plebeians wifhed it, the noife was fo great, it was impoffible to hear or take the voices regulaily.   The Senators ap-peared; the people much aftonifhed, open-ed a paffage and let them approach the tribunal where *Gracchus* was; he would fain have made his efcape ; but a man of the name of Satureius gave the fignal by ftrik-ing the firft blow, and the tribune was foon overwhelmed by numbers. As foon as this was over, the Senate arrefted an hundred of the principal friends of Tiberius, and declared a greater number, who had retired and hid themfelves, banifhed from Rome. The people overcome by fear, dared not to gather up the remains of their broken idol. The brother and family of *Gracchus* could not obtain permiffion to render him fepulchral honours, and his body was thrown into the Tiber.

Caius Gracchus, the younger brother of Tiberius, was at this time, engaged in the war againft the Numidians, in the fuite of his uncle Scipio. Who would not have thought that the example of his elder brother would have ferved him as a leffon, and have prevented him from acting the odious and frequently ufelefs part of reformer of the State: it happened the contrary. After the misfortune of his brother, he remained fome time in fecret, employed himfelf in adorning his mind, and learning eloquence, in which he fuccecded fo well, that on his return to Rome, and Tiberius being almoft forgotten, he made a great

figure

figure at the bar; maintained with great ability some very interesting caufes, which he gained with general applaufe. He was fent queftor into Africa, where he rendered important fervices to his General; for he not only managed the military cheft with judgment and œconomy, but the Roman troops in that country, being in want of many conveniencies of life, which they could not procure of themfelves, he prevailed upon Micipfa, king of Numidia, whom he had made his friend, to procure them every thing they could defire. He returned to Rome after three years queftorfhip; and it was in vain that his enemies ftrove to cavil with him about his adminiftration; the general wifh of the troops fupported him. He then conceived the dangerous ambition of becoming tribune, as his brother had been. At the name of *Gracchus* the people called to mind Tiberius, and in fpite of all the oppofition and intrigues of the Senate, *Caius Gracchus* was elected,

He contented himfelf for fometime with haranguing gracefully and with elegance; he delighted the Romans, and alarmed the great

great, who were not deceived in thinking
that he would foon make a ftorm break over
their heads.   The Senate having decided
two important caufes contrary to his advice,
he complained of it loudly, and formed a
company of three hundred Roman knights,
which company was called the Counter
Senate;   becaufe it took upon itfelf to criticife and reform, under the authority of the
people, the judgments given by the three
hundred Senators;   and to protect thofe
people, who appeared to be unjuftly oppref-
fed.   This eftablifhment made the Senate
tremble, and not without reafon, as it gained Caius the greateft popularity, which
urged him to form feveral other excellent
eftablifhments, fuch as public granaries,
bridges and ftreets, till he became the idol of
the people: the Senate confidered the beft
way to check his defigns, was to oppofe to
him another tribune, who appeared to be ftill
more zealous than himfelf; his name was
Drufus: but *Gracchus* unmafked him, and in
order to furpafs him entirely, brought forward the project of the Agrarian law, which
had been fo fatal to his brother.   Scipio, the
fecond Africanus, although coufin to *Grac-*
chus,

chus, was at that time his moft cruel adver-
fary : he enjoyed all the confideration and
efteem which the honour of putting a final
period to the Punic war, and to the exiftence of Carthage, could give to a Roman
citizen.   *Gracchus* without being alarmed at this great renown, made head againft
him, with as much ability as audacity, aid-
ed by Fulvius Flaccus, whom the protection
of *Gracchus* had raifed to the confulfhip.

Whilft thefe things were paffing, Scipio
was found dead in his bed; this fudden
death caufed fufpicions to fall upon *Gracchus*
and his friends, and perhaps the tribune did
not take pains enough to deftroy them;
thinking that he had no more rivals fo
formidable as Scipio had been, his audacity
encreafed; and the fenate found that this
fecond tyrant was not lefs dangerous than
his brother, and that it was full as neceffary
to cut off the head of the fecond hydra,
as it had been that of the firft.   In a great
affembly of the Roman people, *Caius Gracchus* made a propofition to deftroy the elevated benches for the confular perfonages
and principal fenators; the Senate fet immediately

mediately a price upon his head, and the people defended him no more than they had done Tiberius. *Gracchus* made propofitions of peace ; he was attended to for the fole purpofe of gaining time enough to judge how far he would be fupported. As foon as it was known that he would be entirely for-faken by his friends, he was purfued ; and the laft of the *Gracchi*, being without re-fource, refolved upon putting himfelf to death. The Roman people mourned the lofs of their hero, without ftriving to avenge his fate. Two ftatues were erect-ed to the memory of the brothers ;—even temples were confecrated to them, and the fenate fuffered, with a malicious fmile, thefe vain honours to be paid to their memories. The people are freqently ungrateful to thofe who endeavour to liberate them from flavery, as they generally fufpect that their pretended deliverers act as much from motives of private intereft, as for that of the public ;—they are often right : even the *Gracchi* were not free from this fufpicion : however, another of lefs confequence, may be formed againft them, which is that of rafhnefs, imprudence and inconfideratenefs.

It

It feems to me, that they abufed their good fenfe, zeal and abilities : fuppofing even that they were fincere, they were feverely punifhed for it.—Yet thefe examples have not prevented them from having about feventeen hundred years after their deaths, fome imitators : fuch were in the fixteenth century, the *Count Jean-Louis de Fiefque,* a Genoefe, and in the feventeenth, *Cardinal de Retz.*

ESSAY

ESSAY XVII.

CHARACTER OF COUNT DE FIESQUE,
AND CARDINAL DE RETZ.

JEAN LOUIS DE FIESQUE, Count de Lavagne, of one of the moſt illuſtrious houſes of Genoa, was reſpected on account of his birth, riches, the graces of his perſon, and the agreeableneſs of his wit; and being no more than twenty-two years of age, was imprudent enough to ſtrive to imitate the Gracchi, and finiſhed his career as unhappily as they had done. The hiſtory of the revolution which he attempted to bring on at Genoa, and to which he fell a victim, was written in Italian, in 1629, by Auguſtin Maſcardi, in the manner of that of Catiline, by Salluſt. Maſcardi introduced into his hiſtory, in imitation of Salluſt, harangues or diſcourſes, which were ſuppoſed to be delivered by the conſpirators, deliberating with their chief, upon the ſucceſs of the conſpiracy they had formed. The *Cardinal de Retz*, whilſt he was yet very young, found this hiſtory in Italian ſo intereſting,
that

that he tranflated and embellifhed it; and applied himfelf with an affiduity, which proves he was highly pleafed with the cha-racter of the hero, and that he would gladly have taken him for a model : the Cardinal feems to acknowledge this, by fome paffages in his Memoirs. Yet what could he find to flatter himfelf with in this refemblance ? and to what end did he think to arrive, by pre-tending to imitate the *Count de Fiefque?* This would be difficult to difcover, if it were not known that there is no reafoning with the paffions, and that brilliant actions are, for the moft part, rather the effect of a violence of character, than the confequence of any project formed with reflection.

The confpiracy of *Fiefque* was briefly as follows: *André Doria* after having been a long time attached to the fervice of Francis the firft, became diffatisfied with this mo-narch, his minifters and favourites ; and abandoned the French party, as much per-haps to vex the Court which he had betray-ed, as from a true patriotic zeal. He had re-ftored to the City of Genoa its ancient li-berty ; and eftablifhed there an ariftocratical government, of which he was the real chief.

André

André Doria, old and refpectable by his victories, was not perfonally expofed to the jealoufy of his fellow citizens; but he had a nephew whom he looked upon as his adopted fon, called *Jannetin Doria*, who was young, lively and haughty: it was on him fell the hatred of thofe who thought that in a Republic there ought to be a kind of equality among all the Members of the ariftocratic party. The *Count de Fiefque* held out this principle when talking to his friends; he excited them to revolt; though in public he fhewed the higheft efteem for *Jannetin Doria*, whofe fifter had lately been married to the brother-in-law of the *Count de Fiefque*.

At a moment when it was leaft expected, *Fiefque* convoked an affembly of friends at his own houfe, and difcovered to them a plan of revolt, in which there was more audacity than wifdom. He had found means to purchafe four row-boats, which were in the port of Genoa, and which he had armed, as he pretended, for a cruife againft the Mahometan pirates. He had gained over fome foldiers of the garrifon, and going out at midnight with the confpirators, he attempted to furprize the palace of the Republic;

but

but he did not fucceed: from thence wifhing to gain the port, and to go on board one of his row boats; he had no fooner fet his foot upon a plank than it turned under him: he fell into the mud, and the weight of his arms bearing him down he was fuffocated. His partifans knew nothing of his death for fome hours afterwards, and the revolt continued the remainder of the night: the gates of the city were fhut, and Jannetin Doria was maffacred in attempting to defend them.

Old Doria was gone from Genoa, and the Senate was ready to capitulate with *Fiefque*, when it was perceived that this chief of the revolt did not exift. His name, which during a whole night, and part of the following day, had ferved as a word of rallying to the partifans of liberty or of a new flavery, was profcribed the day following. Old André Doria returned to put the laft feal to the condemnation of his enemy. He made one of his relations, Jerome de Fiefque, fuffer the greateft torments, and banifhed the others, to the fifth generation, from the States of the Republic. The chief branch came to eftablifh itfelf in France, and to form

G   there

there a confiderable houfe : the laft of the
Fiefques died unmarried in 1708.   There
were in the thirteenth century two Popes of
that family, and afterwards a great number
of Cardinals.   The younger branches returned to Genoa, where they exifted not
long ago.

Jean Francois Paul de Goudi, wrote at
feventeen years of age, the hiftory of the
Count de Fiefque; but he did not fo foon
find means to fhew his talent, or rather his
turn for intrigue ; for it was not before he
was twenty-eight years of age, that he was
named coadjutor of the Archbifhopric of
Paris, poffeffed by Jean Francois de Goudi,
his uncle. Lewis XIV. afcended the throne
the fame year, and the troubles of the
Fronde did not begin till five years afterwards, in 1648.   The Coadjutor fignalized
himfelf till the year 1652, when he was
arrefted, and put into prifon ; firft at Vin-
cennes, afterwards in the Citadel of Nantes,
whence he made his efcape in 1655. He wandered for fometime in different parts of Europe, and having made his peace with the
Court, in 1661, he refigned the Archbifhopric

of

of Paris, and kept nothing but the Abbey of Saint Denis; he lived afterwards in a very becoming manner, having recovered from thofe errors into which the examples of the Gracchi, of Catiline and the *Count de Fiefque* had thrown him. Yet he was pleafed in his old age, with the remebrance of the ftir he had made in his youth. Having a good memory, he related with fatisfaction the particulars of his turbulent and agitated life; he has even written them, and his work is well known under the name of Memoirs of the *Cardinal de Retz.* I may fay it is a family work, becaufe my near relations have preferved the manufcript, from which it was printed in the year 1717. I dare moreover affure the reader, that if this manufcript had been loft, I fhould have found it in good prefervation in the converfation of my uncle, M. de Caumartin, bifhop of Blois: this prelate, from whofe converfation I learned the ftile of the wits in the time of Louis XIV. had been brought up, if I may be allowed the expreffion, in the lap of the *Cardinal de Retz,* who had permiffion given him, a fhort time before his death, to refign in his favour the Abbey

of

of Buzay, which the Cardinal himfelf had
been invefted with when he was very young.
My uncle kept it 'till his death. My maternal
grandfather, (father of the bifhop) was the
intimate friend of the Cardinal; my grandmother, who lived to a great age, had
known him particularly; therefore I have
on all fides excellent traditions about this
famous perfonage, and I can take upon me
to fay, that he was really a turbulent man;
a man of intrigue, without motive or object,
making a noife for the fake of doing fo;
and that he was very awkward in the choice
of his means, although he had in other
refpects fome excellent qualities. Such men
are difagreeable to meet with, and dangerous
to follow, when they meddle with public
affairs; but when they are quite retired
from them, they are fometimes delightful
in converfation.

I mean to give fome touches of the character of the *Cardinal de Retz*, and of his
adventures, more from my own private
knowledge and reflections, than from what
is already publifhed.

The

The *Cardinal de Retz* had for his preceptor *M. Vincent*, who has since been beatified,
and will, without doubt, soon be canonifed,
under the name of *Saint Vincent of Paule*.——
If it were true, that thofe who are charged
with the education of young people, have
an influence upon their character and conduct in the world, the *Cardinal de Retz*
ought to have been the moft mild; charitable and pious of all prelates; but, either he
did not profit by the leffons of his bleffed
preceptor, or did not hearken to him.   His
father and mother on the contrary, loved
M. Vincent to adoration; and it is perhaps
for this reafon that their fon thought little
about him.   It happens but too frequently,
that children take a pride in acting contrary
to what they have feen practifed by their
fathers and mothers.

Madam de Goudi had a part in all the
charitable eftablifhments which muft im-
mortalize M. Vincent : the Foundling Hof-
pital, the Grey Sifters, and the Miffionaries
of Saint Lazarus.   How happy would fhe
have been to have become the mother of a
refpectable and an edifying prelate; but her

G 3   fon

fon did not afford her this fatisfaction, although he was promoted to the firft dignities of the church.

Her hufband, father of the *Cardinal de
Retz*, after having been General of the
Gallies, became a widower, entered the
congregation of Oratorians, and was admitted a father of that order. He was bu-
ried in the church of the feminary Saint
Magloire, in 1662.

The fon ought to have begun where the
father ended; but he took quite another
route :—although he was at thirteen years
of age, a Canon of Nôtre-Dame, and in-
cumbent of two abbeys, he fhewed, on
leaving college, inclinations quite oppofite
to thofe which the profeffion he was deftined to required; and it may be faid, that
he did every thing in his power to lofe the
Archbifhopric of Paris, which was to him
almoft a fure heritage, having been held by
his grand and two proximate uncles. Before
he arrived at the age of feventeen years he
had fought three duels, and been concerned
in two affairs of gallantry which had made
some

some noise —Neverthelefs his family was determined to make him the coadjutor of his uncle, and he was obliged, notwith-ftanding his conduct and inclinations, to remain in the church, and make, whether he would or not, a great fortune therein.

The young *Abbé de Retz* intrigued at Court,—and againft whom ? Againft the Cardinal de Richelieu :—and for why ? This is what he would have had much difficulty in explaining, for it could be of no fort of ufe to him. It was at this time that he tranflated the hiftory of the confpiracy of *Fiefque*; he fhewed his work to the Abbé de Boifrobert, and accompanied it undoubt-edly with fome reflections, which gave this great wit, devoted to the Cardinal de Riche-lieu, to underftand, that the *Abbé de Retz* was well enough difpofed to become facti-ous and a confpirator.   Boifrobert told this to the firft Minifter, who faid publicly, that he faw plain enough the little Abbé would fome day become a dangerous being.   This alarmed M. de Goudi, his father ; but the fon was on the contrary delighted with it : he found himfelf highly flattered, by being

treated

treated at his age, as a man dangerous to
the firſt Miniſter, who made France and all
Europe tremble.   To ſupport this fine character, which he pretended already to act, he
diſputed the firſt place of Licentiate in the
Sorbonne, with the Abbé de la Mothe Hou-
dancourt, (related to the Cardinal and protected by him,) and obtained it. Richelieu,
Proviſeur and Reſtaurateur of the Sorbonne,
was equally aſtoniſhed and amazed ; he
threatened the doctors who had voted againſt
his relation ; they all went trembling to
the *Abbé de Retz* to inform him of it,
who anſwered them generouſly, though
haughtily, that rather than be the cauſe of
diſputes between the gentlemen of the Sorbonne and their protector, he would reſign
the place, and be contented with having
merited it.

So haughty a conduct alarmed the family
of Goudi.   The Abbé was ſent into Italy :
he diſtinguiſhed himſelf at Venice by his
gallantries, at Rome by his uncouth beha-
viour, and ſoon returned to Paris, to ſupport again the dangerous and uſeleſs part of
enemy and rival of the Cardinal de Richelieu.

lieu. Sometimes he attached himſelf to women who were diſpleaſing to the Cardinal, at other times, he paid his addreſſes to his miſtreſſes, and even took them from him : at length he entered into a conſpiracy, which had nothing leſs in view than the aſſaſſination of Richelieu. It appears that this proꞁ ject did not at all frighten the young Abbé, he thought himſelf a little *Fieſque* : he was about the ſame age, twenty-two years old, which was the age of his model when he was killed ; but fortunately the conſpiracies of the French Abbé did not break out ſo ſuddenly as thoſe of the Genoeſe Count ; he had the happineſs of ſeeing all his projects miſcarry one after the other, without any accident or danger to his perſon. After this, he was given to underſtand, that he could do nothing more unprofitable than to unite himſelf to turbulent men, with whom he could gain nothing, but might, on the contrary ruin his fortune. He found that it was neceſſary to change his manner of proceeding ; he aſſociated with devotees, without becoming one himſelf; and with eccleſiaſtics who were reputed holy, before he led an exemplary life : he undertook to

2 ·   bring

bring about extraordinary converfions, before he was himfelf converted; and he found
the moft efteemed clergy, and thofe who
held the firft rank in the church, very favourably difpofed to receive him as a prodigal fon, without waiting till he returned
from his errors.

The good M. Vincent himfelf took pleafure in believing, that the inftructions which
he had formerly given him, were not feeds
fown on bad ground; the devotees thought
it an honour to reckon him of their number,
and without putting him to fevere proofs,
they took him to the coadjutory of the
Archbifhopric of Paris.   It was neceffary to
begin by reconciling him to the Cardinal;
this was brought about : it was mentioned
in his favour, and as an act of converfion on
his part, that he did not enter into the confpiracy of Cinq-Mars.   Nothing more was
neceffary to prove that he had renounced all
intrigue; but it appeared by what followed
that he was not yet cured of it.

Every difpofition was made to procure
him the Coadjutorfhip of Paris, when the
Cardinal

Cardinal de Richelieu died. Lewis XIII. died foon after : had he lived, he would probably have finifhed the affair. This honour was referved for the Queen, Anne of Auftria, who began her regency by giving her confidence to people of the greateft incapacity : they made her commit another fault, by prevailing upon her to infure the Archbifhopric of Paris to a perfon as turbulent and dangerous as the future *Cardinal de Retz*.

Mazarine, who foon found means to difplace thefe firft favourites of the Regent, would not pei haps have been guilty of this fault ; but after all, the *Cardinal de Retz* made him more afraid than he did him harm : the policy of thefe two perfonages was of a very different nature ; they had, perhaps, both of them bad hearts : they were neither of them refpectable on account of their virtue and honour ; but Mazarine had his views and purfued them, his head never failed him ; if he was not very brave, he was neither rafh nor inconfiderate : if he was not a great man, he was an able and dexterous one. The *Cardinal de Retz*, was

neithei ;

neither; for a man is not great, when he has not great views; and of what use are talents and address, when a man has no determined object to pursue.

The *Abbé de Retz*, being Coadjutor of Paris, retired to Saint Lazarus, near his old master, M. Vincent. It may be conceived that the good old man gave him the best advice he was capable of: he feigned to profit by it, but this was on his part mere policy. He acknowledges in his Memoirs, that he employed the hours destined to meditation, in reflecting, not upon the manner of living like a good Bishop, but upon that of taking advantage of his character and place, and of doing evil methodically. I have known many turbulent men like him, who, when they had time on their hands, formed plans of conduct detestable in their object, but excellently combined, and very likely to succeed, if they had been followed. The Coadjutor appeared for some time to act agreeable to his plan: he preached in Paris, and put into his sermons, (as my uncle assures me,) both sense and erudition, according to the taste of the age, and even an

appearance

appearance of piety, which he learned without doubt from the good M. Vincent. The people of Paris were delighted to fee their Archbifhop in the pulpit: he affected to perform other religious duties, in difcharging the epifcopal functions of his uncle in his abfence.

Having thus prepared the way, the Co-adjutor waited only for an opportunity to break out, and to reap fome advantage from the prudence he had obferved in his conduct, and which he was incapable of continuing for a long time; but great opportunities did not offer for the fpace of four or five years: And in the mean time he had fome difputes about his rank, in quality of Diocefan of Paris: he maintained them with audacity, and proved to the Cardinal Mazaine that he was not a contemptible enemy. On the other hand, it would have coft too much to have gained him over, for it appeared that his pretenfions were nothing lefs than to fill the place of the Cardinal.

In the mean time, the great indifcretions committed by the Queen, enflamed the minds

minds of the Parifians: it was then that
the Coadjutor played his great game ; he
gained the people fecretly, by charities to
the poor, without explaining what he wanted with them.   Sometimes, he went to the
Queen, to inform her Majefty of the bad difpofition of the people ; at othertimes he told
the Parliament of thofe of the Queen and
her Minifter.   The Coadjutor manœuvred
in this manner till the famous day of the
barricades, when he fhook off all difguife.
There is nothing more curious than the details contained in his Memoirs, upon the
commencement of the war of Paris, and its
confequences.   The weaknefs of the Queen
and of thofe who were about her; the artful,
but illiberal manner of treating the Cardinal ;
the ridicule and folly of feveral Members of
Parliament, and the inconfiderate turbulence
of, the people of Paris, are therein defcribed
in the moft lively and true colours.

The Coadjutor ufed but little diffimula-
tion, in the mifchievous and foolifh part he
acted in that affair, which continued during
the years 1648 and 1649.   After a trifling
interruption, it began again in 1650, and
lafted

lafted till the year 1651; and he there appeared in it more turbulent, rafh and inconfiderate than ever. The defcription of
the ftrange fcene which paffed in the great
hall of the palace, where he was to affaffi-
nate the prince, or be affaffinated by him,
would appear to us apocryphal, if it had
not been public, and tranfmitted to pofterity
by people of all ranks, who were witneffes
of what paffed; but it will always appear
inconceivable that the principal actor fhould
relate it with a franknefs and *naiveté*, of
which we have no example.

The Coadjutor obtained in 1652, the Hat,
which conftituted the whole glory of his
life; but he would have obtained it much
fooner if his conduct had been different from
what it was. He is not the only man in
the world who has taken every imaginable
pains to deftroy a fortune which appeared
certain, and to render problematical the beft
founded hopes. If he did not lofe the Hat,
which could not well efcape him, every ftep
he took from the moment he had it, tended
to make him lofe the efteem and confideration of the public; and to deprive him of
that

that repofe which he did not enjoy again till ten years afterwards, in the moft filent retreat, and profound inaction.

I obferved at the beginning of this article, that Meffieurs Caumaitins, my relations, had had fome part in the publication of the Memoirs of the *Cardinal de Retz*; it confifted in their entrufting to fome indifcreet perfons, a copy of thefe Memoirs, which had been found in the Convent of Commercy, in Lorraine, where the Cardinal had paffed fome years, and of which he was Seigneur; not that it depended upon any of his benefices, but becaufe it was a part of the inheritance of his mother, Marguerite de Silly de la Rochepot. The good women who were in poffeffion of thefe Memoirs, did not know either the merits or demerits of them; I believe they were even ignorant of the lady to whom they were addreffed · I know no more of her than they did; but it is certain that it was in the beginning of the Regency of the Duke of Orleans, in 1717, that the firft furtive edition of thefe Memoirs appeared. The Regent afked my father, who was ftill Lieutenant of the Police, what
effect

effect he thought the book might produce:
" None that ought to make your Grace
" uneafy," anfwered M. d'Argenfon ; " the
" manner in which the Cardinal de Retz
" fpeaks of himfelf,—the frank difcovery
" of his character,—avowal of his faults,
" and the information he gives of the ill
" fuccefs of which his imprudence was the
" caufe, will encourage no one to imitate
" him : on the contrary, his misfortunes
" are a leffon to the rafh and turbulent. It
" cannot be conceived why this man has
" left his confeffion in writing ? if it has
" been printed with the hope of procuring
" him the abfolution of the public, this
" will certainly be refufed him."—My father might be right in his judgment, of
the effect which thefe Memoirs ought to
have produced, yet they had quite a contrary one.

The appearance of finceiity which runs
through this work, feduced and delighted
mens minds. Although the ftyle be neither pure nor brilliant, it was read with
pleafure and avidity ; and what is ftill more,
there were people who were fo enraptured

with

with the character of the Cardinal de Retz,
that they thought serioufly of imitating
him; and as the Cardinal had not been difgufted with the characters of the Gracchi,
of Catiline, and the Count de Fiefque, nor
with the unhappy fate which befel them;
fo his difgraces did not difcourage thofe
who were inclined to take him for a model,
although they had not perhaps his fpirit of
intrigue. Government perceived this in the
year 1718, and the Regent fpoke of it again
to my father, who was become Keeper of
the Seals; a new remedy was fought for
the bad effects which the Memoirs had produced. It was propofed to print the Memoirs
of Joly, who had been his Secretary; they
were alfo in the library of M. de Caumartin,
who made fome difficulty in giving them
up: the Cardinal is treated more feverely in
them than in his own ; but the Regent was
determined to ruin entirely the reputation
of the Cardinal de Retz, to make known
his real character, and to difguft thofe who
were difpofed to imitate him. The Memoirs of Joly did not produce this effect,
being written in a manner lefs pleafing than
thofe of the Cardinal, they brought an odium
upon

upon the author : he was looked upon as an
ungrateful and faithlefs fervant, who injur-
ed the reputation of him who had for a confiderable time given him bread: the Franknefs of the Cardinal had, on the contrary,
interefted people in his behalf; and notwithftanding every thing that was done, men of
turbulent difpofitions continued to love him,
and to imitate his conduct at the rifque of
every thing that could befall them; and no
perfon ever declared himfelf in favour of
M. Joly.

ESSAY

E S S A Y   XVIII.

HENRY OF LORRAINE's CHARACTER,
AND ATTEMPT ON THE SOVEREIGNTY
OF NAPLES.

MUCH about the time when the Cardinal de Retz was ufelefsly employed in intrigues, a confiderable perfonage of the family of Lorraine, undertook to fupport the revolt of a country to which his anceftors had really had fome pretenfions : but titles are not fufficient to pretend to great poffeffions ; force, abilities, and fortunate events, are neceffary to recover and preferve them.

Henry of Lorraine, Duke of Guife, grandfon to Henry the fiift, who was affaffinated at Blois, in 1588, full of vivacity, enterprifing but unfteady, being at Rome in 1649, heard of the Neapolitan revolt, and thought himfelf deftined to take advantage of it ; he remembered the part his anceftois had acted in France, under the reigns of

Francis

Francis I. Henry II. and thofe of the children of the laft. He imagined it would be ftill more eafy for him to fucceed in a leffer theatre: with this idea he refolved to put himfelf at the head of the Neapolitans, and eafily obtained the honour of being their commander. Until he could give them fuccours of men and money, he could not hope for the fupport of any power, except that of France, and it was rather on account of the hatred fhe bore the Spaniards, and a wifh to encreafe their difficulties, than with the idea of making him a powerful fovereign, that fhe would protect him.—— Government was not forry to keep at a diftance the man who bore the great name of Guife, which fixty years before had fhook the crown upon the head of the weak Henry III. but it was thought advifeable not to buy this abfence too dear.

The Duke of Guife was endowed with all the gifts of nature; tall and erect, his features regular, his phyfiognomy happy and graceful; theie was a noblenefs in his countenance, manner and converfation, which captivated the heart; his mind was

H 3   adorned,

adorned, if not by means of ferious ftudies, at leaft by a great deal of reading; he fpoke feveral languages in their greateft purity, efpecially the French and Italian: he was brave even to intrepidity and temerity,— knew enough of the art of war, although he had not been commander in chief,—and of politics, although he had never been charged with any important or difficult ne- gociation. He feemed born to have what was faid of his grandfather and great grand- father, applied to him : " That in a numer- " ous court where the princes of Guife ap- " peared, the reft of the nobility feemed in " comparifon to be nothing more than com- " mon people." But otherwife he had de- fects, which are but too common to thofe of his birth and rank : he thought himfelf fo deftined to great affairs, that he under- took them inconfiderately, and fupported them with more haughtinefs than care and attention : he perceived when it was too late, the faults he had committed, but he would never avow them, and ftrove rather to hide or defend, than repair them. Until he was thirty-two years of age, the time he went to Naples, love had been the misfortune of

of

of his life. His father, who had retired
into Tufcany to avoid the perfecutions of
the Cardinal de Richelieu, (who took care
not to fuffer in France, a man, whom it had
been propofed in the States General of the
League, to make a King) had made him
renounce the Archbifhopric of Rheims, to
marry in 1639, a princefs of Gonzague;
from whom he feparated two years afterwards, to marry at Bruffells the Countefs
of Boffut, widow of a Seigneur of the houfe
of Hennin.

On his return to France in 1643, after
the death of Lewis XIII. he became violent-
ly in love with Mademoifelle de Pons, who
joined to the advantages of the moft illuftrious birth, had every charm which can render a female agreeable. Knowing that he
could not tempt her otherwife than by the
offer of his hand and brilliant fortune, he
undertook to make at Rome his fecond marriage void, as he had done the firft; but he
found in this fome very great difficulties:
he brought his caufe before the Rota, the
firft tribunal of the capital of the Chriftian
World, at the time the revolt at Naples

H 4   began

began, in 1646, under the government, or
rather the tyranny of the Duke of Arcos.
This Vice-Roy had impofed burthenfome
taxes upon the articles of confumption ; the
populace undertook to get the impofts taken
off, and had at firft for its leader a man of
the loweft extraction, his name Thomas
Aniello.   As vile a chief as he was, he foon
became too confiderable to be defpifed : after
fpeaking in a haughty tone without being
attended to, he forced the palace of the
Vice-Roy, pillaged it, feized him by the
muftache, and the Duke of Arcos thought
himfelf happy in retiring to the Caftle of
Saint Elme.   It was then neceffary that
Spanifh haughtinefs fhould have recourfe to
all the artifices of Italian policy. The Vice-
Roy employed the Archbifhop and fome
Seigneurs of the country, whofe names were
dear to the Neopolitans ; but the people perceived that fome of thefe betiayed them,
and that others acted with duplicity. They
perfifted in their revolt, which became more
and more dangerous, on account of their
being more animated and miftiuftful. They
declared Mas or Thomas Aniello their chief,
and this man was for fifteen days in the
month

month of July 1647, abfolute mafter in Naples: nothing could be more ridiculous than this kind of royalty; the exterior appearance of the monarch, and that of the court, exhibited the moft ridicuous farce ; but thofe who faw it played too near, muft have trembled, of whatever defcription or party they might be, if they had any thing to lofe. The Vice-Roy was wholly intent upon deftroying Mas Aniello: he endeavoured to get him affaffinated, in which he could not at firft fucceed: it is thought that he contrived to give him a potion which had an effect upon his brain; perhaps the greatnefs of the enterprize and the uncertainty of fuccefs had this effect. However this may be, Mas Aniello, after committing great follies, was maffacred by his own fervants: the people were delighted with it the firft day, treated his body with indignity, and foon after regretted his lofs.

The Vice-Roy feeing the rebels without a commander, thought he could undertake any thing: he was guilty of new indifcretions, and the people perceived themfelves

in

in want of another chief: they appointed
one whom they took from a quite different
clafs, this was the Prince of Maffa, of the
houfe of Toralte. He had fignalifed himfelf in war; but the Court of Madrid being
jealous of his reputation and abilities, had
obliged him to live in his own country as
a fimple individual: he was now old and
much afflicted with the gout. As it was
known that he was greatly difpleafed with
the Spaniards, the people called out loudly
for him to become their general,—he accepted this delicate commiffion; but he
foon perceived that he could not well command thofe who did not know how to
obey. He obtained twice for the people conditions reafonable enough; in order that he
might have nothing more to do than to
take fuch meafures as were neceffary to
oblige the Vice-Roy to fulfill them: but the
people neglected the means of making themfelves refpected. The Prince of Maffa ftood
his ground for three months, notwithftanding all the difagreeable circumftances attached to his fituation; he wifhed that the
people and the nobility fhould be united
againft the Spaniards their common ene-

mies; but on the contrary, thefe two claffes equally difcontented, fufpected each other: finally, he thought that the beft thing he could do would be to difengage himfelf from a burthen which lay heavy upon him, and to place it upon the fhoulders of a ftranger who had neither relations nor friends in the city; and who could not be fufpected by the populace which had mutinied.

Things were in this fituation when it was learnt that the *Duke of Guife*, who was at Rome, had views upon Naples. He appeared to be the moft fit man to command a revolt, not as a fovereign, but as the protector of a rifing republic. The Duke accepted the command upon this footing, and took for his model the Count of Naffau, who, in defending the rifing republic of the United Provinces, brought things to fuch a pafs as to eftablifh and maintain it.

Whilft he was taking thefe meafures, . and writing to France to obtain fuccours from Anne of Auftria and the Cardinal Mazarine, the new republicans drew up a manifeft, begging the fupport of foreign powers;

ers ; but in a little time after, they maffacred the Prince of Maffa upon the moft falfe
and unjuft accufations.   After a fhort anarchy, the people elected for chief *Gennare*
(or Janvier) *Aunefe,* a man of low birth,
and without any other merit than that of
bravery, and a great hatred againft the
Spaniards ; befides he was ugly to a ridiculous degree, brutal, irreligious, and had
none of thofe mental qualities which make
men amiable.   Aunefe having audacioufly
poffeffed himfelf of authority, preferved it
in fpite of all murmurs and difcontent, when
the *Duke of Guife* having received anfwers
from France, dictated by the Cardinal Mazarine, and in which the Duke was amufed
with hopes, in order that he might amufe
the rebels, he refolved to fet off for Naples,
where he arrived like a true hero of knight
errantry.   He embarked without much fuite,
in a felucca, paffed undifcovered in the day
time, through the Spanifh fleet which block-
ed up the port of Naples.   But as foon as
he appeared in the city, his noble air and
manners left the Neapolitans no room to
doubt, that he was the heir of thofe princes
of the houfe of Anjou, who had reigned for

fo

fo long a time over the two Sicilies : he declared, that he returned to the inheritance
of his forefather, not to govern as a tyrant,
but to protect his people, who were become
republicans. He announced to them that a
French fleet was to fail from Toulon, to fuccour
Naples, and he was declared Generaliffimo,
even over Aunefe, though he acted conjoint-
ly with him. Thefe two perfons of fo different a turn and character acted, for fix weeks
or two months, feemingly in concert; but
it plainly appeared, that Aunefe was the man
of the people, and that the Duke was more
fit for the illuftrious and great. All his
manners were noble; he was gallant with
the women, and generous to the gentlemen
of the country : this alone, would perhaps
have ruined him.

At length the French Fleet arrived, and
appeared ready to engage that of Spain.
This circumftance encreafed the credit of
the *Duke of Guife*; they offered him the
title of King, which he refufed; but he
confented to be proclaimed Generaliffimo
and Duke of Naples, with a fovereign
power, which at firft was to continue for
feven

feven years, but was foon afterwards declared perpetual. Aunefe appeared to comply, and feemed to be no more than a private fubject, or an officer of the new fovereign. The Generaliffimo ordered money
to be coined, upon which were put his
name and arms. The moft brilliant time of
the *Duke of Guife* at Naples, was the laft
month of the year 1647, and the two firft
of 1648 ; but the French fleet foon retired,
without having come to an engagement with
the Spaniards, or having done the Neopolitans the leaft effential fervice : the French
left fome of their officers in Naples, and
things were in this fituation when the fleet
difappeared. The confidence of the Neopolitans was foon diminifhed; in vain did
the *Duke of Guife* and the French, who were
attached to him, perform prodigies of valour :
Aunefe ftrove fecretly to deftroy their reputation, in which he fucceeded. The Prince
and the ancient chief of the people foon
fought each other's life, perceiving that the
ruin of one was neceffary to the fafety of
the other. The Spaniards made offers to
the *Duke of Guife* ; but he knew they were
only feigned, and made to render him fufpected.

pected. They gained fecretly the perfidious Aunefe ; this traitor gave them poffeffion of the Tourion of the Carmes, a kind
of fortrefs, of which he was mafter ; and
whilft the *Duke of Guife* was employed in
attacking diftant pofts, Naples returned to
the dominion of Spain : this was in the
month of 1648.

Guife fupported to the laft his courage,
firmnefs and generofity : he made ufelefs
efforts to get into Naples, and was at length
taken prifoner, after having defended himfelf like a lion. The Spaniards triumphed
at his capture, and whilft they paid him the
honours due to a prifoner of the firft rank,
they deliberated in council, whether or not
they fhould take away his life. A Machiavelian politician voted for this odious refolution : but Don Juan of Auftria, and the
firft Spanifh nobility had generofity enough
to think differently : the Duke was fent
into Spain, where he remained four years a
prifoner. At the end of this period, the
Spaniards who ftrove to foment the troubles
of the Fronde, with which France was agitated, thought that the *Duke of Guife* was

an

an inftrument proper to augment the diftur-
bances in the kingdom ; and that he would
act againft France with as much audaciouf-
nefs and activity as he had done to fupport
the revolt of Naples.   They were deceived
in their opinion ; *Guife* was incapable of con-
tributing to the evils of his real country,
however difcontented he might be with Mazarine, who had fcandaloufly deceived him ;
he would not revenge himfelf by betraying
the young King, who at ten years old could
not be fufpected of having had any part in
the wrongs his minifter had done.

During the imprifonment of the *Duke of
Guife* in Spain, Mazarine made an attempt
which proved more fruitlefs than that of
Guife ; he had fent out a fleet, in which the
Prince Thomas of Savoy, whofe fon had
married the niece of the firft Minifter, had
failed.   The wifhes of this Prince were to
reign over Naples, and Mazarine was more
warm in his effoits to aid him, than he had
been to fuccour the *Duke of Guife*.   But the
man he protected had not the merit of him
whom he had abandoned, and things were
                                          not

not in fo favourable a fituation : this fecond enterpiize failed.

Guife being returned to France, propofals were made him to attempt a third expedition. Government armed at Toulon in 1654, another fleet deftined to bring about a new revolution in Naples. *Guife* did not hefitate to embark; but he was as badly feconded in this laft expedition as he had been in the firft; and it was equally unfuccefsful, although the duke took the city and the caftle of Caftellamare, of which he kept poffeffion for fome time. Difcouraged by fo many misfortunes, and difgufted with every kind of ambition, Henry of Lorraine was promoted in 1655, to the place of great Chamberlain of France; and he confined himfelf for the remainder of his life, to the peaceful functions of this great office of the crown. He performed the duties of his office at the king's marriage, and at the entry of the queen Marie Thérefe into Paris, with all the dignity, magnificence, and gracefulnefs of a defcendant of the dukes of *Guife*, in the preceding century; he commanded, or rather conducted one of

I the

the tournaments in the famous carousal of
1663; and appeared worthy to be upon a
footing with the great Condé, who immediately preceded him.*   He muſt at this
moment have recollected all the greatneſs
he enjoyed during ſome months at Naples;
but he had bid adieu to all ſerious affairs, as
well in love as in ambition; he thought no
more of Mademoiſelle de Pons; yet he
would never be reconciled to his legitimate
wife, formerly the Counteſs of Boſſut.
This lady ſurvived him; ſhe lived till the
year 1670. The duke died in 1664, at fifty
years of age without poſterity.

We have the Memoirs of the duke of
Guiſe during the revolt of Naples, written
by different hands, and with oppoſite intentions.   The two works appeared in a
ſhort time after the death of the hero. The
author

* In this magnificent Carouſal, the duke of Guiſe commanded the tournament of American ſavages , his troop was
the moſt ſingular of all, and as brilliant as any of the others.
The Duke, under the title of *King of* America, had painted
upon his eſcutcheon a Lion couchant, and at the top an
Eagle, with theſe words for device, *Altiora præſumo.* " I
" undertake the greateſt things."

author of the firſt was the Count Raymond
of Modena and Avignon, who, being attached to the duke, went with him to
Naples, where he became Major General of
his troops, and defended the city of Averſa,
between Naples and Capua, againſt the
Spaniards.   It appears that *M. de Guiſe* had
a great friendſhip for this officer, but that
towards the end of the time he ſtayed at
Naples, he had reaſon to complain of him.
Modena, apparently to juſtify himſelf, ani-
madverted freely upon ſome of the faults of
his general, and diſcovered certain defects
which the duke might have in his character.
The work of the count of Modena appeared in 1667, under the title of *Hiſtoire des
Revolutions de la Ville de Naples (en* 164-).
The following year, *Saint Yon*, an old
ſecretary of the duke's, publiſhed another
in oppoſition, under the title of *Memoires
de M. le Duc de Guiſe*.   This work is written
in the name of the prince himſelf, whether
the manuſcript may have bee.. found among
his papers, or that the Saint Yon may have
given it this turn, in order to make the
memoirs more intereſting.   He acquits the
duke of all the indiſcretions which are im-

I 2   puted

"puted to him in the preceding work, and reprefents him in the moft favourable light, yet in fuch a manner, that it appears as if the prince himfelf fpoke, and was modeft enough in giving his own eulogium. This makes thefe memoirs interefting, and marks them with the characters of truth. The memoirs written by Modena, are not fo much fo; yet who knows if it be not the latter which contain the real truth? Who can fay, which of two ocular witneffes, that have been equally in a fituation to know what paffed, and yet have given contrary teftimonies, is to be preferred? Their contradictions can only be founded upon prejudices; but who can difcover the effects of them, efpecially after fuch a length of time!

ESSAY

E S S A Y   XIX.

CARDINAL AMBOISE's MINISTERIAL
CONDUCT

ON reading the life of the *Cardinal Amboise*, I found great room for reflection upon the glory and reputation of kings and their minifters.   There are reigns which owe every thing to minifters, fuch as that of Lewis XIII. under the adminiftration of Richelieu ; and there are others wherein kings and minifters have concurred fo well together, as to make the people equally obliged to them ; fuch were the reigns of Henry IV. and Lewis XIV. It may be faid, that Sully would have done nothing fo well had he had any other mafter than Henry IV. and that Henry would not have been fo great a monarch without Sully. Thus Colbert would never have had fuch extended views, nor have executed the great things he did, if Lewis XIV. had not infpired and fupported him.   It appears to be proved by the reign of Lewis XII. that fometimes a

I 3   good

good king alone acts well, and that a minifter is no more than the executor of his wife
decrees.   Yet the minifter partakes of the
glory, merit, and wifdom of his mafter;
efpecially when the latter is prudent enough
not to be jealous of the reputation of his
minifter.

The *Cardinal Amboife*, had in my opinion,
no other virtues than thofe of his mafter;
and Lewis XII. poffeffed fuch as acquired
him the flattering title of *Father of his
people*.   George *d'Amboife* had wit, abilities
and addrefs; he ufed them principally to
make his fortune, and it was not his fault
that he did not make it ftill more confiderable than it really was; but I am of opinion,
that all the merit of the reign of Lewis XII.
is due to the monarch, and the blame to the
firft minifter.   Lewis XII. was a mild and
good man, but fearing to act according to his
own manner of thinking, he afked advice
of others; and I fufpect the *Cardinal Amboife*
of being more artful and political in his
counfels, than candid and zealous for the
real interefts of his prince and country.   In
order to be well convinced of this, it is neceffary

ceffary to examine one after another, the events of the reign of Lewis XII. it will not be very difficult to diftinguifh the intentions of the Sovereign from thofe of the *Cardinal*.

George d'Amboife, was the youngeft of nine fons which were borne to *Pierre d'Amboife*, Seigneur of *Chaumont*, firft gentleman of the bed chamber to Charles VII. and Lewis XI. All of them lived long enough to become very confiderable in the ftate. Three were the roots of as many branches; five were bifhops, and the laft was grand mafter of the order of St. John of Jerufalem. They had eight fifters, two of whom were abbeffes, and the other fix married to the greateft Seigneurs of the kingdom. *George* attached himfelf early in life to the houfe of Orleans. He had fcarcely finifhed his ftudies when he was made chaplain to Lewis XI. although he was not yet in holy orders; his youth did not prevent his being elected in 1475, *Byfhop of Montauban*. Towards the end of the reign of Lewis XI. the court being divided into factions, he joined the party of the

I 4   houfe

houfe of Orleans which he never afterwards quitted. Madame de Beaujeu, eldeft
daughter of Lewis XI. to whom this
monarch on his death bed, had confided the
care of the young king Charles VIII. and,
I may fay, the regency and government of
the kingdom, foon became acquainted with
the fentiments of the young bifhop of *Montauban*, for which fhe could not forgive him.
The prelate was juftly fufpected of being
the accomplice of fome perfons who attempted to make themfelves mafters of the
perfon of Charles; he prattled with him,
making him recite his prayers, or rather he
pretended to make him do it.   The young
monarch expreffed to him fome defire of being releafed from the power of his eldeft
fifter.   The bifhop informed the duke of
Orleans of it; the king's efcape, and confequently the difgrace of Madame de Beaujeu, were determined upon, when in the
interim, fhe was advertifed of what had paffed.   She immediately caufed the young
bifhop, who had juft been elected archbifhop of Narbonne, to be arrefted.   The
duke of Orleans would have been in the
fame fituation, had he not taken refuge in
Bretagne.

Bretagne. However, the imprifonment of *Amboife*, was not of long duration; he protefted his innocence; to piove which, he appealed to the king himfelf, who not wifhing to make aepofitions againft him, he got rid of the affair.

Lewis, Duke of Orleans, was taken prifoner at the battle of *St. Aubin*, and conducted to the great towei of *Bourges.* The archbifhop of Narbonne, conftant in his attachment to the duke, ufed every effort to procure him his libeity; and when his place of chaplain to the king was reftored to him, he had recourfe to the fame means as before. He perfuaded Charles VIII. that it was equally juft and conducive to his intereft, to pardon the firft prince of the blood, and to take him out of piifon unknown to Madame de Beaujeu. The king followed his advice, and went himfelf to open the gates of the tower of Bourges for the Duke of Orleans. This prince was not ungrateful, for he contributed to the marriage of the king, with the heirefs of Bretagne, although he was himfelf much enamoured with her, and that fhe had an
equal

equal paſſion for him.　After the marriage, Madame de Beaujeu, became Duchefs of Bourbon, quitted public affairs, and left the court.

The duke of Orleans had the government of Normandy, and ſoon afterwards found means to change *Amboife* from the archbiſhopric of Narbonne, to that of Rouen ; and declared him at the ſame time, his Lieutenant General, and Commander in Normandy. *Amboife* employed himſelf at firſt in reſtoring tranquillity to this province, which was infeſted with thieves and high-waymen; in this he feconded the intentions of the duke of Orleans ; he regulated alſo his diocefe with zeal and wifdom; but he foon thought himſelf obliged to go to Italy, upon the fervice of the duke his protector; he accompanied him into the Milanefe, and never left him during the two laſt years, 1494 and 1495, which the prince paſſed there.　The laſt year was terminated by the fiege of Novara, which Lewis XII. courageoufly fuſtained. *Amboife* gave him not only political but military advice; it is even faid, that he fought in perfon, as well as

feveral

feveral other bifhops. On his return to France, he retook the adminiftration of Normandy. It cannot be denied, that he caufed complaints and murmurs, and that he was accufed of being a tyrant ; but his prince defended him againft this accufation, which undoubtedly he thought an unjuft one, becaufe it was very far from his own way of thinking. Charles VIII. died in 1498. Lewis XII. afcended the throne, and *Amboife* was made his firft minifter, with fo much the more confidence and power, as the good king, who was willing to forget the injuries which had been done to the duke of Orleans, made it his duty to reward thofe who had ferved him. Let us examine at prefent what paffed during the firft twelve years of the new reign, and to the death of the Cardinal ; let us alfo examine the part which both the one and the other had in them.

The firft fervice which the new Cardinal did his mafter, was to diffolve his marriage with the fecond daughter of Lewis XI. and facilitate the means of his efpoufing the widow of his predeceffor. It muft be allowed,

lowed, that this fervice was great, and at once conformable to good policy, and the real inclinations of Lewis XII; but to bring it about, it was neceffary to manage the worft Pope that was ever at the head of the chuich of Rome (Alexander VI); and this was carried fo far, that the king thought himfelf obliged to receive with the gieateft honours *Cæfar Borgia*, baftard of that unworthy pontif, and to let him marry Charlotte d'Albret, one of the greateft matches in the kingdom, and to confei upon him dignities, and make him grants in France. If there were any political ieafons which authorifed this conduct in Lewis XII. they were certainly diffeient from his way of thinking; but the minifter who perfuaded him, had more confideiable perfonal interefls in view; he wifhed to form himfelf a party in the facred college, and conceived aliçady the pioject of fucceeding Alexander VI. upon the pontifical throne This ambitious idea made *Amboife* engage his mafter in the Italian expedition. Anne of Bretagne, was almoft thrown into defpair by it; but her obligations to *Ambo.fe* were too confideiable to permit her to contradict,

tradict, openly, his opinion, or to oppofe his intereft with the king.

The firft campaigns were favourable, Lewis triumphed over Ludovico Sforza; but the latter caufed foon after a revolt in Milan ; he was punifhed for this and taken prifoner, as well as his brother the Cardinal Afcanio. *Amboife* hoping to obtain voices in the next conclave, procured the liberty of his brother Cardinal; in which it cannot be denied, that he committed a great fault, as he gave a chief to the party in oppofition to France. The Cardinal was made governor of the Milanefe and he pardoned, in the king's name, the people of Milan, their revolt ; this parade was ftill neceffary to his plans of ambition. He was afterwards employed to accommodate a difference between the republics of Pifa and Florence; he gave his judgment in favour of the latter, and befieged the former in perfon.

Alexander VI. was ftill alive, but very old, and as mifchievous as ever; but *Amboife* not wifhing to lofe fight, for a long time, of the court of France, returned to it in quality of Legate, which gave him an opportunity

portunity of drawing immenfe fums from
the clergy and people, without its being
known: he poffeffed but one benefice, which
was the archbifhopric of Rouen; but he
difpofed of others in favour of his relations
and friends, and to Italian Cardinals whom
he kept in his intereft.   He determined
Lewis XII. to engage again in a war in
Italy; upon the faith of a treaty with Ferdinand of Arragon, one of the moft perfidious of princes.   This was an unfortunate war for the French; they were deceived, and could not fail of being fo, by the
king of Arragon, the pope, and his worth-
lefs fon Cæfar.   Many of the French diftinguifhed themfelves by heroic but ufelefs
actions.   It became neceffary at length to
declare war againft Ferdinand; a frefh army
was fent into Italy, and *Amboife* managed
fo well, that the pope was reftored to his
former confidence in this fecond expedition.
The Cardinal was at Rome with the French
troops when Alexander the VI. died; he
then made known the project he had formed of fucceeding him.   He entered the conclave, was deceived and duped by the Italian
cardinals.   Francis Picolomini, nephew to
                                        pope

pope Pius II. was elected under the name of Pius III. and he lived but twenty-five days. The hopes of *George d'Amboise* were perhaps renewed by this event; but they were foon deftroyed a fecond time in a more open manner.   Julian II. was elected, and the Cardinal *Amboise* ran the rifk of lofing his life. The new pope was the declared enemy of the firft minifter, as well as that of France.   The French loft once more the kingdom of Naples, and all Italy.   Borgia, whom *Amboise* thought might be of ufe to him, was taken prifoner and conducted into Spain, from whence he made his efcape. He commanded afterwards a French army againft the king of Arragon in Navarre, where he was killed, leaving no other re-putation behind him, but that of an odious and abominable heroifm, which has dif-honoured even his machiavelian panegyrift.

Amboife, forced to content himfelf with his place of firft minifter in France, engag-ed the king again in new treaties and wars, of which this monarch was the dupe. Ferdinand of Arragon, married Germaine de Foix, niece of Lewis XII. but he was

I   not

not less his enemy on account of the marriage; this alliance became another, means
which the king of Arragon acquired, of de-
cciving the king of France.

The year following, 1506, it happened
fortunately, that *Amboife* permitted a fault
to be repaired, of which he had been the
author. The king and the queen Anne had
promifed their daughter Claude in marriage
to Charles, commonly called Count of
Luxembourg, and who was afterwards
the Emperor Charles the fifth. This foreign
prince would have gained, by his intended
marriage, the dutchy of Bretagne, and pretenfions to the Milanefe. The States General were affembled, who demanded loudly
of the king that the alliance fhould not
take place, but that the princefs fhould be
married to Francis of Angoulême, prefumptive heir to the crown, who reigned
afterwards in the name of Francis I. It
may eafily be judged, that the Emperor
Maximilian was provoked at feeing fo fine
an occafion efcape; however, he diffembled,
and *Amboife*, on his part, flattering himfelf
without reafon, that he fhould regain the
pope,

pope, undoubtedly with the idea of fucceeding him, perfuaded the king to aid
Julien II. to feize upon Bologna.   Julien
was ungrateful, as might have been expected.

The Genoefe revolted againft Lewis XII.
who repaffed the mountains to fubdue them;
he treated them with that mildnefs which
was natural to his character.

In 1508, was formed the famous league
of Cambray.; a great and important nego-
ciation, of which all the honour would have
fallen upon the Cardinal of *Amboife*, if any
honour could have refulted from it ; but it
was at the fame time the moft unjuft and
ill contrived treaty that could poffibly have
been made.   It is remarkable, that in the
council where this league was determined,
upon, there was but one man who had
courage enough to fhew the injuftice of it,
and the dangerous confequences it might be
attended with ; this was Stephen Poncher,
keeper of the feals, and who died archbifhop of Lens.   His opinion made an impreffion upon the wife and judicious Lewis

K   XII.

XII; but, unfortunately for France, the Cardinal got the better of him. The king put himself at the head of his army, and gave battle at Agnadelloa, contrary to the advice of his council, and even of the cardinal. The good prince imagined that God was for him, fo much was he deceived upon the juftice of his caufe. He gained this battle, but his affairs were not benefited by it. The predictions of Stephen Poncher, were but too well verified. Julien II. leagued himself with the enemies of France, and even with the Venetians, in order to crufh the French.

In the middle of this difafter, *Amboife* conceived a new project of ambition; he refolved to depofe Julien II. and occupy his place, or at leaft be declared Patriarch and Sovereign Pontiff in France. Death put an end to his ambitious defigns; he expired at Lyons the 25th of May, 1510. Four days before he died, Lewis XII. paid him a vifit, when *Amboife*, fhedding a torrent of tears, made to the monarch a general and minifterial confeffion; he acknowledged to him, that he was going to leave a confiderable fortune, in the

acquifition

acquisition of which he had to reproach
himself with many things; he said positive-
ly that he had taken nothing from the sub-
jects of the king; but confessed that he had
for a long time past received a pension of
fifty thousand ducats from different princes
and republics of Italy; and thirty thousand
ducats from the Florentines alone. He had,
moreover, received considerable presents, and
amassed immense sums; he beseeched the
king to permit him to dispose of all he was
possessed of, and the good Lewis XII.
granted him even more than he asked.

He made use of this liberty in his last
testament, the first article of which is singular enough, and is as follows: "I bequeath
" to my nephew, George of Amboise, my
" Archbishopric of Rouen, and all my
" moveables, which are valued at two mil-
" lions of gold, together with the furni-
" ture of Gaillon, and the convenience of
" the house, such as it is. *Item*, to my
" nephew Monsieur the Grand Master,
" chief of my arms, an hundred and fifty
" thousand ducats of gold; my handsome

K 2   " cup,

" cup, valued at two thoufand crowns ;*
" one hundred pieces of gold, each of them
" worth five hundred crowns ; my gold
" plate, and five thoufand marks in filver
" plate. *Item*, all my patrimony to the
" fon of the Grand Mafter."

He left confiderable legacies to his other
nephews and fifter; t n thoufand livres to
the four mendicant orders, to fay maffes
for the iepofe of his foul; and wherewith
to marry an hundred and fifty girls, in honour of the hundred and fifty pfalms of
which the pfalter is compofed. His funeral
was the moft fumptuous which had ever
been given to any prelate; his heart was
left with the Celeftins of Lyons; and his
body cairied to Rouen, accompanied by
eleven thoufand piiefts, twelve hundred
prelates, twelve hundred gentlemen, &c.

Hiftorians add to the recital of thefe
obfequies, a great eulogium of this Cardinal
minifter: they fay, that *during his admini-*
ftration,

---

* Wheiever crowns are fpoken of in this manner, half
crowns are to be underftood.

ſtration, every kind of happineſs reigned in the ſtate ; that France was never ſo populous, fruit-ful, rich or well cultivated as under his prudent management ; ſo much ſo, that as long as he lived, war was baniſhed from the kingdom and carried on in other places. This eulogium is juſtly due to the reign of Lewis XII. but is it equally ſo to the adminiſtration of the Cardinal *Amboiſe* ? Lewis would not by any means charge his people with new impoſts, but the Cardinal made him undertake ex-penſive wais ; he propoſed to him a means milder in appearance than that of encreaſ-ing taxes, but whoſe conſequences may be ſaid to have become more pernicious; this was the ſale of offices. The chancellor Duprat, is generally accuſed of being the author of this venality: it is true that he was the firſt who regulated the ſale; but the Cardinal *Amboiſe* began to introduce it, and it was only more dangerous before it became general and regular. Its abuſes might be greater and more profitable to the miniſter who granted the perniſſion, and through whoſe hands the money paſſed.

K 3   The

The Cardinal *Amboife* ruined the Marſhall de Gié of the houſe of Rohan; and it is generally agreed, that it was purely on account of his being jealous of the favour he was in with the young Francis, heir to the crown : this kind of conduct in a courtier and miniſter, is not leſs odious on account of its being rather common. *Amboiſe* might have hoped to outlive his maſter, for he was about the ſame age; but the monarch was of a much weaker complexion. The Cardinal not having ſucceeded to the government of the church, continued to govern France. There is reaſon to believe, that under another king, he would have made a leſſer ſhew of goodneſs and virtue; but it was neceſſary to render that homage to the virtues of Lewis XII. and appear to ſecond his good intentions; they were pure in the heart and character of this father of his people, but I think them very ſuſpicious in thoſe of his favourite. One of the virtues of Lewis XII. was gratitude, and he would have been very ſorry to have been wanting in it. He had great obligations to *Amboiſe*; from hence came the repeated acts of complaiſance and deference to his advice. Lewis

was

was œconomical and exact in his affairs, and *Amboife* appeared to be the fame in order to pleafe him. Lewis XII. has been accufed of avarice, but it appears that gifts, penfions and ordinary appointments never fuffered the leaft delay during his reign. He was liberal to the Cardinal only; yet the mini-fter was adroit enough not to obtain any very remarkable favours, but made his fortune fecretly. Several minifters have been as wife, able, and referved as *Amboife*; no king was ever fo good, fo juft, and fo well dif-pofed as Lewis XII.

K 4

ESSAY

ESSAY XVII.

ON THE CHARACTER AND MEMOIRS OF SULLY.

I MAY boaſt of having made known the merit of *Sully*, to many people who did not before ſufficiently eſteem this Miniſter of Henry IV. His Memoirs have been wiitten under the title of *Economies Royales*, by four of his Secietaries, whom he had retained after his retreat, and who made a part of his numerous couit: Although theſe Memoirs contain excellent things, which make us undeiſtand how great a part *Sully* had in the glory and happineſs of the reign of Henry IV. they aie badly written, are incoherent, and chaiged with diſagreeable calculations and details. An edition in folio which is called *V. V. Verts*, is particularly eſteemed, becauſe there are in it ſome anecdotes of particular families, who deſired afterwards they might be ſuppreſſed. I engaged, at leaſt indirectly, a man of ſenſe, and who writes well, to digeſt the Memoirs of of *Sully*, and to render them more pleafant. to read.* I am perfuaded, that when this great man fhall be better known, people in general will be as enthufiaftic as I am, in their admiration of him. I am become paf-fionately fond of him; I have got his por-trait, framéd, and have placed it before my fecretáire, to have it continually before my eyes, in order to call to mind his features, principles and conduct. I approve of the noble and fimple manner in which he made his fortune, by the beft of all means: by ferving well his mafter he could not fail of pleafing him; by pleafing him he deferved to obtain confiderable gratuities, but he ne-ver fucked the blood of the people: he ne-ver received any thing from foreigners to betray his prince and country. It cannot be faid that a man who contrived to fave his king thirty-fix millions of livres out of his treafures made depredations upon the finan-ces. I even admire his retreat; it was as great and noble as the means by which he made his fortune: he had a numerous fa-mily,

---

* The Memoirs of Sully, arranged methodically, by the Abbé de C. Eclufe, appeared in three volumes in 4to. in 1747.

mily, lived in his castles like a prince, was respected by his relations, and gave subsistance to those who became old in his service. I see nothing in all this but what is highly praise worthy. It was just, that he should make a figure according to the titles he had acquired by having deserved them: he remembered the good he had done, and wished still to serve the state; but he did not wish to be harrassed with the cares of it. A Minister out of place is no longer stunned with the buzzing of flatterers, who strive to persuade him to grant unjust favours: but he judges calmly and in peace the conduct of his successors, and of the good or bad success with which their measures are attended. He is no longer before the curtain; but if he remains in his country, the theatre is not at so great a distance from him as to prevent his deciding upon the merit of the actors.

I even like the manner in which, politically speaking, *Sully* understood his religion: he was a Calvinist, and without doubt, he was so from conviction; but very far from being either a fanatic or rebel,—even after the death of Henry IV. he refused to put
himself

himself at the head of the Huguenot party,
as soon as a revolt became in queftion. It was
not required of him to facrifice his opinion
in matter of faith; and on his part, he never
made his manner of thinking a pretext to
difturb the public repofe. His firft profeffion was that of a foldier and engineer, and
the firft fciences he ftudied were thofe of
war, gunnery, and fortification. He learnt
them well, and in the exercife of them he
never loft that coolnefs and combination
which are equally neceffary in war, and in
the adminiftration of affairs. It was undoubtedly a long time before he fufpected
that he was deftined to be a Minifter of State
and Superintendant of Finances. But let
us not deceive ourfelves in thinking that po_
litical principles require much ftudy; when
a man has a turn for great affairs, he foon
furpaffes his mafters in this kind of ftudy:
moreover he obtains a perfect knowledge of
them by practice. With refpect to the adminiftration of finances, it is a matter of
calculation; it is neceffary to form a plan,
and it foon appears whether or not profit
will arife from purfuing it. A financier
muft not be daunted by the multiplicity of
branches

branches which he has to make fruitful.—
When he has found a central point, it is the
bufinefs of clerks to combine thefe proceedings with the principles of the Minifter;
but they muft be conftant and invariable,
and have been formed before he entered into
place; for it is too late to tamper when once
he is charged with the moft important adminiftration.

M. de Sully has been reproached with being too fevere; but who knows if he were
fo by character, or by a kind of neceffity,
which the conduct of his mafter Henry impofed upon him? This Prince, the beft who
ever lived, was weak, often in love, accuftomed moreover to feek expedients and refources, fuch as are found in the midft of
civil wars, and to recompenfe his partifans,
by giving them the fpoils of his enemies.
If Sully had left him to act he would have
done more harm to his affairs than his Minifter could have done good; but it was
very neceffary that Sully fhould be negative,
becaufe Henry IV. was generous, and that his
generofity ftood in need of being kept within
bounds. In matters of bounty, the King and

I   the

the Minifter fhould always underftand each other, that either one or the other may appear difficult; according to the natural order of things, the mafter fhould be fo; but when he will not, the Minifter is indifpenfably obliged to put on that character. The beft means of diminifhing the embarraffments of both, is to agree upon certain principles never to be departed from; for if once either the King or the Minifter counteract them, they will be importuned for the moft unjuft gratifications, and will make themfelves enemies by the moft reafonable refufals.

The character of *M. de Sully* was fomething like that of Cato; but we need only read his Memoirs to be perfuaded, that his Catonian firmnefs was founded upon the real interefts of the ftate, and that neither humour nor malice had any thing to do with it. It even appears that he was a man of feeling, and feveral articles in his Memoirs prove it. We have reafon to believe that his anecdotes are true, becaufe they were not contradicted by any cotemporary author; confequently we ought to believe what he fays of himfelf; part of it is as follows:

he

he believed that it was better to gain the esteem of little people, and to console them, than to be complaisant to the great: he knew that these frequently abuse the attentions which are paid them, and that the suffrages and applause of the former are the real foundation of the reputation and satisfaction of a good Minister.

He studied but very little during his military or political life: he read in his retreat, but it was not, said he, so much to store his mind as to improve his reason. He protected and rewarded men of letters, but they had very little access to him: he listened to every advice which was given him, but he looked upon no particular one as an infallible inspiration, and did not adopt it till after mature reflection How could he, who had so frequently resisted the orders of his master, submit himself blindly to those of others? He introduced the greatest order into his private affairs; he said, that the manner in which a Minister conducts his own affairs, shews how he will conduct those of his master. In fact, although a
man

man charged with the affairs of ftate may
have but little time to think of domeſtic details, he may always lay down certain principles for the government of his houfe and
private affairs, as well as for the objects
which are intereſting to the nation, and
confign the one to his ſteward as he does the
other to his fecretaries and clerks. There
are none but little minds which trouble
themfelves with minutiæ; great geniuſes
adopt juſt and clear principles, and regulate
their actions accordingly.

Nature had given *M. de Sully* an excellent
conſtitution; his vifage was majeſtic, mild
and agreeable; that feverity which appeared
in his conduct was not written in his countenance; a proof that it was not natural to
him, and that it was owing to circumſtances.
He was temperate, flept little, and endured
every kind of fatigue: the fatigues of war
had accuſtomed him to thofe of adminiſtration.

The reputation of *M. de Sully* was never,
as I have before obferved, fo great as it
deferved

deferved to be ; but it will, on this account, be more brilliant and folid, when particular and perfonal prejudices being diffipated, men fhall judge of his adminiftration by the great effects it produced.   It was under him that the finances began to be regulated, commerce extended, and population encreaf-ed.

ESSAY

ESSAY   XXI.

CHARACTER OF CARDINAL FLEURY, AND SULLY, COMPARED.

WE have at prefent a prime Minifter *M. le Cardinal de Fleury*, who poffeffes a part of the virtues of *M. de Sully*— his principal qualities appear neverthelefs to be of an inferior kind : but perhaps this difference is wholly due to their fituations and the circumftances of the times in which they lived. One was a military man, the other is an ecclefiaftic : *Sully* had feen and experienced all the miferies of a civil war; he had order and œconomy to re-eftablifh in every department ; *M. de Fleury* has only to maintain that order which is already wifely eftablifhed : finally *Sully*, met with contradictions from his mafter, and thinking himfelf obliged to refift them, he was more attentive to oppofe nothing but the public welfare to authority, which, except in this cafe, ought always to be decifive. The Cardinal meets with no oppofition, except upon

L   trifling

trifling fubjects. I am perfuaded that he
would refift ftronger ones; and it is perhaps a misfortune for him that he has not
had fuch to encounter.

Sully was the Minifter of the nation, becaufe he loved it, and faw that it ftood in
need of affiftance, and that it was neceffary
to repair its loffes, and make it enjoy happinefs under a good King. Richelieu, on the
contrary, was a brilliant Minifter, and feared by a King, whofe abfolute authority he
eftablifhed, becaufe it was confided to him
and remained in his hands. *Cardinal Fleury*
is at the fame time Minifter of the King and
of the nation, and the time will come, when
juftice will be done to him as well as to *M.
de Sully.* It is faid, that his genius is not
great, but we are in an age which does not
require a man of that defcription: he has at
leaft an amiable mind, a great knowlegc of the
world and the court, is agreeable and polite,
even gallant with decency ; nor does he act
inconfiftently with the gravity of any of the
characters with which he is invefted. His Minifterial qualities are, juftnefs of thinking,
folidity in his views and intentions, franknefs
                                    and

and fincerity to ftrangers; a policy refined enough, but not deceitful. He knows how to avoid the fnares laid for him by courtiers, without ufing perfidious and machiavelian means; he takes care to hazard no ufelefs expence, and efpecially not to lead the nation on in the purfuit of chimerical objects; he fhews much difintereftednefs and moderation in his perfonal expences; he avoids all kind of pomp, thinking it more noble to live above it; his conduct in this refpect is the fhield which he oppofes to thofe who afk him extraordinary favours, which would only ferve to feed their luxury. Finally, this Minifter feems calculated to encreafe our happinefs without changing it: this is all we can defire: for France is at prefent in a fituation to fay, *Let the Gods take nothing from me—this is all I afk.*

L 2   ESSAY

E S S A Y   XXII.

ENCOMIUM OF M DE CHAUVELIN, SUBMINISTER TO FLEURY.

THERE is at this time rifing under the eyes of the *Cardinal Fleury* a new Miniſter, whoſe merit and abilities it is not eaſy to appreciate, becauſe he does not act oftenſibly ; and whilſt in ſecret with a ſuperior, it is difficult to judge to which of the two, the ſuccefs of many affairs ought to be attributed.   At preſent, he has but the rank of what was called, under the Cardinal de Richelieu, a *Sub-miniſter* : but if he be obliged to act according to the ideas of others, or at moſt improve them, it may be imagined, that on account of his extenſive knowlege, his application to buſineſs, the manner in which he decides upon matters, the attention he pays to what is ſaid to him, and his manner of anſwering, ſhews that he will one day be a very ſuperior man, if his authority become ſo great as not to be reſtrained, except by that of the King, which has

never

never yet appeared to be very embarraffing. He has the department of foreign affairs, although he has never been employed in any embafly ; but he knows the world by means of geography and hiftory; the Courts of Europe by relations on which he can depend; and in truth, when a perfon is not profoundly ignorant, and has difcernment enough to judge of men, and to appreciate their interefts, even thofe of the day and moment, he may do without much travelling. What is a minifter of foreign affairs, who has been in all the Courts of Europe? Thofe who have been moft employed, have nothing but old memoirs of fuch courts as they have formerly been fent to. *M. de Chauvelin* is a Magiftrate and Keeper of the Seals, and as he has difcharged the functions of magiftracy in a diftinguifhed manner, he knows well the laws and rules of the Kingdom: it is in this that he is very ufeful to the Cardinal, who has never had an opportunity of ftudying them. He gives him information upon thefe objects, and who knows to what a degree he guides him in his proceedings? M. le Chancelier d'Aguefleau, although virtuous and learned, is rather obfcure, and decides

L 3 , with

with difficulty. A man in his fituation ought to determine quickly, but regularly : generally fpeaking, great magiftrates would be good minifters; they apply to bufinefs, they hear and decide, they feize the point of difficulty and that which is to fix their opinion, they underftand the principles, and know how to apply them : and has a minifter any thing more to do ?

[*Note of the Editor*—The author wrote the two preceding articles as well as all the others in 1736, but his death not happening till 1756, he had time in reading them over again, to make reflections founded upon pofterior events: they are in his manufcript upon feparate fheets, but it is not known precifely in what year he committed them to paper,—they are as follows :]

At the end of the year 1736, all the eulogiums which I had written of *M. le Cardinal de Fleury* and of *M. Chauvelin*, the hopes I had conceived of the benefit which might refult from a good underftanding between them, were proved to be juft and well-founded. I wrote, as I do at prefent, for my own amufe-

amufement, or at moft for the ufe of my
children after my death, that which I faw,
believed and thought, without prejudice,
and having no intereft to deceive any body.
The Cardinal covered himfelf with honour, by concluding a peace which procured
to the King Lorraine, a province full of
riches and refources, and which coft the
nation little or nothing to acquire: our military men had diftinguifhed themfelves ; we
had been every where fuccefsful, although
our Generals had fometimes committed great
faults. The Kingdom was not exhaufted
either of money or treafure ; France enjoyed
an interior calm and was renowned abroad ;
but the courtiers played the Keeper of the
Seals a trick, or rather the Cardinal, of
which he felt the cruel effects for the fix laft
years of his life. They perfuaded him that
the intended fucceffor to his place and authority, was tired of waiting ; that he had
an ardent defire to poffefs what he looked
upon to be his inheritance ; and was capable
of making his fituation difagreeable, in order
to oblige him to give it up fooner than he
otherwife wifhed to do. The Cardinal, who
perhaps a few days before he entered the miniftry,

niftry, had no great ambition for his place,
was ten years afterwards afraid of lofing it :
fo true it is that men foon accuftom themfelves to fovereign power.   He ftrove to difcover if what had been told him was true
and I can eafily believe that fome affirmative
proofs were given him. this was done without much difficulty ; but he forgot that he
was eighty years of age, that an affiftant became daily more neceffary to him ; and that
without fome fuch aid, he muft neceffarily
be the tool of intrigue ; that even in the
courfe of ordinary affairs he would have nobody to point him out expedients, and whom
he would be able to make what is called a
right hand man.   He thought he revenged
himfelf upon a traitor, and he ruined a man
who was neceffary to him : he took extraordinary meafures which proved his credit
with the King, of which nobody had the
leaft doubt.   His Majefty had never had a
fingle converfation in private with *M. de
Chauvelin*, his manner was difpleafing to
him ; but the courtiers more artful than
the firft Minifter, faw that as the Cardinal
could on one hand obtain every thing of the
King, they fhould afterwards be able to obtain

tain whatever they pleafed of the Minifter; even things the moft contrary to the principles and welfare of the ftate.

The Emperor Charles VI. had acted in favour of France, with no other idea than that of engaging her to become guarantee of his pragmatic fanction, or the act which was to infure the fucceffion of his ftates to his eldeft daughter. The Cardinal had promifed him this, and the reputation which the Cardinal had till then enjoyed, of being virtuous and fincere, made the Emperor eafy upon the effect of that promife; therefore, Charles VI. died in 1740, in the pleafing perfuafion that his daughter and his fon-in-law would inherit his crowns; and that if any power fhould difturb them in their poffeffions, France would fly to their affiftance. The Queen of Spain was the only difcontented perfon, becaufe fhe had no eftablifhment in Italy for her fecond fon: however unjuft this pretenfion might be, it would have been poffible to fatisfy her, without undertaking to deftroy the new Houfe of Auftria. But the man who, like a wife and great politician would have been able to make,

make this arrangement was in exile at Bourges. More dangerous and lefs delicate negociators, or rather intriguers, deranged the head of the firft Miniftcr, who was eighty-fix years of age, and the deftruction of the Houfe of Auftria was refolved upon : he was taught to look upon this as a thing fo eafy of execution, that he would have reproached himfelf feverely, if he had let flip fo favourable an opportunity of effacing even the remembrance of Charles Vth's pretenfions to univerfal monarchy. The poor Cardinal was fo convinced of the truth of what was propofed to him, that his only objection was the great expence France would be put to by the enterprize : he feared, leaft it fhould exhauft her treafures, and overturn his fyftem of œconomy. He was given to underftand, that France had only to fhew herfelf, or that at moft, it could only coft her a few men and a little money : he fuffered himfelf to be prevailed upon ;—he gave more than he was willing to do, but much lefs than was neceffary. He died difgraced in the eyes of all Europe, betrayed by one part of his allies, and detefted by the other, having neglected to conciliate himfelf the friendſhip of thoſe whom he ought by all means to have made ſure of, ſuch as the King of Sardinia, &c. He left France in the greateſt diſtreſs, engaged in a naval war, without his having taken meaſures either to prevent it or carry it on. Solon ſaid to Crœſus, that no man could be called happy before his death ; and may not it equally be ſaid, that a Miniſter is never certain of being to the end of his life, a wiſe, virtuous and able politician.

ESSAY

E S S A Y XXII.

ON BENEFICENCE.

MY good friend the Abbey de St. Pierre, who has laid fo many plans for the good of the public, has never had the fatiffaction of even feeing one of them fucceed. His fuccefles are confined to eftablifhing the reputation of a fingle word, which is *beneficence*. But is this word as generally underftood, as it has been enthufiaftically adopted? No: every one interprets and practifes this virtue according to his own manner. Upon the whole, beneficence implies as much as charity; but this old devout expreffion, with which our pulpits ring, appears no longer proper for our men of the world, who pretend to have no farther need of thinking of God to do good actions. Let us not difturb thefe gentlemen in their fyftem of beneficence; if they be really defirous of following it, let them fatisfy themfelves.

felves. I remember to have heard a very fevere devotee complain to a Jefuit, a man of great fenfe, that her daughter in-law, was humane and geneious, but had no merit, as fhe faid, in her good actions, becaufe fhe did not do them in the fight of God. *Let her alone, Madam,—let her alone,* faid the cunning Jefuit, *fhe will gain Paradife without fufpecting it.*

Well, let us be beneficent, fince we blufh to be charitable; but let us beware of deceiving ourfelves in the manner of exercifing our beneficence; let us regulate it according to time, place and circumftances. There are acts of beneficence adapted to every fituation : that of kings, refembles the beneficence of particulars in the principle only; but it is much more extenfive in its effects. The individual does fervices to men one by one ; the monarch, by a ftroke of his pen, makes thoufands happy. People in place may do good in proportion, each according to his ftation. In the firft moments, we ought only to confider the degree of fufferings and mifery, or the danger of him whom we wifh to fuccour.

But

But except in unforeseen cafes, it is neceffary to be more circumfpect. There are
fervices which a man might render, thinking himfelf difpofed to do fo by beneficence,
and which might be mifunderftood ; fuch
are thofe which would do more harm to
others, than good to thofe he wifhed to
oblige. The conclufion is ; that it is not
fufficient to defire to be beneficent, it is
equally neceffary to know how to be fo.

ESSAY

E S S A Y   XXIV.

ON SELF-LOVE.

SELF-Love is not generally to be blamed; in the firſt place to condemn it, would be ineffectual, ſince we cannot entirely diveſt ourſelves of it.   It is neceſſary that a man ſhould love himſelf, but, as one of my friends, a man of great ſenſe, ſaid, in every thing which is good and honourable, as he loves a virtuous woman whom he wiſhes to marry, and not as an unhappy wretch whom he ſtrives to debauch.

ESSAY

ESSAY XXV.

IDEAS OF HAPPINESS VARIOUS AMONGST PHILOSOPHERS.

THE end of philofophy has ever been to make men happy; but the different fects of philofopheis have fought this end by different ways. The Stoics pretended, that the only means of finding it was to refift every evil, to become infenfible of mifery, pain, chagrin and inquietude. They might be right; in fact, when we are free from all evil, hapinefs comes of itfelf; but how great is the difficulty of being thus exempt, efpecially when we do not think of preventing mifery, but wait its arrival with unconcern and a ftoic firmnefs. The Epicureans, on the contrary, fought happinefs and even pleafures; but perhaps the more pleafure is fought after, the lefs it is found. Let us be of neither one fect or the other, but wifely put away from ourfelves, that which may become prejudicial; let us pave the way to happinefs and to foft and peace-

ful

ful pleafures in which it really confifts; but do not let us be anxious to call for it, neither fatigue ourfelves by running after riches and voluptuoufnefs ; thefe are like birds which only require their nefts to be prepared, and which come of themfelves to depofe their eggs in them.

To increafe the happinefs of thofe who are about us, appears to me an excellent means of prolonging our own.

M   ESSAY

E S S A Y   XXVI.

ON THE DOCTRINE OF CHANCES APPLIED TO LIFE

THE Englifh are known to be great cal-
culators, great bettors, and to wifh to
reduce every thing to analyfis and probability. We have already tranflated into
French their calculations upon the probabi-
lities of the duration of human life, the
analyfis of all the games of chance, and
rules for gaining at them, as well as in
lotteries, in fpite of the decrees of fate.
One of my friends, who has been fometime in England, has carried this fpirit of
calculation ftill farther than even the Englifh ; he makes a problem of every thing to
have the pleafure of refolving it ; he meafures the extent of his pleafures, his pains,
his friendfhip, and his hatred. With refpect to love, he agrees that, when it is
real, it is commenfurable. Not content
to

to have found out new rules for games of chance, he has undertaken to calculate how much is to be afcribed to hazard, and how much to the fkill of the player in games of commerce, efpecially at * tiictrac and piquet. After having amufed myfelf with his re-fearches upon this fubject, which he be-lieves to be an important one, I afked him if he could alfo calculate what part foitune had in the life of men who had made moft noife in the world, confidering on one hand the fituations they were in, and on the other their perfonal merit. The fame principles may be applied to them, faid he, as to playeis at piquet. This idea made me finile; I amufed myfelf with it for fome time as we continued our walk, (for we were in the country) ; and we brought upon the carpet feveral perfons with whom we weie both acquainted. On our return to the city, I committed to paper a part of what had been advanced in this fingular converfation, and which is as follow :

The

* Something like Backgammon.

The fum played for, fignifies nothing to the fkill of the player, nor to the chances which may derange all his meafures; it is fufficient that he be interefted in the game, fo as to give it his whole attention. In like manner thofe to whom nature has given the greateft talents, employ them in places where they firft drew breath, conformable to their fituation and the circumftances they have to encounter. All the ability of a village parfon, who plays ever fo well at piquet, gains him nothing more than a few crowns at the end of the year, even with the affiftance of aces; whilft he who plays againft rich financers with the fame fuperiority, fometimes encreafes his income fome thoufand guineas. The fimple monk, born with a great difpofition to intrigue, difcards his rival, parries the ftrokes of his adverfaries, does nothing without reflection, and at length fucceeds; and to what? to become fuperior, and govern a community, or at moft a province of monks. It is by the fame means that a courtier becomes a favourite, a prime minifter, and governs defpotically a great empire. The republican

who

who wifhes to rife above equality, and become mafter of his countrymen, follows
the fame route. Wherever ambition, intereft, or gallantry is concerned, it is only
neceffàry to be prudent, like as at play, not
to fuffer the head to turn, and to make a
proper ufe of all the advantages which fortune prefents to us. But as it is remarked,
that there are players at piquet, whofe chief
excellence is to difcard well, others whofe
fuperiority confifts in playing the cards, and
fome who are wholly attached to betting,
knowing the gain this produces at the end
of the *partie*; fo there are men of ambition
whofe only care is to remove all obftacles
to obtain their end; others, wherever they
may be placed, ftrive to take advantage of
their fituation, and finally, fome who wifh
to confolidate their fortunes, and infure
their reputations, perfuaded that they have
done nothing well if they do not crown
their actions by fomething brilliant.

After all, many games are won contrary
to every rule, and others loft, notwithftanding all the art of the moft fkilful players;

M 3   in

in the fame manner there are events which difconcert the greateft connoiffeurs; but thefe are real phenomenons, and notwithftanding fuch extraordinary inftances, it is neceffary to follow thofe principles of conduct which are generally received and approved of.

ESSAY

ESSAY XXVII.

CARDINAL ALBERONI'S ORIGIN AND CHARACTER.

THE Cardinal *Alberoni*, is one of thofe phenomenons of which I have juft fpoken,
and may be compared to the great player,
M. Wall, whom we know at prefent in
Paris, and who has made his fortune, as it
is reported, with an orange which was
given to him ; he played it againft a crown,
hazarded the crown againft others, and
gained infenfibly a confiderable fum. By
hazarding fortunately he has realifed feveral
millions of livres. *Alberoni* ftaked lefs and
gained more ; at leaft in dignities and reputation. He was the fon of a gardener, and at
firft a ringer in the cathedral of Plaifance.
The bifhop took a liking to him, and finding him active and intelligent, made him
his fecretary, and gave him a canonry. He
had occafion to know the duke of Vendôme
in Parma, and he pleafed him by mean-

M 4 neffes

neffes of which an Italian prieft alone is capable; the duke attached him to his fervice, brought him to France, and took him afterwards into Spain. Vendôme wanting a faithful and difcreet agent near the Princefs des Urfins, fent her *Alberoni*. This Italian, as pliant in appearance as audacious in reality, perfuaded the princefs, who governed Philip V. in the moft abfolute manner, during the time that this monarch was a widower, that fhe ought to make him marry the Princefs of Parma. This marriage was accomplifhed, and the difgrace of the Princefs des Urfins was the confequence. *Alberoni* took upon himfelf to lead the new queen. She procured him the cardinal's hat; he became her firft minifter, and confequently that of the king her hufband. He difplayed immediately the whole extent of his views, both in Spain and elfewhere; he re-eftablifhed the king's authority in the Government, and made ufe of it to correct many abufes, and to begin feveral important eftablifhments which deferved to be encouraged. The population and commerce of Spain were interefted in them. He made a military reformation, and put the army

upon

upon a more ufeful and regular footing.
He had never been more than fecretary to a
general, but had feen enough of armies, to
judge of what was neceffary to eftablifh in
them order and difcipline; this is what a
minifter ought to attend to.   His duty is to
fee that troops are well regulated, and in a
good ftate, before the general who is to command is charged with them.   *Alberoni* employed himfelf fuccefsfully alfo in the adminiftration and   regulation of   finances.
This interior arrangement was neceffary to
prepare for the execution of the great views
which he had abroad.   Thefe were no lefs
than to make Spain the arbitrefs of Europe,
to infure her Italy, and to give employment
enough to the Emperor, to England and
Holland, (which were then called maritime
powers) to prevent them from oppofing his
defigns.   For this purpofe, he formed alliances in the north, and even one with
the Turks.   It unfortunately happened,
that particular circumftances made France
an enemy to the Duke of Orleans who was
regent.   He carried on with ability,
audacious intrigues to infure Philip V.
the crown of France in cafe that the
                                    young

young King Lewis XV. fhould die. But
with whatever prudence fo many great
enterprizes were formed and carried on,
fome of them croffed each other in fuch a
manner, as to make it impoffible that they
fhould all fucceed.   Peace was made between
France and Spain, and *Alberoni* fell a victim
to it.   He fupported the difgrace and perfecution, which were its firft confequences,
like a great man : in fact he was one.   He
faw that he was a victim from circumftances, and not on account of any fault he
had committed.   His defire had been like
that of Richelieu, to ferve his mafter ; but
time, place, and even his mafter were
very different.

Alberoni, at length enjoying tranquillity
in Rome, obtained the legation of Romagna,
and diftinguifhed himfelf again by undertaking a conqueft for the Pope as Temporal
Sovereign ; this was the little Republic of
St. Marino, a village fituated near Rimini,
upon an eminence.   The enterprize had all
the appearance of a parody of the heroic
comedies which *Alberoni* had performed in
Spain, twenty years before.   At leaft this

I   com-

comparifon ought to be applied to him, drawn from piquet players,—that a ruined gamefter, although able, conducts himfelf in the fame manner when playing at fixpence a fifh, as he formerly did when playing for guineas a point.

Since it is agreed, that all the books we have printed under the title of *Teftamens politiques*, are nothing but hiftorical romances, there could not be a better, than the political Teftament of *Alberoni*.*

* Note of the Editor. It has been fince publifhed and is tolerably well written.

ESSAY

E S S A Y   XXVIII.

CHARACTER OF THE PRINCE OF CONDÉ.

THE great *Condé* was born with fo ftrong
a military genius, that, by a foit of
natural impulfe, I will fay almoft in-
ftinct, he chofe the beft pofts, ranged his
troops in the moft advantageous manner,
fupported the different bodies of his army
by each other, made them attack with
vigour, fought courageoufly at their head,
never loft his compofure even in the heat of
battle, faw every thing which happened,
and took advantage of every incident in fuch
a manner as not to let the leaft favourable
one efcape him.   This hero in war was but
a very middling politician at court.   He
knew not how to act opportunely.   The
honour he had acquired gave him at firft
fome weight ; but his capacity being tried
in councils and intrigues, he was found inferior to his reputation.   He was incapable
of application and reflection ; he committed imprudences, had feveral weakneffes,
                                        and

and was even frequently guilty of injuftice. War had hardened his heart, and he began rather late to cultivate his mind. If the advantages of birth had not given him the command of armies, whilft he was yet in the flower of his age; if the time in which he lived had not been full of troubles and continual wars, but pacific like our own, his military talents would have been loft, and *M. le Prince de Condé*, would never have borne the furname of Great.

Condé, being made a tool of by the Cardinal Mazarine and the Spaniards, into whofe ftates he had been obliged to retire, returned to France after the peace of the Pyrenees: he found himfelf as great a warriour as ever, and it appeared that he had loft none of his military merit. He beat at Senef, the fame enemies of France, at the head of which he had fought Turenne, at the battle of Dunes; this proves more ftrongly, that he was born with thofe talents which make great generals, and not with fuch as would be ufeful to kings in their councils, and are neceffary to minifters.

2   ESSAY

ESSAY   XXIX.

CHARACTER OF MARSHAL TURENNE.

M. *De Turenne,* of a lefs illuftrious birth, and whofe reputation in war was not fo brilliant as that of the Prince of *Condé,* had, perhaps upon the whole, as much military merit. He placed it in the moft advantageous point of view, becaufe his talents were diftinguifhed and procured him employment. He had, perhaps, others which his extreme modefty and referved character hindered him from making known ; he was thought capable of being at the head of a party becaufe he refufed it. But if his military fuperiority was balanced by that of *M. de Condé,* the qualities of his mind were always looked upon to be fuperior to thofe of his rival. He was as compofed in the cabinet as in the field, and this hero in war was a mild and amiable individual in fociety. He did not become a Catholic till

it

it was too late to fufpect his change of
religion, to proceed from motives of ambition or intereft.   His death was equally
regretted by the foldiers and people; an
eulogium which no General had merited
fince the glorious ages of the Roman Republic and Empire.

ESSAY

ESSAY XXX.

CHARACTER AND MILITARY SERVICES
OF THE DUKE OF VENDOME.

THE *Duke of Vendome* was born, like the Great Condé, infpired with the fcience of war: he had the fame courage, the fame coolnefs in the midft of the greateft dangers, the fame juft and rapid *coup-d'œil*; but thefe advantages were counterbalanced by great defects. I have never feen him perfonally, but I have had occafion to fpeak of him to fo many military men who had ferved under his command, that I am not deceived in what I have juft faid of him.

After having ferved as a volunteer under the Great Condé, as Colonel and a General officer under Marfhal Luxembourg, the command of the army was given to him at the beginning of the war for the Spanifh fucceffion. He was fent into Italy in 1702, and during three or four of the firft campaigns, he fupported the honour of the

King's

King's arms, and gained four battles, two
of them before the defection of the Duke
of Savoy, and two afterwards; yet he had
to do with the famous Prince Eugene, who
underſtood the art of war better than any
man of the age in which he lived; provided in the beſt manner for every thing which
could happen, knew better than any body
how to ſubſiſt an army; and conducted it
with wiſdom, coolneſs, and reflection, into
ſuch ſituations as were capable of rendering
it the moſt uſeful. *M. de Vendome* was not
ſo profound in his deſigns, made fewer reflections and combinations in preparing for
his operations: he was too neglectful of detail; but in critical and deciſive moments,
he awoke, as it were from a trance; ſeemed
to recall his whole genius; took meaſures
equally wiſe and vigorous; and ſhewed more
heroiſm and judgment than even the Prince
Eugene would perhaps have done in a ſimi-
lar ſituation. The French ſoldiers, whom he
did not ſubject to too ſevere a diſcipline, had
ſo much confidence in his meaſures, that they
would have riſked every thing to have with-
drawn him from any diſagreeable ſituation
into which he might have fallen. They fear-

N   ed

ed nothing when they faw him at their head; and were perfuaded that to go into battle under his command was to be led on to glory. It is generally believed, that a perfidious policy recalled him from Piedmont, and fent him into Flanders; and that when there he had not time enough to repair the faults which the Marfhall Villeroy had committed. He was afterwards fent into Spain, without any body to fecond him, without an army or any kind of fuccour; but his name and reputation, added to the former confidence of the French who had ferved under him fome years before, made up every deficiency: he reconducted Philip V. almoft driven from his poffeffions, to Madrid; purfued the enemies, forced them to evacuate Spain, and retire into Portugal. This was the fruit of the famous battle of Villa Viciofa, in 1710. Covered with glory, (which feemed to feek him rather than he to run after it) with honours, which he thought himfelf, as he really was, fuperior to, and with riches which he neglected and defpifed, he died at Vinaros in Catalonia, of an indigeftion, a kind of death which appears little worthy of one of the greateft and moft

able

able Generals of the age, but which anfwered otherwife well enough to his private life; for it muft be agreed that this made a great contraft with his military one. His character was mild and beneficent; he was a ftranger to envy, hatred and revenge; he prided himfelf in thus refembling Henry IV. he was neither haughty, vain nor oftentatious; and fully perfuaded that nobody could have a defire to be wanting in refpect to him : effectively, he never had reafon to think to the contrary. The princes of the blood only could difpute with him in France the fuperiority of rank, and he never had the leaft difference about it but with them; and even thefe, were always terminated in the moft honourable and becoming manner.

Such was the *Duke of Vendome*, confidered in the moft favourable light. Let us at prefent examine what he was, according to other Memoirs, perhaps as faithful, in a lefs advantageous point of view. He was of a middling fize, and had a vigorous conftitution ; his figure and air were noble, his look and converfation graceful : he had great na-

N 2 tural

tural fen'e, which was but little cultivated ;
he was even profoundly ignorant in the art
of war, which he had never ftudied or reflected upon; brave even to intrepidity, daring when he could get the better of his indolence ; he was generally fuccefsful by
what may be called an effect of his happy
ftar ; he knew as much of the world and
the court as he did of war, and in the fame
manner, by routine, and without any regular
principles ; notwithftanding this, he pleafed
every body, though he was no courtier, except to the King alone ; and he made all the
reft perceive that he was the fon of Henry
IV. and that he ought not to cede, except to
the legitimate defcendants of that monarch.
This kind of vanity pleafed Lewis XIV.
who having, like his grandfather, natural
children, wifhed to make them equal to
the princes of the blood.   The *Duke of Vendome* was not exceffively polite, and was referved with thofe whom he thought capable
of oppofing him ; but he affected to be familiar and popular with the loweft rank of
officers, with the foldiers, and thofe of his
fervants, whom he believed incapable of
abufing his goodnefs.   Obftinate and inac-
ceffible

ceffible to the counfels and reprefentations
of thofe who would have been attended
to by any other man; he fuffered himfelf
to be governed by fuch only as were extravagant in their praifes of him, and in their
admiration and refpect for his perfon and
qualities. As foon as it was perceived in
the army that this was the means to obtain
his confidence, there were found in the
moft diftinguifhed military rank, men bafe
enough to flatter his weakneffes, in hopes
that he would put them in a fituation to
make their fortunes. He carried, particularly in the decline of life, libertinifm, flovenlinefs and indolence to fo great an excefs,
that it is inconceivable thefe defects were
not more prejudicial to him. In the midft
of the court of Lewis XIV. fometimes gallant, fometimes a devotee, he made no fecret
of his moft indecent and culpable pleafures;
and Lewis XIV. dared not reproach him
upon a kind of debauch, which, during the
whole time of his reign, would have ruined
any other fubject. Every thing, which the
courts of Verfailles would have blufhed at,
was openly braved in the little court of Anet.
Thofe who ferved under him in his Italian

N 3 cam-

campaign have affured me, that he had by
mere indolence miffed more than twenty
times the fineft opportunities of beating the
enemy; and that he had by negligence as
frequently expofed his army to be deftroyed : but happily thofe who commanded the
wings and in the rear, were more attentive
and vigilant.

Every body has heard talk of the cool of
the morning of *M. de Vendome,* an expreffion which is ftill made ufe of to defcribe a
march made in the heat of the day : this
comes from the cuftom *M. de Vendome* had,
of announcing in the evening, that he
would march very early the next morning ;
but when the moment indicated for departure arrived, he lay fo long in bed, that it
was generally noon before he was in motion ; the warmeft climates and feafons
made no difference in this refpect.

The greateft advantage he had over Prince
Eugene, was in defeating his calculations,
by making none himfelf. As he never
took his departure from any place at the
time he had previoufly fixed upon, no fpy
could

could give intelligence of his motions. He held no councils with his general officers, fo that no body ever knew what he meaned to do; he began a campaign without any fettled plan, and gave himfelf but little trouble about thofe fent him by the court; therefore his defigns might well be faid to be impenetrable. His audacity and penetration in great operations repaired all his faults. It was only in the campaign he made in Flanders in 1708, where he had under his command, the Duke of Burgundy, prefumptive heir to the crown, that his obftinacy in not taking every poffible advantage, made him lofe a battle, and all the fruit of a campaign which might have been happily terminated. The French army was encamped near Oudenarde; it was eafy to take poffeffion of that place, which was badly fortified, and to cut off all fupplies from the enemy; but to effect this, it was neceffary to anticipate them, before they could perceive it was poffible to diftrefs them. *M. de Vendome*, was frequently advertifed of this, but as it did not come from thofe, who by their meannefs had gained his

N 4 con-

confidence, he took no notice of what was said to him upon the subject.

Marlborough, who commanded the enemies army, soon saw that *M. de Vendome* had only his motion to make, and that it was necessary to oppose him. But he could not approach Oudenarde, without making a considerable circuit, and he might arrive there too late for his purpose: the Duke of Burgundy went himself to prevail upon *M. de Vendome* to act without delay; he could not make him shake off his indolence, nor persuade him to quit the place he was in. Finally, M. de Biron, Lieutenant General, who commanded a *corps de reserve*, sent word, that the enemy approached and went himself to confirm this advice. *M. de Vendome* refused obstinately for some time to believe it: at length M. de Biron ran to to his corps, and put himself in the best possible posture of defence. The general had permitted him to do this upon condition only, that the enemy was near charging. The order was imprudent enough, but Biron was obliged to execute it; for the engagement began immediately between his advanced

advanced pofts and the enemy, which came to reconnoitre them. Marlborough reinforced thofe who had begun the attack, and Biron did the fame to his advanced pofts. It became neceffary for *M. de Vendome* to march, and it was in this manner that the battle of Oudenarde began. Notwithftanding the valour of the French troops, the efforts of the king's guards, and the perfonal bravery of the duke of Burgundy, the ground not being favourable, becaufe it had not been chofen, neither were the manœuvres prepared, the fuccefs was not advantageous to us. Some troops were neceffarily facrificed to favour the retreat of the army, which was made to Ghent. The duke of Burgundy did not remain in that city, but retired with the head of the army, behind the canal of Bruges. *M. de Vendome* on the contrary, ftopped at Ghent to repofe himfelf after the fatigues of a day, whereon he had given greater proofs of bravery, than of judgment. As foon as the duke of Burgundy was fixed in his general quarters, he wrote to the king, informing his Majefty of what had paffed; but he was delicate in what he faid about the duke of *Vendome*, know-

knowing that the king loved him ; *M. de Vendome* wrote alfo, and affured the king that he had gained the battle, and that if his fuccefs had not been complete, it was not his fault. Lewis XIV. was pleafed to believe him, although France and all Europe were informed to the contrary. *M. de Vendome*, did not lofe the favour of his mafter which he ought to have done ; on the contrary, the king believed that the duke of Burgundy would never make a good officer, and that it was ufelefs to continue to fend him to the army. If he judged by what paffed before, and at the battle of Oudenarde, this great monarch was deceived. The fiege of Lillo, which the enemies undertook the following year, proved clearly what was the confequence of the lofs of that battle : neverthelefs, *M. de Vendome* was fent the next year to fave Spain ; and whofe prefence alone procured an army, which regained Philip V. his capital, beat the enemy at Villa Viciofa, and gave the young king the moft magnificent bed which was ever prepared for a fovereign, being compofed of the enfigns of his enemies ; but it was only neceffary to excite the enthufiafm

thufiafm of the Spaniards and of the French who were in Spain. The name of *Vendome* had this effect. His reputation, juftly or unjuftly merited, frightened Staremberg and Stanhope, and his daring character and determined bravery did the reft. Yet his end, which is fo brilliant in hiftory, was melancholy and unhappy. After having paffed the year 1711, in triumphing over the enemies of Philip V. he had no fooner received at Madrid all the honours which this king could confer upon his liberator,—the title of Highnefs,—the pre-eminence over all the Grandees of Spain,—in fhort, all the diftinctions formerly enjoyed by the famous Don Juan of Auftria, than he grew tired of this Spanifh greatnefs; and leaving the court of Madrid, and the conduct of the army to his Lieutenant Generals, he retired to a burgh of Catalonia, called Vinaros; furrounded there by a fmall circle of flatterers and *debauchees*, he gave himfelf up to that kind of voluptuoufnefs which was fo agreeable to him. He glutted himfelf with fifh, which he was extravagantly fond of; whether it were good or bad, well or ill dreffed, it was the fame thing to him; he he drank thick bodied and heady wine; and at length brought on a kind of indigeſtion, or rather an illneſs, the conſequence of repeated indigeſtions, which might undoubtedly have been cured by diet and exerciſe. His diſorder was treated in quite a contrary manner; and he had very ſoon no hopes left of being reſtored. The moſt honeſt of his Courtiers then abandoned him; others took his furniture and equipage; and it is aſſerted, that ſeeing a few moments before he expired, ſome of his under Valets ready to take away and divide his bed cloaths, he aſked them as a favour to permit him to draw his laſt breath in his bed.——He was only fifty-eight years of age when he died. The Princeſs des Uiſins, who had at that time the greateſt influence with the king of Spain, got orders for his body to be laid in the Royal Tomb of the Eſcurial. The moſt elegant funeral orations were delivered in honour of him, both in France and Spain. Theſe have ſerved to deceive poſteiity with reſpect to his real character; and no hiſtorian whom I have heard of, has yet given himſelf the trouble to undeceive it.

I have

I have heard feveial anecdotes, related by perfons who lived with *M. de Vendome,* of his cynical flovenlinefs, and which are of fo fingular a nature, that I would mention them if they were not more difgufting than ridiculous. It was by applauding his filthinefs, that the Cardinal *Alberoni* made his fortune : fo true it is that men fucceed in this by every kind of means, and the Italian priefts and monks are not fcrupulous about any.

The duke of *Vendome* had a younger brother, who pofleffed all his good qualities and his defects, but in a lefs proportion. On this account he has acquired lefs honour, and his memoiy will be lefs revered by pofterity. But M. le grand Prior of *Vendome,* was fufferable in the world and in private fociety ; he was even looked upon, towards the end of his life, as an amiable voluptuary; and he died at the age of feventy-two years, beloved and regretted by men of fenfe, who were fond of his company, and pleafed with the friendly reception they ufually met with from him in his houfe. I have frequently feen him at the

the temple; fome of my friends were intimately acquainted with him, and I know others of his affociates who are of the moft refpectable characters: on the contrary, if the duke of *Vendome* had lived to a greater age, and had peace been made, his talents, or rather his good fortune in war, would have become ufelefs to the ftate; his debauched and difgufting manner of living, would at length have rendered him contemptible in the eyes of every honeft man; and as great as he was by birth and military renown, no body would have affociated with him.

The grand Prior ferved in Candia againft the Turks, with his uncle the duke of Beaufort, fo much known at the time of the Fronde, and who terminated by that expedition his tempeftuous life. It was a fine aprenticefhip for a knight of Malta. This campaign faved him one caravan: he was ftill young when he made it, but feventeen years of age; and foon after his return to France, he followed Lewis XIV. to the conqueft of Holland; and diftinguifhed himfelf at the paffage of the Rhine, and in the

campaigns

campaigns of the two following wars, one of which was terminated by the peace of Nimeguen, and the other by that of Ryfwick. He was wounded at the battle of Marfeilles, and made Lieutenant General in 1693. He ferved with his brother, and fometimes under him, but never after the year 1705. He fhewed the fame bravery as his elder brother,—the fame military talents; perhaps they were greater, becaufe he was lefs opinionated and indolent. He was not commander in chief, confequently the fucceffes of his brother did not contribute to his reputation: but who knows what part he had in thefe, and that if his advice had been followed, the duke of *Vendome* would not have gained more honour? The libertinifm of the grand Prior, was not lefs exceffive than that of the duke, although it was in certain refpects, more decent. His pleafures kept him from his duty, and from being at the battle of Caffano in 1705. He was difgraced on account of his neglect; after which he retired to Rome, and fpent fome years in travelling in Italy. The king was determined to deprive him of his benefices, but he refigned them to fave appearances,

pearances, and a penſion was granted him. Having unhappily been made priſoner by the Imperialiſts, in croſſing the country of the Griſons, he could not return to France before 1712, the ſame year in which his brother died in Spain. It is poſſible that the fault he had committed ſix or ſeven years before, might have ſpared him a great deal of mortification and embarraſſment; at leaſt he was not a witneſs to the campaign of 1708, wherein his brother behaved ſo ill, nor to his miſerable death at Vinaros. He ſurvived him fifteen years, and was the laſt of the houſe of *Vendome*; but he had received the order of Malta. His brother married a Princeſs of Condé; but not being dazzled with the honour of this alliance, he took no means to give nephews to the great Condé, nor to perpetuate the illegitimate race of Henry IV. The grand Prior, for his part, thought of nothing but enjoying, like a true epicurean, the encreaſe of his fortune. Nevertheleſs he made in 1715, once more, a truce with his pleaſures, to fly to ſuccour Malta, which was threatened with an invaſion by the Turks; he was declared Generaliſſimo of the forces of his order.

order. This is the only time he had fuch a
title, and that he was commander in chief.
Malta was not befieged, and the grand
Prior returned to his delicious retreat of the
temple, when he died in 1717. He had,
like his brother, good natural fenfe, and
few advantages of education ; but he made
a better ufe of his wit than the duke did,
and fometimes challeng d in verfe, the Abby
de Chaulieu and the Marquis de la Fare.   I
never knew the latter, who died in 1712;
but I have fometimes converfed with the
Abbé de Chaulieu, who died in the year
1720, eighty-feven years of age.   I faw
him at the court of the Duchefs of Maine,
where he was in love with Mademoifelle
Launay, her femme de chambre, at prefent
her companion, under the name of Baronefs
of Staal, fhe died in 1750.   The Abby de
Chaulieu was deeply fmitten with her, although blind ; and certainly Madame de
Staal was very well calculated to infpire
fuch a paffion, for fhe was neither handfome nor defirable, but was well recompenfed by her wit and underftanding.   Voltaire, whom we formerly called Arouet,
was of the grand Prior of Vendôme's fociety;

O   and

and from that time, I always heard him call this prince his song-making highness, with the same tone of ease he always assumed with men of rank.

The grand Prior was for a long time in love with Mademoiselle Rochois, a famous actress at the Opera; and this passion did him honour, compared with that kind of debauch adopted by his brother. He appeared decent also, if opposed to the duke; yet there was a good deal of negligence in his dress, especially in the decline of his life. He took a great deal of Spanish snuff, and had the best it was possible to procure: his only snuff box was a pocket lined with leather, destined to that use, into which he put his hand, and besmeared his nose with the snuff he took out. A great quantity fell upon his cloaths, with which they were always disgustingly covered; it is said, that his valets de chambre made great profits by scraping off this snuff, putting it into leaden boxes, and selling it as newly arrived from Spain.

ESSAY

ESSAY XXXI.

MEMOIR OF THE MARQUIS BELLE-ISLE.

WE have at prefent in France, a man advancing rapidly towards a moft brilliant fortune, who, on beginning the world had every thing againft him, but whofe happy ftars have furmounted all obftacles. The oftentatious device, which his grandfather, M. Fouquet took, may be applied to him ; a fquirrel climbing a globe with thefe latin words: *Quo non afcendet?* Whither will he not climb ? The fuperintendant foon faw his pretenfions vanifh : the fuccefs of this man appears to be more certain ; no body can be more attentive and induftrious than he is in every thing he undertakes. His conduct will be better appreciated, or rather the favours of his protecting Deity, when it is known from whence he is originated. His father was fecond fon to the Superintendant, and born after the difgrace of this minifter. The hatred with which Colbert had infpired·

Lewis

Lewis XIV. againſt the name of Fouquet, prevented the Marquis of *Belle-Iſle* from becoming any thing. Yet he found means to marry a woman of faſhion, who, in truth, was without fortune · ſhe was of the houſe of Levis, ſiſter to the duke of that name. Her family was diſpleaſed with her on account of her marriage, and was a long time without ſeeing her; the new married couple went to live with the biſhop of Agde, younger brother to the Superintendant in diſgrace. This prelate was a great reſouce to his family.

It was in this kind of retreat that the preſent Marquis of *Belle-Iſle*, his brother, called the Chevalier, and ſeveral ſiſters were born. At the death of the biſhop of Agde, it was neceſſary for *Monſieur* and *Madame de Belle-Iſle* to return to Paris, to the good Madame Fouquet, widow of the Superintendant, whoſe charity was ſo univerſal, that ſhe was looked on as a ſaint. She died and left *Monſieur* and *Madame de Belle-Iſle* in very narrow circumſtances. The Iſland of *Belle-Iſle*, from whence the marquis took his name was very poor land, produced but
a ſmall

a fmall revenue, and even that may be faid to be fequeftrated in the hands of the king, who had a garrifon there. However the prefent marquis has found means to reap great advantages from his poffeffion, or rather from his pretenfions to that ifland. He was at firft deftined to the profeffion of arms, but certainly he could not begin that career with the fame advantages as men of quality do: however he found refources in the name of his mother, and in the credit of his maternal relations. He obtained a regiment of dragoons, ferved in the army of Flanders, and was in Lifle when it was befieged by the enemies, and defended by the Marfhal de Boufflers. He attached himfelf to this general, and was fortunate enough to pleafe him. He foon became neceffary to him, and having been wounded, the marfhal obtained him for the rank of brigadier, in preference to others who applied for it, among whom was the Marquis of Maillebois, fon to M. de Defmarets, comptroller general of the finances, and nephew to Colbert. This was the firft victory which the family of Fouquet obtained over that of Colbert, after the difgrace of the Superintendant.

At

At length, being continually protected by
the Marſhal de Boufflers, he was promoted
even before the death of Lewis XIV. to the
place of *Meſtre de Camp*, general of dragoons, which was the object of ambition in
ſome of the firſt men of the court. After
the death of the king, *M. de Belle-Iſle*, conducted himſelf, during the whole courſe of
the regency, with inconceivable propriety
and addreſs, never loſing fight, for an in-
ſtant, of the object of his ambition and
fortune. He was well with every body in
the time of trouble and faction, and made
himſelf uſeful to all parties. I have ſeen
him make his court to my father, and gain
his good graces. He was not deceived by
the ſyſtem of Mr. Law ; nor did he embark
in it like many others who hoped, at firſt,
to draw therefrom immenſe riches, but who
were in the end ruined. After the over-
throw of this adventurer and his ſyſtem,
M. de Belle-Iſle, reaped the fruit of his
prudence.

During the little Spaniſh war of 1719,
he ſhewed great zeal for the regent, againſt
a king who was grandſon to Lewis XIV.
and

and his zeal made him Marechal de Camp, and Governor of Hunninguen. He contributed to determine the regent to give the title of firſt miniſter to the Cardinal Dubois; but death deprived him of this perſonage, who was otherwiſe incapable of the leaſt gratitude for his good ſervices. M. le Blanc was ſecretary at war, without ſupport or counſel; *M. de Belle-Iſle* made himſelf maſter of his mind and his department; the death of the Duke of Orleans, at length checked his career. The Duke of Bourbon, took upon himſelf the premierſhip, without *M. de Belle-Iſle's* being able to ſeize the moment and means to prevent him. M. le Blanc was arreſted; government was determined to proſecute him; *M. de Belle-Iſle* was himſelf confined to the Baſtille. He was exiled the year following, and perſecuted during the whole adminiſtration of the duke, by perſons whoſe beſt friend he is at preſent. At length the duke was diſplaced, and the enemies of *M. de Belle-Iſle* impriſoned and exiled in their turn. The Cardinal Fleury came into place; he had been the intimate friend of the Ducheſs of Levis, aunt to *M. de Belle-*

O 4   *Iſle,*

Isle, who made ufe of this old connexion to gain the confidence of the new firft minifter. He fucceeded in his attempt : M. le Blanc was reftored to his place, and *M. de Belle-Isle* continued to enjoy the greateft credit until the death of the Secretary of ftate. He faw that it was impoffible to have the fame influence under his fucceffor, and that on this account, the beft thing he could do would be to ferve in the war. He was made Lieutenant General, and commander of Metz and the Evêchés, or bifhopricks he made a great difplay of the advantageous arrangements undertaken for the ftate in his new command. At the beginning of the war, he poffeffed himfelf of Treves, which is an open city. He fpoke in great terms on the utility of this conqueft : that of Philipfburgh was not due to him, although he ferved well at the fiege. He was created *Chevalier des ordres du Roi* in 1735, and from that moment the cardinal took his advice upon the conclufion of the peace. This old man thought perhaps, that he was obliged to him for having acquired Lorrain, becaufe *M. de Belle-Isle* infifted upon the importance of this acquifition propofed

pofed by others. May it pleafe heaven, that after having applauded a good refolution, he may not hereafter make him take a worfe! However this may be, there is every appearance that the fortune of *M. de Belle-Ifle* will not remain in its prefent fituation. Although he has fcarcely done any thing but intrigue, he is thought very capable of being a great general and a great minifter: it will be neceffary to examine this matter.

He is tall and thin; his conftitution has always appeared to be delicate, his ftomach weak, his heart affected, fince the wound he received at the fiege of Lifle. He appears obliged to be exceeding careful of his health, which he really is, to as great a degree as is poffible; but as foon as he feels himfelf animated by the defire of acquiring glory, and of infuring fuccefs to a plan of ambition or intrigue, the activity of his mind gives him that ftrength which the weaknefs of his body refufes: he is continually at bufinefs, fleeps but little, and tires the moft indefatigable of his fecretaries, dictating to feveral at a time. In a word, he is like fire, he devours every thing and

refifts

refifts every thing; he carries on feveral intrigues at the fame time, never lofes fight of
one of his threads, and takes care that they
do not crofs each other. In an age where
ftrict probity, real merit, and wife and folid
views are not the beft recommendations, a
man who knows how to ufe at once docility
and affurance, cannot fail of fucceeding. A
proof that his ideas are neither enlightened
nor really great is, that his ftile is weak and
unanimated, that he neither writes correctly
nor forcibly, and has no eloquence even in
fpeaking; but he always appears to be certain of fuccefs, he never hefitates in giving
affurances of it; and he perfuades the more
on account of its being believed that he ufes
no art in doing it. He makes that which
he has done, appear to greater advantage
than that which he means to do; thofe who
follow his advice, if they receive benefit from
it, think themfelves obliged to him; if the
contrary be the cafe, they blame themfelves
only. If *M. de Belle-Ifle* fhould be charged
with a great adminiftration, it may be feared,
that his exceffive love of detail, and of every
kind of project, will induce him to adopt
many plans which he will not be able to
execute fully; and that he will never have
time

time enough to make a reform. He will certainly be fond of adventurers, being a little fo himfelf ; and will never diftinguifh thofe who might be really ufeful to him.

M. de Belle-Ifle married in 1729, a lady of the houfe of Bethune, well made, beautiful enough, and fuch a one as is neceffary for a man like him ; fhe was fometimes a coquette, with a great deal of art, addrefs, and decency ; at others a devotee, always cajoling without meannefs, and fenfible without pretenfion : her hufband who knows equally her virtues and defects, fhews a great attachment to her ; and effectively, having no other paffion than ambition, he has no other miftrefs than his wife who feconds his views. The coquetry of the wife, and the ambition of the hufband equally fucceed, becaufe they flow from their natural fource, and coft nothing to thofe who employ them.

The *Chevalier de Belle-Ifle,* brother to the Count, has, according to people who have been a good deal in the company of them both, more folid and extenfive views in his

s   plans

plans than his brother ; but he has lefs complaifance, is lefs docile, and· poffeffes fewer means of pleafing : he has perhaps more knowledge of the art of war, of policy and adminiftration, but he does not know fo well how to enhance the value of his thoughts and actions. Ambition is common to them both, and the chevalier is modeft enough to appropriate to himfelf, no more of the honour of great fucceffes, than what belongs to a younger brother ; but it is fuppofed, that being always hid behind his brother, he is of great ufe to him, and that he will feverely feel his lofs, if he fhould die before him. The chevalier writes the memoirs of the count, rectifies his plans, and prefides over his domeftic affairs ; they enjoy in their family affairs, every thing in common. The chevalier having better health than his brother, gives himfelf up more to pleafure ; but he does not on this account lofe fight for a moment, of their common ambition and political intrigues.

The beft thing which the two brothers have done, is the exchange of the miferable
Ifland

Ifland of *Belle-Ifle*, for the *Comté* of Gifors, that of Vernon, and the foreft of Lyons and Audelis. *M. de Belle-Ifle* has a fon, born in 1732; if he lives he will be as great a man as his father and grandfather would have been, if M. Fouquet had died in place, with as much power as Cardinal Mazarin had.

ESSAY

E S S A Y XXXII.

RESPECTIVE EXCELLENCIES OF GENIUS AND JUDGMENT IN BUSINESS.

VIVACITY of thought is vulgarly called wit. It is but too frequently judged that men of dull, and rather heavy fenfe, and who have not a brilliant and eafy flow of words are fools; this is certainly a miftaken notion. To be a man of wit, is to have juft ideas, and fooner or later, to apply them rationally. To be a fool, is to be incapable of judging; the inconfiderate judge precipitately, and are deceived for want of reflection and attention.

Setting out from thefe definitions, the perception of a man of great fenfe is equally quick and juft. A man of genius has fomething more; he rifes above that which is fubmitted to the ordinary judgement of men; he is full of imagination, has great forefight, is inventive without exceeding

pro-

probability, becaufe he never departs from a certain bafis, which bafis is fentimént and reafon. None but fools foar imprudently, and at the rifk of every thing. A man of genius feizes immediately an idea, and carries it as far as poffible. A man of good fenfe takes his refolution after ferious reflection; but nothing is worfe than to be inceffantly undetermined.

In the courfe of ordinary affairs, there is a certain flownefs of decifion, the ufe of which is admirable, becaufe it feems to put men who are not above mediocrity, upon a level with thofe of the greateft abilities. I have feen adminiftrators and minifters who had this kind of merit only, fucceed perfectly, and for a confiderable length of time But if they had had great and unforefeen difficulties to encounter, they would not perhaps have acquitted themfelves much to their honour. Thefe men ought, on entering into place, to inftil into themfelves well approved principles; and after having confulted perfons capable of furnifhing them with fuch, to abide by, and firmly to look upon them as

their

their compaſs : yet ſome exceptions muſt neceſſarily be made, for there is no general rule without them.   A man of an enlightened mind, ſees immediately where they lie ; but however great his ſenſe and genius may be, he can never diſpenſe with fundamental principles.

The beſt, in matters of adminiſtration, are thoſe which have been adopted in councils, and made uſe of for a length of time ; becauſe they are the fruit of the reflections and experience of a great number of people ; and that perſonal intereſts and conſiderations have leſs influence therein, than in thoſe which have been formed by an individual.

But every man, in whatever place he may be, ought to lay down certain rules for his private conduct ; with reſpect to theſe, they ſhould be reflected upon in retirement, and perhaps the beſt way is not to conſult any body about them.

It is not only neceſſary to deviate at certain times from the beſt ~~principles~~, but in ~~. . . . .~~ the

the end, they muſt be abandoned, or at leaſt modified. Many things become worſe by uſe, but thoſe who manage prudently throw nothing away, without being fiiſt aſſured, that no farther uſe can be made of it.

It will not be difficult for me to give examples of the different kinds of abilities, I have juſt been ſpeaking of, and of miniſters in whom I have obſerved them; I will do this preſently. In the mean time, let us reaſon a little upon the manner by which men in place ought to act, ſo as to be equal to the numerous objects committed to their care, in a kingdom ſo extenſive as that of France.

When men have occupations of too uniform and monotonous a kind, relaxation is abſolutely neceſſary, if not by real amuſements, at leaſt by varying their employment: magiſtrates apply themſelves at intervals, eſpecially in their vacations, to literature, or to their domeſtic affairs; miniſters who have buſineſs every day in the year, but of different kinds, relax their minds by paſſing from one thing to another.

P　　　　　　　　A de-

Detail which would be fatiguing of itfelf, is enlivened by another with which it is connected. It is faid, that Cardinal Richelieu applied to bufinefs no more than fix hours a day; the reft of his time was taken up by giving audiences which were not all equally ferious and tirefome ; by intrigues, and finally by pleafures, for the great Cardinal partook of them. I imagine, that independently of Marion de Lorine, and the Abby de Bois Robert, the compofition of his theatrical pieces, and his rivalıty with Corneille, were real amufements to him : how could he have looked upon them other-wife ?

The learned Abby de Longuerue, with whom I have been a good deal acquainted, amufed himfelf in the middle of his library, without deviating from his fearch after knowledge. He has frequently told me, that he took up one book after another, and varied his ftudies; that it was in this manner, having a ftrong memory and great facility in reducing to order what he read, he had learned a great deal without fatiguing himfelf. This facility becomes habitu-al;

al; we perceive that we are infenfibly become more learned than others. We gain
a kind of confidence in our own knowledge,
which leads to pronounce upon every thing
which prefents itfelf; and when this decifive manner is not carried to impertinence
and pedantry, otheis accuftom themfelves to
believe you, acknowledge your fuperiority,
and leave you to engrofs the whole converfation. We allow men their erudition,
when they are not overbearing; and their
extenfive knowledge when they attribute it
to memory only, and not to a fupeiiority of
underftanding: but a man of projects, who
difplays them, and fays publicly, that they
are fuperior to all that have ever been invented, and who will take to himfelf the
honour of the greateft difcoveries, is commonly looked upon as a quack, who wifhes
to fell his drugs; but no purchafers are
found; for men would fear being poifoned if
they tafted them.

Minute exactitude and punctuality are
virtues of the fecond order; but it becomes
modeft people to obferve them. There are
even cafes, from which if we deviate, we

fhould appear to infult thofe who are dependent upon us. It feems that we ære laying fnares, by requiring them to obferve rules which we do not ourfelves follow. We bring upon us their hatred, and perhaps make them doubt of our capacity; for people who have no other merit than that of induftry, think it a very great one. Without having fo great an opinion of exactitude, let us at leaft believe that it has its value. Lewis XIV. did not difdain to be punctual; he never failed a minute in his appointments; and as great as he was, it was perhaps this perfonal exactitude which gave him a right to take notice of the leaft want of it in people about him, and to reproach them with it.

I have frequently heard it faid, that *we ought not to fuffer others to do that which we can do ourfelves*; for my part, I am of a contrary opinion, and maintain it. *We ought to fave ourfelves the trouble of doing that which may be done by others*, but although it be not neceffary to do every thing, nothing ought to be difdained. To be attentive to every thing which is done in our name, to

adopt

adopt ceitain principles ; to give them to thofe whom we employ ; to take care that they never deviate from them, to be fure of what they do ; finally, to know how to gain proper affiftance, this is what diftinguifhes the ftatefman, the man capable of conducting great affairs. To know how to govern fecondary caufes, and not to be governed by them, is a fublime art. How happy fhould I be, if I could find people who could and would think and wiite for me, fay all that I have to fay, and execute every thing I would do! But as there are exceptions and bounds to every thing, there are ceitain cafes wherein it is eafier to do the bufinefs ourfelves than by others : God forbid, that by this I fhould give the advice of an indolent man ; my opinion is founded upon reafon and experience. It is a good thing to apply habitually to bufinefs ; but it is ftill better to look fo well into that which is done for us, as to enable us to difpenfe with a part of our application ; but it is neceffary to have been a great deal employed, to be able to direct the operations of others.

P 3   ESSAY

ESSAY XXXIII.

CHARACTERS OF STATESMEN EXEMPLIFIED.

THERE are certainly no ministers but thofe of great abilities, who know how to prefcribe to their fecretaries, what they ought to do. I knew in France an ambaffador, a man of great merit, who became afterwards minifter of a great department in his own country. Under the pretence that his writing was bad, he never wrote a fingle letter with his own hand; he figned his name only; but he explained his intentions fo clearly to his fecretaries, who were intelligent people, that they reduced them to good and clear language. He reafoned with them, told them his motives, encouraged them to make objections, and even to difpute with him, with decency and refpect. When he had cleared up every thing, and thought he had convinced them, they fet to work and his difpatches were admirable.

It

It is certain that political affairs are frequently forwarded more by converfation,
than by means of correfpondence. This is
the great difference between minifters and
men of letters. Thefe do better in retirement and contemplation becaufe they have
to refer to books; but the others ought to
live in the great world and converfe with
men, becaufe they have men to govern,
whilft literary men have only their ideas
and phrafes to arrange. A minifter of the
fiift order, in a great court, fhould know
how to hearken with patience, attention,
and mildnefs; to anfwer calmly, and exprefs himfelf gracefully. Secretaries want,
on the contrary, nothing but good fenfe to
underftand, and a good ftile in their writing. This is what makes it impoffible that
a fecretary fhould fupply the place of an
ambaffador, becaufe he cannot enjoy the
fame advantages at the court in which he
refides; he cannot know fo well the character of perfons with whom he has bufinefs,
without the freedom of mutual converfation.

P 4

It

It is a queſtion difficult to reſolve, to know if a good ſecretary can become a great miniſter. This depends to a certain degree, upon the country and circumſtances ; but he vould ſucceed with great difficulty in a monarchical ſtate. Miniſters ſhould be acquainted with the court, and enjoy when they go into place, ſome conſideration ; they ſhould not be accuſtomed to tremble when in the prefence of courtiers, and they ought to know how to avoid all their ſnares ; for theſe gentlemen wiſh for nothing more than to ſhackle miniſters, ſometimes by ſeducing them, at otheis by alarming their fears. Moreover, a good ſecretary ought to have no ideas of his own, but to know how to turn to a good account thoſe of the miniſter he is under ; the miniſter ought, on the contrary, to think for himſelf ; for the advantage and intereſt of the ſovereign and the ſtate. A man who arrives at a great employ, without the advantages of birth, and never having filled an important ſtation, muſt neceſſarily be embarraſſed about the countenance he ought to put on ; if he be firm, he is accuſed of inſolence, and is ſaid to have forgot himſelf ; if he

pre-

preferves the manner of his former ftate, he is defpifed and treated as if he were ftill in it.

On the other hand, would it be well done to fill up the places of adminiftration with military men, and thofe of the firft rank ? Lewis XIV. did not think fo; but was of opinion, that it was his intereft that the greatnefs of his minifters fhould depend upon his confidence. A much ftronger reafon is, that men of the firft rank, and thofe in the army, do not often contract when young, the habit of applying to bufinefs; that they are ignorant of all the forms of it, and that moft departments require a perfect knowledge of thefe. The real bufinefs of a fecretary of ftate, being to give a regular form to all the decifions of the king and his council. Minifters ought to be brought up to adminiftration, becaufe they are nothing more in reality, than the adminiftrators of affairs. The details confided to their care, are lately become immenfe; nothing is done without them, or by any body elfe. It is to be wifhed that their knowledge were as great as their power; if it be not, they are

obliged

obliged to leave every thing to their clerks, who become masters of affairs, and consequently of the state. It is by a knowledge of forms, that subalterns are arrived at governing their principals, and to make use of a vulgar expression, *that journeymen are become masters.*

I will give my opinion freely upon ministers, whom I have seen for the last thirty years at the head of affairs in France, and of some others more ancient whom I have not personally known, but upon whose characters, &c. I have had memoirs sufficient to enable me to speak decidedly about them.

The Chancellor le Tellier, father of M. de Louvois, died some years before I was born, which was in the year 1693; M. Boucherat was elevated to that great dignity, which would have been much above his capacity, if the times had been more difficult: but the power of Lewis XIV. was so well established, the parliaments were so submissive, the right of remonstrating had been so restrained, or rather taken

away

away from the fuperior courts, that there
was no danger in giving the place to a
magiftrate, almoft become the oldeft member of the council; in confiding to him no
other cares than thofe of filling up the offices of magiftracy, which venality and
right of inheritance facilitated the means of
doing; of fealing edicts and declarations,
and creating impofts and new offices, fuch
as minifters thought proper to expedite.
Therefore M. Boucherat held his place very
peaceably until the year 1694, when he
died at eighty-four years of age. He left
daughters only; his fucceffor was M. de
Pontchartrain, who was afterwards in
1689, comptroller general of the finances,
and in 1690, marine fecretary of ftate,
and of the department of Paris. It was he
who, in 1697, perfuaded my father to charge
himfelf with the care of the police of the
capital. M. de Pontchartrain took the
chancellorfhip as a retreat; in fact it might
be looked upon as fuch at this time, when
every thing was in fuch a ftate of fubmiffion. He was very happy to find the king
difpofed to make M. de Chamillart his fucceffor in the comptrollerfhip, and M. de
Pontchartiain

Pontchartrain his fon, in his other departments. Neither one nor the other was worthy of fucceeding him; but at length they eafed him of the moft important cares, and fatiguing details. It was however neceffary that he fhould give advice to his fon, in whom he had not all the fatisfaction he had hoped for, which determined him to retire in the year 1714, from all public affairs. Lewis XIV. was become old, and ready to fink into the grave; M. de Pontchartrain was exactly of the fame age. Moreover, he wifhed prudently to avoid being obliged to carry into parliament, an edict which declared the legitimate princes capable of fucceeding to the crown. M. Voifin was charged with this commiffion, which was executed with all the fubmiffion generally fhewn to the orders of Lewis XIV. even to the death of this monarch, which happened in the month of September, 1715. —M. Voifin, about as good a chancellor as M. Boucherat, died very à-propos, in the month of February, 1717, and was replaced by M. d'Aguefleau. I will fpeak of this gentleman in his turn, as well as of the other minifters of the prefent reign; in the

mean

mean time, I muft again obferve, that of the
three laft chancellors of Lewis XIV. M. de
Pontchaitrain was certainly the moft able.
He had been a long time counfellor of the
parliament of Paris; abandoned by his relations the Phillippeaux de la Vrilliere, a
branch of which vegetated in the place of
fecretary of ftate ; and was neverthelefs jealous of the Phillippeaux of Pontchartrain,
who were defcended from the firft who had
held that employ by means of Mary of
Medicis. M. de Pontchartrain was after-
waids, for twenty years, firft prefident of
the pailiament of Bretagne : he not only
made himfelf efteemed in that province, by
his equity and knowledge, but he gave
proofs of firmnefs, ability and addrefs in
managing the Bretons, who have ever
been very difficult to govern. It may eafily
be judged, that he had other affairs, when
he was minifter of the finances. But they
ceafed to give him trouble the moment he
became nothing more than a minifter of
juftice. The chancellorfhip was very eafy
in his time; the chief magiftrate being too
much taken up with paffing edicts of finance, and creating offices, had no time to
make

make wife regulations; alfo, if he had no
trouble he had no honour.

Let us now confider the adminiftration of
finances under the late king. The great
Colbert died in 1683 ; he was fucceeded by
M. Pelletier, a very worthy man, and who
had behaved perfectly well in every department he had filled ; but he was not fit for
that of the finances, efpecially in time of
war, which happened as foon as he went
into office.   Supplies were difficult to obtain, and confequently burthenfome ; M.
Pelletier made ufe of fuch as occuried to
him, which he diftributed with all imaginable juftice and equity ; but he could not
prevent the impofts he had laid on from
doing a real injury to the ftate.   He had no
opportunity of making ufeful arrangements,
after having been obliged to employ the
moft pernicious means.   The Chancellor
Le Tellier, who was alive when M. Pelletier went into adminiftration, was right in
faying to Lewis XIV. that the new comptroller, although an honeft man, and had
great application, was unfit for the finances :
he gave a bad reafon for this, by adding,
                                                    that

that he was of too mild a difpofition. His Majefty replied, that it was precifely on that account he had made choice of him: this was a fine and noble fentiment ; but the king and the chancellor were equally deceived in their opinion of the defects of M. Pelletier. This appeared clearly, upon his being fucceeded in 1690, by M. de Pontchartrain, who was not over mild, although equally equitable in the ufe of means to which he was obliged to have recourfe, undoubtedly with regret ; and which were the more cruel, by reafon of his being obliged to encreafe them very confiderably : the people cried out, but they fubmitted, for the king's authority was uniformly and generally eftablifhed. M. de Pontchartrain was fortunate enough to get rid of the finances in 1690, and they were given to M. de Chamillart, of whom the king was very fond, which indeed he merited in fome degree. This minifter, without being either weak or quite incapable of bufinefs, was not equal to his place : but who would have been equal to it in fuch unhappy times ? What could a comptroller do but repeat, and augment the burthens, and double

double burthens of the people : this is what
M. de Chamillart did; he funk under the
weight of affairs, retired from the miniftry
in 1708, and died in 1721. M. Defmarets,
nephew to M. Colbert, took his place ; the
choice of this gentleman was perhaps the
beft that could be made : but did M. Colbert, himfelf get well over it in 1708, 1709,
and fome of the following years ? No. It
is only neceffary to read the memoir which
M. Defmarets prefented to the regent, to
become acquainted with all the difficulties
he had to encounter : this memoir is a
melancholy proof of the defolating evils
with which France was at that time afflicted; it expofes the fituation the kingdom was
in, and no good Frenchman can refrain
from weeping at the recital. M. Defmarets
fays therein, that the king affured him he
knew the ftate of his finances ; that he did
not expect from him impoffibilities ; and if
he fucceeded, he would do him the moft
important fervice, but if he was unfortunate in his endeavours, he fhould not im-
pute to him the leaft blame. Nothing
could be more reafonable ; for it would have
been impoffible to have re-eftablifhed the

finances

finances as circumftances then were. M.
Defmarets did his beft; he continued in
place, until after the death of Lewis XIV.
and died in 1721, the fame year with M.
de Chamillard: he left among other evils,
two many-headed moufters, which it was
neceffary to deftroy—notes of the State and
notes of the Mint —We fhall fee what became of thefe in the following reign.

The adminiftration of foreign affairs, the
moft important of all departments, had been
entrufted in 1679, to M. Colbert of Croiffy,
brother to the great Colbert; he died in
1690: his fon, M. de Torcy, had had the
reverfion of his office and department given
him the year before; but at the death of his
father he was found too young to replace
him, although he was thirty years of age:
he was put under the direction of M. Amaud,
of Pomponne, who had already filled the
department from 167., to 1679, when he
was obliged to retire, although accufed of
nothing but negligence: he was otherwife
moft polite and refpectable; but like the
family of the Amauds, fufpected of Janfenifm, which was at that time a crime at

Q   Court,

Court. M. de Pomponne, guided his son in law three years; after which, the latter was in a fituation to fhew what he was and what he could do; he kept his place until the death of Louis XIV. His conduct fince that epocha has been that of a true philofopher, and ought to be an example to the old minifters. For my part, who am not yet become one, I mean to gather from the converfation of this refpectable man, principles of conduct for the time when this fhall happen, and for that, when I fhall be fo no longer. If ever the memoirs which he has done me the favour to communicate to me be printed, his manner of thinking, and the qualities of his mind, will be feen without difguife; and M. de Torcy will be looked upon as a claffical author, proper to inftruct Minifters of foreign affairs, both for the time prefent and to come. They will be taught how to act in cafes of the greateft delicacy. Thofe which M de Torcy had to encounter were certainly very embaraffing, but in all the misfortunes which befell the old age of Lewis XIV his minifter of finances was moft to be pitied.

The

The war department had been given, at
the death of M de Louvois, which happened in 1691, to M. de Barbezieux, his son,
who held it ten years. This secretary of
state, who had good natural sense, a great
aptitude to business, a quick and lively con-
ception, and a great habitude of detail, to
which he had been in the early part of his
life formed by his father, had also great
defects. He had been spoiled in his youth,
by every body, except his father; he was a
libertine, dissipated, and impertinent; he
sometimes treated the military too lightly,
who, according to their custom, spared
nothing, not even meannesses, when favors
were to be obtained by them, and complained haughtily the moment nothing more was
to be hoped for. He went to his offices
from necessity, but was always treated with
great respect, because the son of M. de Louvois, who had, as we may say, created
them, could not fail of inspiring veneration,
and even attachment Lewis XIV. who knew
all the defects of M. de Barbezieux, complained of them privately, and spoke to him
sometimes in a sharp and particular manner;
but he suffered him to remain still in place,

Q 2   because

becaufe he faw how important it was to preferve in his deportment, the fyftem and principles of M. de Louvois.   M. de Barbezieux
never entered the council of ftate ; it is faid
that he burned with rage to fee M. de Chamillard, whom he had often made wait in
his father's and his own anti chamber, a
member of it. But, according to all appearances, the ruinous and mortal alliance
which M. de Barbezieux wifhed to make,
of a life of libertinifm and diffipation, with
the bufinefs and multiplied expeditions
which the fituation of France required,
(Lewis XIV. having accepted the teftament
of Charles II. and fent the Duke of Anjou,
his grandfon, into Spain,) was what brought
on the violent illnefs which carried him in a
few days to the grave. M. Fagon, firft phyfician to the king, pronounced his illnefs
mortal, the firft moment he faw him after
he was attacked by it. He informed the
king of it, who feemed but little affected at
it. M. de Barbezieux died the fifth of January 1701, and the unhappy Chamillard
was immediately charged with his department, in addition to that of the finances.
I could here make great and juft reflections
upon

upon the incompatibility of thefe two departments. Moreover they could not be
more improperly united than in the perfon
of M. de Chamillard ; but a glorious reign
of fifty years had infpired Lewis XIV. with
the prefumption not only to believe that he
knew how to chufe his minifters, but that
he could teach them their duty, and direct
their operations : he certainly deceived himfelf. It depended on him alone to unite in
the fame perfon the two important employs
of Colbert and Louvois, but, it was not in
his power to fupply the want of their abilities. It is not that M. de Chamillard was a
man without merit ; he gave, early in life,
proofs of a rare probity, from which he
never varied. But, if a want of probity renders the greateft talents ufelefs, and even
dangerous ; on the other hand, this great
virtue, being alone, fupplies not the want
of them, nor that of knowledge. Finally, at
the end of fix or feven years, M. de Chamillard funk under the weight of bufinefs,
which he difcharged as well as he could, but
to which he was never equal. He quitted
firft the finances, and foon afterwards the
war department. Lewis XIV. incorrigible

Q 3

in

in his opinion of being more able than all
his minifteis, made M. Voifin his fucceffor, who knew lefs of affairs than M. de
Chamillard. The gicat proofs which this
minifter gave of his abilities in the war department, were not what procured him the
elevated place of chanc llor, which he became poffeffed of in 1714; this was the
price of his compliance with the abfolute
will of his mafter, who, far from having
learned any thing from his misfoitunes, con-
foled himfclf by believing he fhould find
refources in the choice he made of his mi-
niflers. M. Voifin was, till the death of
the late king, at the head of the magiftracy,
and of military affairs ; cares very different
in their objects, which ought not to be in-
trufted to the fame perfon, but whofe principles are not fo wide of each other as might
be imagined. There are maxims common
to every kind of adminiftration ; men who
are without them are incapable of any. On
the other hand, there are particular ones,
according to the nature of affairs and circumftances, which occur. M. de Seignelai
replaced M. Colbert, his father, in the marine department only; with the defects

2   which

which fons of minifters generally have, when they become minifters themfelves, which are felf-fufficiency, prefumption and levity. He had, however, certain talents, and fupported the honor of the French marine, which was, in fome meafure, created by his father ; but he deviated from the principles upon which it had been formed : it was with a view to commerce, to make it flourifh, to extend and encourage it, that M. Colbert engag'd Lewis XIV to build fhips. He was controller general, and made the marine department depend upon commerce and the finances ; his fon, who had wit, ambition, and audacity, confined to the marine department alone, looked upon it in quite another point of view : the finances were in other hands ; he faw how defirous Lewis XIV. was of conquefts, and of ruling in Europe It was by taking advantage of thefe difpofitions in the king, that M Louvois gained the confidence of the monarch ; M. de Seignelai wifhed to rival the minifter of the war department ; he undertook to make the arms of France as powerful by fea as they were by land ; he bombarded Genoa, crufhed the Algerines, had ambafladors

Q 4   from

from Siam brought to France, in the king's veffe s, and l d them about Verfailles. The year following he cannonaded Tunis and Tripoly, and gave brilliant entertainments to the king, in his caftle of Sceaux; finally, he attacked the Dutch by fea, and undertook to re eftablifh James II. upon the throne of England, from which the Prince of Orange, his fon in law, had driven him. In 1690, the laft year of his life, he faw the king's fleet gain two battles in the channel. At length he died, and, after his death, Lewis XIV. re-united once more, and very properly, the adminiftration of the marine to the finances; but M. de Pontchartrain was much embarraffed in finding refources in one to fuppoit the other.

This gentleman became chancellor, and left the marine department to his fon, whom he had married to Mademoifelle de la Roche, Foucaud de Roye, who died, leaving him an only fon, the prefent Count of Maurepas. I dare not give the portrait of M. de Pontchartrain, junior; this I leave to others, who had bufinefs with him during his adminiftration, and are ftill of his acquaintance.

ance*. I have been affured that he has
pointed out the danger of inheritance in
places of confidence and adminiftration ; and
that the public, far from regretting his going out of office, thought themfelves happy
on getting clear of him, at the death of the
king.

Little need be faid upon the department
and hiftory of Meffieurs de Philippeaux de
la Vrilliere, de Chateau Neuf, and of Saint
Florentin : thefe were the furnames of the
fons of that family of fecretaries of ftate,
which may be traced back to the firft race
of our kings   It is to be believed that Paul
Philippeaux de Pontchartrain had merit, or
und.rftood, at leaft, political intrigue;
fince after being twelve or fifteen years clerk
to M. M. de Rovol and de Villeroy, he was
made, in 1600, fecretary to Mary of Medicis, in her coactive power.   This queen had
confidence enough in him to make him fecretary of ftate, as foon as fhe became regent.   He died in 1621 ; his eldeft fon, who
was counfellor in the parliament, fon in law
to

* He was alive in 1736, the time when thefe Effays were
written.   He died the year following.

to the famous Advocate General Talon, did not succeed him ; his place went to his younger brother, Raymond Philippeaux de Herbaut, who was at firft fecretary to the privy-council, afterwards treafurer of the cafual revenues, and at length of the favings. He died in 1629 and his office remained to the younger branch in prejudice of the elder, which did not return to it until eighty years afterwards. M. d' Herbaut was replaced by Lewis Phillippeaux de la Vrilliere, who was fixty-two years fecretary of ftate under the reigns of Lewis XIII. and XIV. ; but he made fo little ftir at court and in the ftate, that we fhould not know he ever exifted, were it not for the great number of edicts, declarations and letters patent he figned, and did not his name appear on the lift of fecretaries of ftate. He inherited the fortune of the famous Particelly d'Emery, his father-in-law, who, after having.been the moft terrible partizan, and cruel extortioner under the reign of Lewis XIII. became in the adminiftration of Mazarine, fuperintendant of the finances. Baltazar Phillippeaux, who was counfellor, clerk of the parliament, left the church to fucceed his father,

father, and died in 1700; he was called
M. de Chateau Neuf. His fon took again
the name of la Vrilliere, and it was this
gentleman who figned, perhaps, the moft
difpatches; for, at the beginning of the regency, the Duke of Orleans, wifhing to difcharge all the fecretaries of Lewis XIV.
kept M. de la Vrilliere only, becaufe he appeared to him a man of little confideration.
The adminiftiation of affairs in general was
given to different councils, but every thing
neceffary to be figned by order came under
his pen; he died in 1725. His fon, the
Count of Saint Florentin replaced him;
but his department has been put upon the
fame footing as that of his father, under
Lewis XIV. The lift of affairs entrufted to
him appears of confiderable length in the
Royal Calendar; in reality nothing of importance devolves upon him; he figns and
difpatches, as did his father and grandfather.

ESSAY

E S S A Y   XXXIV.

THE ADMINISTRATION OF THE REGENT
¡DULY EXEMPLIFIED.

IF I were not fure of writing for myfelf
only, I fhould tremble at giving my
opinion of the minifters of the prefent reign.
Some of them are yet alive, and others belong to families now in favor : on the othe
hand, if I write not at prefent what I have
feen and known, important and inftructive
truths, will, perhaps, efcape pofterity.   I
will therefore explain myfelf with the liberty of a man who neither hopes nor fears,
nor has any intereft in the fuccefs or failure
of any party, and who fpeaks to a pofterity,
perhaps, very remote.

The Regent had no fooner taken the reins
of government than he propofed a form of
adminiftration quite different from that of
Lewis XIV.   Whether it was from a fpirit
of innovation, which is almoft inevitable at
the

the beginning of a reign, or from a wish to
avoid the reproach caft on the late king and
his minifters, of being defpotic and arbi-
tiary, he confided each part of adminiftration to as many councils ; gave full activity
to thofe formed in the preceding reign, for
the finances, commerce, and foreign affairs,
and created others for the war and marine
departments ; he was even defirous of _fta-
blifhing one for ecclefiaftical affairs, but
this was attended with great difficulties.
All thefe particular councils were without
prejudice to the council general of the Regency, from which they might be looked
upon as fo many emanations, and that of the
malecontents, which has always been directed by the chancellor   I have already
faid that M. Voifin filled this place at the
death of Lewis XIV. that he died in 1717,
and was fucceeded by M. d'Aguefleau, who
is ftill invefted with that dignity.   If
piety, and all the virtues which derive from
it, probity, erudition, a tafte for letters,
and great fenfe, but of a different kind from
that which adminiftration requires, could
make a perfect chancellor, M. d'Aguefleau
would certainly be one ; but other talents

I   are

are neceſſary to perform the duties of ſo important an office.   The chancellor ought to
unite every thing that conſtitutes a great
magiſtrate, to that which makes a great miniſter ; he has buſineſs continually with
men of the law ; he is their chief, and
ought to underſtand their language, know
their forms, and poſſeſs the art of conducting courts of every kind : he is at the head
of one very difficult to govern, namely the
council.   On the other hand, he is the
king's miniſter, and ought to maintain his
authority, by carefully obſerving to conciliate acts with forms, a negligence of which
might make the beſt concerted enterprizes
fail, and ſuch as would be the moſt advantageous to the king and people.   He ought,
if it be poſſible, to gain the conſideration
and eſteem of the magiſtracy; but he ſhould
not be afraid of it   it is his duty to make
it reſpectable, but not to eſteem any member of it more than he merits ; not to heſi-
tate in reforming unjuſt judgements, and
in puniſhing iniquitous and partial judges ;
but he ſhould ever give his reaſons publicly,
and expoſe the faults he is obliged to repreſs ;
he ought particularly to diſtinguiſh between
                                        thoſe

thofe of ignorance and negligence from fuch
as are of a more ferious kind. Like all the
other minifters, he fhould fometimes make
ufe of the two-edged fword of royal authority ; but it behoves nobody more than himfelf to prove that he has conftantly kept a
watchful eye over it.

M. d'Aguefleau has perhaps too great a
refpeet for the perfons of Magiftrates ; he
always gives them an advantage over him,
and fince the unhappy epocha of the venality of offices, they are far from always
meriting fuch attentions. The Regent
made his Court to the Parliament, at a
time when he thought he ftood in need of
its affiance, by conferring the firft dignity
in the kingdom upon the Attorney General ;
but men of the robe are apt to receive every
thing offered to them as due to their merit,
and to form new pretenfions to obtain ftill
fomething more They fometimes carry
thefe to fuch excefs, that it becomes neceffary to check them, were it only for
form's fake, even when they may, upon the
whole, be juftly founded. This is what
M. d'Aguefleau was by no means fit for,
and

and what obliged the Regent to have recourfe to my father in delicate cafes.   Moreover, M. d'Aguefleau has another great
defeat, which is that of being too flow in
deciding on great affairs.   The functions of
Advocate General, which he has performed,
have accuftomed him to weigh opinions,
and to take his refolution with difficulty ;
he hefitates even afterwards concerning its
rectitude, and feems to wifh he could re-
tract it ; but if this were the time to correct any error, inftead of doing it he would
commit others.   I have feen him, for the
purpofe of coming to a decifion, call to his
aid one of his children, who was young,
and not capable of making his refpectable
father take the beft refolution ; on which
account a lady of his acquaintance, a very
fenfible woman, faid to him one day, " take
" care Mr. Chancellor what you do; you,
" though very learned, doubt of every
" thing, and your younger fon doubts of
" nothing ; you will never do any thing
" well in this manner."   In fact, the confcience of this great Magiftrate is as delicate as his mind is timid, and he torments
himfelf with continual fcruples.

My

My father was of a very different character, knowing how to determine himfelf
with promptitude, and to hold firmly to
the refolution he had taken. Being charged twenty years with the Police of Paris,
he was accuftomed to that kind of detail, to
that fagacity which enabled him to find in
an inftant the point of difficulty, and the
means of refolving it. He was intelligent ; had a long and perfect knowledge of
forms, and knew how to apply them to circumftances, even thofe of neceffity, with
the greateft advantage. He knew the Parliament, as our great Generals know thofe
with whom they have a long time been at
war, as the Duke of Vendôme might know
the Prince Eugene, and the Marfhal Villars,
Marlborough. He did not perfonally hate
this body, he even refpected it, and was al-
lied to the moft confiderable members of it,
by his wife, who was of the family of
Caumartin, and by his grandmother, niece
to the Chancellor de Chiverny. He owed
his robe to thefe alliances. The functions
of lieutenant of the police are a mixture of
civil magiftracy and political adminiftration ;
to fill this place it is neceffary to unite all

R   the

the abilities of a great politician, and I can affert, without prejudice, that my father had them all. Moreover he knew the court, and how to manage men of rank, without offending or fearing them: to this effect he ufed the advantages of his birth, and made a merit of his modefty; whilft prefidental haughtinefs obfcured thofe who bore a diftinguifhed and illuftrious name in our hiftory. He was amiable in fociety, and the moment after his contracted brow and black wig had made the populace tremble, the agreeablenefs of his converfation, and eafy good breeding, proved he was fit to keep the beft company. People were perfuaded that the art of fpying, which he carried to the laft degree of perfection, put him in poffeffion of the fecrets of every family; but he made ufe of his information with fo much difcretion, that he never difturbed the repofe of any body, and preferved every myftery in his own bofom, never proceeding unfeafonably, and always for the welfare of the ftate, and that of individuals. I am obliged to acknowledge that his private morals were not perfectly pure. I knew him too well to fufpect him of being a devotee,

votee, but he made religion and decency refpectable, and fet the example whilft he
was prefcribing laws to enforce the ob-
fervation of them. Such a man was neceffary to the Regent, to make up for the
weaknefs of M. d'Agueffeau, at a time
when government was obliged to keep the
parliament in awe. He was keeper of the
feals in 1718, and the records of juftice for
that year contain remarkable, and I will
dare to add, precious proofs of my father's
fenfe, abilities, and firmnefs of mind.

As long as he thought the fyftem of M.
Law neceffary for the good and intereft of the
ftate. he eftablifhed and maintained the credit
of the bank ; he difcharged, in this manner,
the immenfe debts of the crown, and enriched it with real treafures, either in fpecie or
credit, which is the fame thing, provided
the latter be generally adopted ; for after all,
even riches are matters of opinion. My father employed, like a good citizen, all the
refources which his intelligence and character acquired him, to procure honour to the
Regent and advantage to the ftate. But,
when he was fully convinced that the abufe
of bank notes was carried to an extreme,

and

and it would be betraying the nation to give them an unjuft and forced credit, he refign-ed the places which put him at the head of thefe operations. His retreat finally dif-covered the illufion ; but the mifchief was over, and irreparable, before he retired. The Regent never* withdrew from him either his kindnefs or confidence.   He lived upwards of a year after his retreat, and did not die of vexation ; he had too great a foul to fink under its weight.   He was by no means accuftomed to the management of the finances ; but a ftatefman feizes all the objects of adminiftration in general—knows how to procure affiftance from the *details* he does not perfectly underftand—and to com-mand that to be done which he either can-not or will not execute himfelf.

My father died in 1721.   M. d'Agueffeau, who was recalled in 1720, was fent in 1722 to Frefne, and the feals were given to M. Fleuriau d'Armenonville, one of thofe chan-cellors whofe merit confifted in their pli-ancy in receiving the impreffions of the prime minifter, and of putting the great feal and moft refpectable marks of fovereign au-thority,

thority, to refolutions in which they had themfelves no fhare. After the difgrace of M. le Duc, the adminiftration of royal juftice was put into the hands of two men, equally intelligent and equitable, although of very different characters. M. d'Aguefleau found himfelf again at the head of the council, and M. Chavelin had the feals.

The chancellorfhip was not, like every other department, fubfervient to the council ; but the finances were not exempt from it. M. Demarets was entirely difcharged ; there was no longer a controller-general ; none but the Regent gave orders, as the king had formerly done. M. le Marefhal de Villeroy was named chief of the council of finances, but purely honorary, and the Duke of Noailles prefident ; although the duke had confiderable wit, and as much knowledge as could be expected from a young man of the court, he could not, certainly, conduct this important adminiftration, nor underftand any thing of the details in which it was neceffary he fhould take the greateft part ; he had in his character an indecifion, from a perpetual hefitation, which

R 3   muft

muft frequently have prevented him from
acting well.   I do not believe what I have
heard of the defects of his heart ; perhaps
thofe who have fpoken to me of them were
prejudiced againft his perfon ; it is, however,
certain that, with great fenfe and abiltics,
he could not manage the finances.   The
Marquis d'Effiat, fiift equerry to the
Duke of Orleans, was vice prefident of the
council, and ftill lefs capable of bufinefs
than the prefident ; he did not, however,
like the latter, turn the heads of his fecretaries. Thefe gentlemen had under them
nine counfellors of ftate, to whom different parts of the adminiftration were diftributed ; fome were capable of the details
entrufted to their care, others were not ;
but, if even they all h d the fame capacity
and merit, a neceffary union would not have
reigned amongft them, becaufe no one depended upon another ; and, confequently,
the council did not act upon conftant and
uniform piinciples.   I cannot too often repeat, upon this occafion, that however ufeful councils are, when well directed, and
although after having been confulted upon
general arrangements, fage, meditated, and

wife

wife laws, have refulted from their advice,
they are equally dangerous, when, inftead
of leaving them the care of watching over
authority, it is wholly abandoned to their
difcretion, they then degenerate into mere
bear garden meetings ; they quariel, difpute, no one undeiftands what he is about ;
and hence nothing iefulrs but anarchy and
confufion.   If arbitrary and abfolute authority degenerate into defpotifm, councils to
which nothing is prefented in a prepared
ftate, and wheiein their decifions are not regulated, do ftill more harm to public welfare.   When the abufes of the councils
eftablifhed by the Duke of Orleans were perceived, and it appeared neceffary to abrogate
them, they were given a kind of *extreme
unčtion*, by charging theAbby de Saint Pierre,
who at firft approved of them, to make the
apology.   He acquitted himfelf of this, by
compofing a work, intituled *La Polyfinodie*,
or *L'Avantage de la Pluralité des Confeils* ; to
which he added the following epigraph,
taken from the Proverbs of Solomon : *Ubi
multa confilia, falus*.   He was right to a certain degree, but he was obliged to acknowledge it to be equally neceffary that fome-

R 4   bo

body fhould be charged to prepare queftions before they were fubmitted to councils, and that authority ought to decide when they have been maturely difcuffed.

To return to the council of finance in particular, fome changes were made in 1717, in the members of which it was compofed, but no advantage derived from them. In 1718, my father was made prefident in the place of M. de Noailles ; this gentleman had not perceived of what utility the fyftem of M. Law, well regulated and underftood, might be, in liberating the ftate from its debts, and in re-eftablifhing, at the fame time, the finances and commerce. My father feized this idea, but he comprehended that it was neceffary to direct and put bounds to its effects and confequences ; he gave to this object all poffible attention ; he employed his firmnefs to overcome the obftacles which thofe who were not perfuaded of the utility of the new fyftem, oppofed to its eftablifhment but alas ! it was not long before he was obliged to ufe the fame means to colour and hide the abufes committed by the Regent, in the ufe he made of thefe
                                    refources,

refources, which are truly delicate in their application.

The Duke of Orleans had knowledge, fagacity, and even vigour enough to conceive the merit of a great plan, and to identify his fame with the welfare of the kingdom he had to govern ; but ftrong paffions, and a kind of weaknefs into which they betray men of the moft enlightened underftandings, carried him beyond the bounds he ought to have prefcribed himfelf : they transformed into a poifon what fhould have been a remedy ; my father faw this, explained and repeated it—not to the public, from which a wife minifter always conceals the evil he forefees, but to him who was mafter to the Regent—to him only who could prevent or repair it ; ufelefs efforts ! the bank loft its credit. My father faw it was impoffible to retrieve it ; at length he abandoned, if I may be allowed the expreffion, the ftate to its unhappy fate, contented with not having made a fortune in a critical time, during which fo many others had unjuftly enriched, or imprudently ruined themfelves. The 5th of January 1720, M. Law
was

was named controller-general, and before the end of the year he was obliged to fly precipitately, and quit the kingdom.

M. Pelletier de la Houffaye, chancellor to the Duke of Orleans, was appointed controller-general in his place; but he held his employ little more than a year. In the month of Auguft 1722, he was replaced by M. Dodun, who kept his poft till the year 1726, when the Duke was exiled. Thefe two controllers-general were but of a middling capacity: it was under the firft of them that the great operation of the *Vifa* was begun, of which M. le Pelletier, member of the council of finance in the time of the Regency, and controller-general after M. Dodun, was the real author. He propofed to examine the original of all the notes and debts, at the charge of the ftate, to pay attention to thofe whofe object fhould appear perfectly legal, in order to difcharge them, but to annul fuch as fhould appear confpicuoufly ufurious or exceffive. This plan was good in itfelf, and it were to be wifhed it had been carried into execution with a fcrupulous exactitude; but the leaft

abufe,

abufe, or fufpicion of injuftice, fpoiled the whole. The fyftem of M. Law appeared preferable, on account of its being more expeditious, and as eafy to keep within proper bounds it was fo in fact, but, as I have juft obferved, it was abufed ; and it was not till after it had been renounced, that the idea of the *Vifa* was again taken up, when it was ftill more difficult of execution than at firft ; it therefore became the fource of great abufe and injuftice.

M. le Pelletier was no more to be blamed for the prefent bad proceedings, than my father had been for all the evil which happened towards the end of M Law's fyftem ; but there was this great difference between them, M. d'Argenfon did not abandon the adminiftration of finances until he faw they were ruined in fpite of him, and M. le Pelletier took the title of controller-general after every thing was loft by the *Vifa.* It is, however, important, to remark that the finances of France were foon re-eftablifhed, notwithftanding the cataftrophes of the bank and the *Vifa* ; fo true it is that in matters of finance, public credit and circulation find

I their

their own level, like the water of the fea, after ftoims and tempefts. There are but fome particular foitunes which are loft without refource ; a melancholy and fatal truth for many people in ceitain critical moments, but confolatory to the ftate. In 1726, M. Oiry replaced M. Dodun : the apparently rough and aufteie chara&er of this miniftcr, docs not picvent his being juft, and even œconomical ; he feconds, in this refpe&, the views of the Cardinal de Fleury, who has, moieover, the prudence and addrefs to make what is moft agreeable in the adminiftiation of finances fall to his fhare.

The minifter of foieign affairs was, at the death of Lewis XIV, fubje& to a council as badly compofed as that of the finances. The Marfhal d'Uxelles was piefideat, and had neither a profound knowledge of affairs of this kind, nor real talents for adminiftration ; all his policy was that of a courtier, and, although maifhal of France, his military talent was confined to overawing fubalterns ; forcing them to difcipline by gieat feverity, and dazzling them

them with haughtinefs and pomp. I was
not much acquainted with the qualities of
his heart, which have been the fubject of
much cenfure ; but I remember his figure,
which was very extraordinary ; I know alfo
that he lived in an elegant ftile. His three
affociates in council were the Abby Def-
tiées, the Marquis of Canillac, and the
Count of Chiverny : their heads were not
much better than his own ; but in other refpects, the two laft were men of wit : Chiverny had been ambaffador at the court of
Vienna, and Canillac was the intimate
friend of Lord Stairs, ambaffador from England. The Regent wifhed to form connec-
tions with this power, and to change fo completely the political fyftem, relative to his
particular interefts, that M. de Torcy was
not only ufelefs, but prejudicial to him :
therefore although the Duke of Orleans
could not but efteem him, he left him in
the council of the Regency, and gave him
the fuperintendance of the pofts, without per-
mitting him to enter the council of foreign
affairs ; yet this council had no other guide
or director than Pecquet, its fecretary, and
who had been clerk to M. de Torcy. The
foreign

foreign minifters knew not to whom they were to apply to treat upon bufinefs ; a man who was not, nor ever had been of the council, was appointed to hear them ; this was M. d'Armenonville, ordinary counfellor of ftate, who had been intendant of the finances, and had bought the office of fecretary of ftate of M. de Torcy ; but upon condition not to exercife the functions. In 1718, the Abby Dubois entered the council of forcign affairs ; in 1719, the offices of fecretary of ftate having been re-eftablifhed, a fifth was created for the Abby, and to which was attached the department of foreign affairs. The council had then nothing more to do ; Dubois became the fole inftrument, and the fole organ of the policy of the Regent, of his correfpondence with the courts of London and Vienna, and of his great cavils with Spain and Alberoni. It was during this adminiftration that the treaty of the quadruple alliance, &c. was concluded.

Dubois, who at length became cardinal, was one of thofe men againft whom many things may, in all fafety of confcience be
faid,

faid, and to whom there is neverthelefs fome good to be attributed ; but we ought, however, to be careful of what we fay in his favour, for fear of being thought declared paitifans of a bad charaćter.   Born in the loweft order of the Bourgeoifie of Brive, in Limoufin, he was firft attached to the Father le Teller, confeffor to the king, who gave him an opportunity of acquiring a good education ; afterwards to a vicar of Saint Euftache, whom he was fortunate enough to pleafe, and who wifhing to place in the tuition of the Duke of Chartres, afterwards Duke of Orleans and Regent, a man incapable of giving him umbrage, procured this honour to Dubois.   He was at firft no more than fub-preceptor under M. de Saint-Laurant, to whofe place he afterwards fucceeded.   He pleafed his pupil by flattering his paffions ; but the true *coup de partie* the Abby Dubois made, and by which his fortune began, was his determining the Duke of Orleans to marry Madamoifelle de Blois, natural daughter to Lewis XIV. notwithftanding the great oppofition and repugnance of MADAME.

In thofe delicate affairs, filent and obfcure, intri-

intrigues are the means which are moft advantageoufly employed ; it was therefore Dubois who concluded this great bufinefs. Continuing to make himfelf agreeable, *per fas et nefas*, to his pupil, (now become his mafter) and having endeavoured to infpire him with vice rather than virtue, he enjoyed the greateft credit from the beginning of the Regency ; having moreover much wit and effrontery, and not being held by any confideration capable of reftraining a good citizen, he put himfelf at the head of feveral intrigues, whofe object was the particular intereft of the Duke of Orleans, and not conformable to thofe of the younger king and the ftate. His conduct was that of bafe, but political fpirits ; who, when they find obftacles on one fide, turn to the other. He fpoke naturally very well when he was not embarraffed; but when he treated of affairs with people of whom he was not fure, he hefitated and ftammered, perhaps to give himfelf time to think of what he ought to anfwer. he was deceitful and guilty of the greateft falfehoods, but he did not fpread with the fame effrontery that he conceived them. Capable of the greateft atrocities,

he

he was fometimes convicted of them; then
he trembled, blufhed, and was confufed;
but he was always very far from changing
for the better, or repenting: his manners
and converfation formed a perfect contraft
with his ecclefiaftical habit: he fwore,
blafphemed, and faid the moft indecent
things againft religion: but he ought to be
reproached moft with having perfuaded
his prince, that there was not in the world
either real piety or true probity,—that every
thing confifted in arriving at a propofed end,
by keeping fecret the means made ufe of
for that purpofe. He extended the principles of this bad education to the Duchefs
of Berry, daughter of the Regent. It was
this man whom the Duke of Orleans made
fecretary of ftate for foreign affairs, at a
time when he found himfelf obliged to re-
ftore to thefe offices their functions.

The connection of the Regent with the
Englifh, were managed by the Abby Dubois
and Camillac, with Earl Stanhope and Lord
Stair; but Dubois having poffeffed himfelf
of the real fecret of that arrangement, was
the only perfon who could follow it up. He

S   was

was certainly a penfioner of England, that
is, of the enemies of the ftate, and the
catholic religion ; but as it was for the
Regent he intrigued, he feared nothing
from him. In 1720, this worthy ecclefiaftic was promoted to the archbifhopric of
Cambray, and obtained it with circumftances which, for the honour of religion
I dare not infert. In 1721, he was made
cardinal, and in 1723 was declared prime
minifter, when the Regent was obliged to
give up to the king, at leaft in appearance,
the helm of the ftate. It may eafily be
believed that the Duke of Orleans thought
of making him oftenfible minifter only,
and of being the real one himfelf . yet
who knows that Dubois would not have remained prime minifter if the Regent had
died before him ; but it happened to the contrary, and the Duke of Orleans was obliged
to take this title. M. de Morville, fon of
M. d'Armenonville, keeper of the feals,
who had the marine department, took that
of foreign affairs, and kept it under the authority of the duke of Bourbon, who had
the title of prime minifter after the Duke of
Orleans. This prince had no merit which

I   made

made him fit for this place, his fole recommendation was the greatnefs of his birth;
he was merely oftenfible, and every body
knew the agent by whom he was governed.
M. de Morville was a man of but middling
abilities, yet he had good fenfe, and a juft
judgment: he poffeffed a fecondary merit,
which we diftinguifh by the name of *bon
ecouteur*, (a perfon who hearkens patiently
to what is faid to him); he never fpoke
but in his turn, nor without giving himfelf
time to think of what he ought to fay;
then whatever he faid was to the point.
Men went from his audiences pleafed with
having been attentively heard. He retired
in Auguft 1727; his father gave up the
feals at the fame time, and they were both
replaced by M. Chauvelin, in whom their
titles were united. The father died the
year following, the fon in 1732.

The council of war, eftablifhed under
the regency, had for its chief the marfhal
Villars, already famous for his victories
gained over the enemy, and who feemed to
have reftored the tarnifhed glory of the arms
of France to its former luftre. This gene-

ral's

ral's defects were vanity and prefumption,
or at leaft all the appearances of them;
otherwife, he had a greatnefs of mind, good
fenfe, and marked talents for war. But
however brilliant thefe advantages may be,
they are not fufficient to make a good minifter for the department he held. Therefore the Regent, in placing him at the head
of the council, gave him nothing more than a
public reprefentation, without the real adminiftration. The marfhal flattered himfelf he fhould have the diftribution of favours, but means were foon found to take it
away from him; it was decided that this
diftribution fhould be made in full council.
It would have been a perpetual fource of
frightful diffenfions among the members;
but they liked better to operate each of
them with the Regent, relative to the different military corps over which they were
particularly charged to watch, and leave
him to pronounce the appointment; this is
really what happened, and the Regent difpofed of favours with as much authority as
Lewis XIV. had done. Nothing remained to
the military counfellors, than the care of di-
gefting fome ordonnances and regulations
                                    of

of difcipline : and when they propofed any new expences, they found themfelves fubject to the examination and controul of the two loweft members of the council of war ; men of the robe, who had in their departments, war, finances, contracts, diftribution of funds — the real bufinefs of preceding war minifters, and the only one with which they ought to be charged. One was M. de Saint Conteft, who had been a long time intendant of the frontier provinces ; the other M. le Blanc, mafter of requefts. Treafurers, commiffaries of war, and contractors, knew thefe two gentlemen only ; confequently the whole machine of war turned upon them ; therefore M. le Blanc foon made himfelf mafter of the ground ; and when the fecretaries of ftate were re-eftablifhed, he became one of them. The form of the council of war exifted, however, for fome years ; but M. le Blanc having united all the details of M. de Saint Conteft to his own, was the fpring and pivot of it. He had the fame credit as M. de Chamillard and M. de Louvois ever had before him. Certainly he was not without talents and addrefs for his perfonal conduct,

S 3 and

and he had a great knowledge of the bufinefs of the war office; but the details of
finance and military adminiftration, became
very delicate in the midft of the pecuniary
embarraffments occafioned by the fyftem of
M. Law, and afterwards by the *Vifa*. In
1723, M. le Blanc was difplaced, and fent
to the Baftille, with the intention of profe-
cuting him.   His department was filled
by M. Breteuil, intendant of Limoge, a mild
and pliant man, but extremely ignorant;
every body knows that the effential fervice
which he rendered to the cardinal Dubois,
procured him this piace; he fupported himfelf under the duke, by extreme complaifance to perfons in favour. Meffrs. de Belle-
ifle and de Seichelles, intimate friends and
counfellors of M. le Blanc, were alfo put
into the Baftille, fome months after him.
The ftorm continued to threaten them during the whole adminiftration of the duke;
but as foon as the prince was fent to Chan-
tilly, every thing changed; M. de Breteuil
returned to place, and the faction of Belle-
ifle and de Seichelles fent in their turn the
two brothers, all powerful under the Duke
of Orleans, one to the Baftille, the other
                                        into

into exile. In 1728 M. le Blanc died; M. Dangervilliers, intendant of Paris, who had for a long time occupied the fame poft in the province of Alface, took his place, and M. de Breteuil remained aloof. M. Dangervilliers, fon or grandfon of a famous partifan, who lived under the adminiftration of Colbert, is defcended from a celebrated phyfician and botanift, has wit and talents, with defects, and fome ridicule in his character.

The council of the marine was compofed like that of war, and had the fame fate; the Count of Touloufe was its honorary chief, the Marfhal d'Eftrées, prefident, and it was blended with fome officers and old intendants of the marine, who were charged with all the details. La Chapelle, an old firft clerk of M. de Pontchartrain, was fecretary : as the marine was now reduced to a mere trifle, this council appeared to be of little importance. As foon as the fecretaries of ftate were re-eftablifhed, M. d'Armenonville, who had bought the employ of M. de Torcy, had the affairs of this department, the Abby Dubois being

S 4

charge

charge des affaires etrangeres, as fifth fecretary of ftate.   M. de Maurepas retook the
office of the Pontchartrains, his father and
grandfather; but he had the expediting the
affairs of the King's houfhold, and of Paris
only, under the infpection and orders of his
father in-law, la Viilliere.   This continued
till 1722, when M. d'Armenonville became
keeper of the feals ; M. de Morville being
fecretary of ftate for the marine department.
At the death of the Cardinal Dubois in 1723,
M de Morville took the adminiftration of
foreign affairs, and M. de Maurepas had the
whole department poffeffed by his father
previous to the death of Lewis XIV.   The
marine council had been fuppreffed in 1722;
after having been for fome time in a lan-
guifhing ftate.   The young marine minifter
is more amiable, but ftill more ignorant than
his father was ; he delights in pleafantries,
which may be called the pranks of a young
courtier, rather than malice and acrimony of
difpofition, of which it was faid his father was capable.   But he enjoyed too
foon the charms and advantages of adminiftration, and it does not appear that he is
yet acquainted with its duties and principles.
                                             He

He was but eighteen years of age, when his clerks faid to him, " Monfeigneur, amufe " yourfelf, leave bufinefs to us; if you " wifh to oblige any perfon, make your " intentions known to us, and we will find " proper means to give fuccefs to what- " ever you pleafe. Moreover, forms and " rules are learnt in proportion as affairs " and opportunity prefent themfelves, and " enough of thefe will pafs before your " eyes, to give you in a fhort time more " experience than we have." It muft, however, be agreed, that we may pafs a long life in labouring without principles, and never learn any thing, and that expe- rience is rather the fruit of reflection upon what we have feen, than the refult of an infinity of facts to which we have not paid all the attention they merited.

A council for home affairs was formed in 1716. The Duke of Antin was prefident; the Marquiffes of Biinghen and Brancas were placed with fome counfellors of ftate, *maîtres des requêtes*, and counfellors of parliament ; this council was to be charged with the fame object of adminiftration as the prefent coun-

cil

cil of difpatches. It exifted till the re-eftablifhment of the fecretaries of ftate, that is to fay, about three years ; after which M. de la Vullicre returned to the care of the provinces which had formerly belonged to him. M. d'Armenonville and Maurepas were charged with the reft. The minifters of foreign affai s and that of war, had authority at that time ; it was not till afterwards that they were reftored to their places.

At length, to all thefe councils was added one of commerce, the prefidency of which was given to the Marfhal Villeroy, a man of the world, to whom the Duke of Orleans was little difpofed to give employment and confideration. With him was affociated many counfellors of ftate, and *maîtres des requétes*, to whom was diftributed the care of different branches of commerce; and they were not only charged to watch over them, but to make proper regulations, whereby they might be augmented and improved. Nothing could be more interefting to the ftate, than what might refult from fuch a council ; but it was neceffary it fhould be directed, that there fhould be

an

an unanimity in' its operations, which
fhould all have tended to one end only;
but this is what was wanting in that as well
as in all the other councils: when the
Marfhal Villeroy was difgraced, it was deftroyed, or, at leaft, it remained two or
three years in inaction. It was at length
re-eftablifhed under the name of the royal
council of commerce; the king prefided
there as well as at the royal council of finances, that of difpatches, and at the council of ftate, properly fo called   The names
of a part of the minifters, and of fome counfellors of ftate, are upon the lift of the members of this council; the controller general
of finances, and the fecretary of ftate for the
marine department, are effential members of
it.   There was a board of commerce more
numerous eftablifhed to propofe fuch bufinefs as was to be laid before the council.
The offices of the intendants of commerce,
created under Lewis XIV. were re-eftablifhed, and each commercial city fent a de-
puty to Paris.   All this prefents the idea of
a wife and good adminiftration; but it is,
in reality, upon paper only; the royal
council of commerce never affembled, the
board

board but feldom, the intendants and depu-
ties act with the controller general only,
and know nobody but him ; the latter are
his clerks, the former his clients: finances
and commerce may be faid to be the fame
thing in France, and to move round the
fame axis.

It ought to be concluded, from the fup-
preffion of the councils eftablifhed under the
regency, and the inactivity in which the
principals of the royal councils which decorate our almanacks are fuffered to lan-
guifh, that it is not yet known in France
what advantage may be derived from councils, diftinguifhing well what ought to be
fubmitted to their deliberation, from that
which fhould be left to the daily decifion of
minifters of each department ; and what
ought to be laid before the king, from that
which they may perfonally decide upon in
their cabinets.   All the ordonnances, and
the general regulations, which form the
law, and eftablifh principles in the adminiftration, ought to be deliberated upon in
council, difcuffed, ferioufly examined, and
finally decided therein, as far as agrees with
the

the conftitution of a monarchy, wherein every council ought to be nothing more than a deliberative body. Every queftion agitated there, ought to be clearly propofed, and it is the duty of the minifter to make this propofition. Each minifter ought to be the reporter of the affairs relative to his department, as he is to look to their execution when once they are regulated. I fpeak not of little private affairs with which the board is at prefent amufed, in the royal councils of finance and difpatches, when they are affembled, but of general regulations, for which alone councils, at which the king affifts in perfon, fhould be called together. Minifters are not fufficiently aware of the importance it is to them to have guarantees for thefe regulations. By taking them upon themfelves, they are expofed to become refponfible for every difficulty they fuffer either in the regiftering or execution; they are frequently victims to their imprudence, and thus furnifh occafions of being difplaced. With refpect to favours, councils fhould be acquainted with the principles only upon which the minifter propofes them; but it is highly important even for

minifters,

minifters, that thefe principles fhould be
fomewhere depofited ; they ought to be
their buckler to fortify themfelves againft
unjuft demands : and it is highly neceffary
they fhould thus defend themfelves. For
one favour againft rule and reafon which the
minifter accords to thofe whom he perfonally and really protects, he is obliged to
grant twenty others to peifons protected by
his patrons, and by thofe to whom he cannot refufe any thing ; in that cafe, being
preffed, he knows not what to anfwer. If
he refufes to one what he grants to another,
he creates to himfelf difagreeable cavils.
A wife man, on going into place, ought to
take more meafures to enable him to refufe,
without doing himfelf much harm, than to
give every thing according to his fancy ;
for it is certain he can never bring about the
latter. However, he fhould always refufe
without caprice, and receive with mildnefs
even the moft unreafonable demands ; and,
above all, never promife that which he is
not fure to perform : *Hoc opus, hic labor.*

ESSAY

E S S A Y XXXV.

EXEMPLARY CHARACTER OF CARDINAL ROHAN

I HAVE juft treated, in a long article, an important fubject, to eftablifh occafionally great maxims, and draw interefting portraits. I dare affert their juftnefs and refemblance, having fpoken according to perfonal and certain knowledge only : I have defcribed ftatefmen, or at leaft thofe who fhould have been fo. At prefent I mean to treat of the principles of conduct men ought to follow in private life, and in fociety, always from my own exprience, or the examples of perfons with whom I have been moft acquainted.

The moft perfect model of a great and amiable man of rank is the Cardinal Rohan ; although he is but a man of middling abilities, contracted in erudition and reading,

has

has neither been charged with the adminiftration of the higher departments, nor applied himfelf much to important affairs, he
has a remarkable advantage over thofe who
have been deeply engaged in negociations
and public bufinefs. He has neither the
figure nor features of a prince fit to command armies ; but he is the moft handfome
prelate in the world ; and, when young,
was a charming abby of quality. He maintained his thefis, in the Sorbonne, in a diftinguifhed manner ; his leffon was given
him ; but he retained it with facility, and
delivered it with grace. Having obtained
early the bifhoprick of Strafburgh, and the
Cardinal's hat, he was charged with nego-
tiations at the courts of feveral German
princes, and in the Conclave at Rome, he
always got through them with dignity and
eafe ; and, certainly, if any body has been
able to verify the fingular and proverbial
expreffion, that *men of quality know every
thing, without learning any thing*, it is the
Cardinal de Rohan. His policy was always
paffive ; he accommodated himfelf to time
and place ; to governments and circumftances. With fuch a conduct he might
have

have appeared mean ; but he knew always how to ftamp his actions with a character of noblenefs, in fuch a manner as to be applauded by fools, and pardoned by men of underftanding. He declared himfelf, according to circumftances, in favour of the bull *Unigenitus*, or left the Janfenifts to think as they thought proper. He was made a member of the council of the regency, at the end of the adminiftration of the Duke of Orleans, to infure the Cardinal Dubois the fame rank as the Cardinals Richelieu and Mazarine had enjoyed in the council. It was perceived that Dubois had no right to pafs over fuch a charm after eighty years interruption. The birth of M. de Rohan, and the dignities with which he was invefted, independently of the cardinalfhip, made him fufceptible of it, but he was the forerunner only of a prime minifter very unworthy of that high office ; after all, what could the Cardinal Rohan lofe by this complaifance ? He acquitted himfelf of the ceremonies of the church, to which his office of great almoner obliged him, in the moft becoming manner, without affecting too much devotion : neither is

T   he

he accufed of hypocrify; nor can any reproach him with indecency. He behaves
more nobly at Strafburgh and Saverne than
any German prince, or even the ecclefiaftical electors: his court and retinue are numerous and brilliant; with all this, he preferves that air of decency which the diftinguifhed members of the French clergy
have, and which is not to be found among
thofe of Germany and Italy: he is gallant,
but he finds opportunities enough to fatisfy
his inclination to pleafure with great princeffes, fine women, and canoneffes double
proof, fo as not to demean himfelf by gallantry; or, at leaft, to be accufed of low
debauch. The cardinal, fometimes, in
fpeaking of himfelf, modeftly gives you to
underftand, there muft be in him fome refemblance of Lewis XIV. as well in his perfon as his character; in fact, the Princefs
of Soubife, his mother, was very beautiful;
we know that Lewis XIV. was in love with
her, and the epocha of this *penchant* is near
the year 1674, in which the Cardinal de Rohan was born. If there be any truth in this
anecdote, we may add, that, defcended
from a very great prince, it is poffible other
great

great princes owe to him their exiftence. His politenefs to individuals who go to fee him, whether it be at his bifhopric, the court, or at Paris, proceeds certainly more from habitude than fentiment ; but carries fo much the mark of friendfhip, that, even though perfuaded that it is not fincere, men fuffer themfelves to be feduced by it. As foon as you arrive he feems to have a thoufand things to fay to you, as a confidential favorite, and foon afterwards he leaves you to fpeak to another ; but, whilfthe does what is moft agreeable to himfelf, he feems to think only of leaving you mafter of his houfe, withdraws for fear of embarraffing and importuning you, whilft, on the contrary, you would embarrafs and importune him by prolonging your vifit. In a word, nobody poffeffes the talent of pleafing more than the Cardinal de Rohan ; but it does not belong to every one to make ufe of the fame means. *Every body is not permitted to go to Corinth* ; this old adage may be applied to the ufe of more than one amiable quality ; there are people who may neglect fome one of them ; others who ought to

T 2   collect

collect as many as poffible, and who ftill fucceed with difficulty, notwithftanding all the refources, furnifhed them by nature.

ESSAY

E S S A Y   XXXVI.

ON PUNCTUALITY.

I WILL return in a moment to the art and means of pleafing ; but I wifh to fay a word more upon exactitude and punctuality : thefe are merits of the fecond order ; they feem to belong to fubalterns only ; yet they are fometimes very valuable : I confefs that I am fcrupuloufly attached to them, although I have a ftrong domeftic example to the contrary.   My father was the leaft punctual of any man living ; he never knew what it was o'clock ; charged with an infinity of details, moft of them very important, but of different kinds, he got through them when he could, or when he would, *by fits and ftarts*, tho' interrupted inceffantly by one or the other; but his fure and active genius fupplied every thing : he always found the end of his threads, although he broke them every moment ; and embraced fucceffively an hundred different

T 3   objects,

objects, without confounding them. I admired this wonderful talent, but never perceived that I poffeffed it. I have introduced more method, order, and punctuality in my proceedings, but my brother took the refolution of imitating my father. For my part, I thought it might be prefumptive to follow that route, when nature had not pointed it out. Moreover, when you are not fure of being above proceeding methodically, and wifh, notwithftanding, to attain that elevation, you run a rifk of being unequal to your affairs, and of lofing and difhonouring yourfelf.

ESSAY

ESSAY XXXVII.

ON THE ART OF PLEASING.

MONCRIF, who is attached to my brother, came to communicate to me his project of printing a book, intituled: *De la neceſſité et des moyens de plaire.* " My dear Moncrif," ſaid I to him, " nothing is ſo eaſy as to treat upon the firſt head of thy diſcourſe; all the world feels it; all the world has a deſire to pleaſe, but the means are extremely difficult to be found : it is a difficult, and very delicate matter to indicate the true ones; they depend upon a great number of circumſtances, which make them vary *ad infinitum.*" From this I entered with him into particulars, of which I have ſince committed a part to paper. After hearkening to me attentively, " Sir," anſwered he, humbly, " I will make uſe of the ſage reflections you have juſt communicated to me ; but the plan of my work is not laid exactly in the manner you

T 4   propoſe."

propofe."—" Thy work ! is it already finifhed ?" replied I. " Yes, Sir, it is in the prefs." In fact, in a very little time afterwards, he brought it to me, printed and well bound : I have read it, and this reading has recalled to my mind what a man of wit, a friend of mine, once faid to me, as we were walking in a great library, where there were a multitude of books upon fpeculative philofophy, metaphyfics and morality : *" Here are,"* faid he, *" thoufands of volumes, of which the greateft number ought to be fuppreffed, and the reft new modelled :"*— that of MONCRIF is fo much the more of the latter defcription, on account of its being very unanimatedly written ; it is, therefore, tirefome, although a fmall volume : he finifhes with fairy tales, above the capacity of children, and not interefting enough to men.

Moncrif faid himfelf that the marvellous could not be agreeable, but by the manner of reprefenting it ; that otherwife improbability difgufted and fatigued. His tales are the beft proofs of this truth.

Moncrif's

Moncrif's mother was the widow of a *procureur*, called Paradis. She was a woman of wit, and knew how to ufe it to advantage, and to bring up two children, which her hufband had left her. By the protection of my brother one of them became a fubaltern officer, and, at length, commander of a fmall place ; the eldeft had the greater fhare of his mother's affection, who, to introduce him into the world, made the laft efforts to cloath him well : fhe fent him to the theatres, to the places fet apart for the moft diftinguifhed people, where he might make ufeful acquaintances. Moncrif, following his mother's counfels, became acquainted with me and my brother, amongft others. This has been beneficial to him ; our relations were in place ; my brother made him his private friend and fecretary, upon the moft genteel footing : fome years afterwards he attached himfelf to the Compte de Clermont, Prince of the blood, and he had the flattering title of fecretary to his commanderies ; he had even a lift of vacant benefices depending upon this Prince-Abby ; but he propofed no fubject but with the approbation of certain women

of

of the opera.   He quarrelled with this little court ; but my brother repaired all by
making him reader to the queen, and fecretary general of the pofts.   It is faid he
had learned to fence, and that he was even
received as a fencing-mafter ; what makes
this probable is, that when Moncrif became
reader to the queen, and confequently at
court, his age was enquired after : his
friends wifhed to prove him older than he
appeared to be, and quoted the epocha of
his reception in the coips of fencing-mafters.
M. de Maurepas would aflure himfelf of it ;
and, having had occafion to read the lift
of the members of this community, who
prayed a renewal of their privileges, he
found, in fact, the name of Paradis at the
head.   He afked the Syndics what was become of this mafter : the anfwer was, that
he had difappeared for fome time, and confequently renounced the profeffion.   The
minifter, who, as every body knows loves
a little waggery, related this anecdote to the
king.   According to this account, Moncrif
was eighty years of age.   Lewis XV. having laughed at it a good deal, finding
Moncrif one day with the queen, faid to
                                                    him,

him, *Do you know, Moncrif, that there are people who give you eighty years of age ?* *Yes, Sire,* anſwered he, *but I do not take them.* For my part, I do not believe that Moncrif has been a fencing-maſter ; it muſt rather have been his brother, in whom his mother could not find other talents for ſociety than fencing, which is not a very ſocial one.

I return to Madame Paradis. With wit, reading, an agreeable manner, and addreſs, ſhe procured herſelf a good income. Towards the end of the reign of Lewis XIV. there was more pretenſion to wit in intrigues than at preſent : it was the cuſtom to write gallant notes, which required anſwers of the ſame kind, and the ardour of the cavalier was judged of by the energy of the letters which he got ſecretly delivered : the lover, in the ſame manner, calculated his hopes according to the anſwer. Madame Paradis devoted herſelf to the epiſtolary ſtyle ; being known to ſeveral ladies of the gallant court of Lewis XIV. ſhe aſſiſted them with her pen to make agreeable advances, or give tender anſwers ; and this was no real injury

to

to her fortune, nor to the advancement of her fon. Moncrif appeared to inherit the talent of his mother. My brother having made a journey into Touraine, became intimately and particularly acquainted with a lady of this province. After his return to Paris, he received from her fome letters of gallantry, to which, in politenefs, he could not but return anfwers. He charged Moncrif to wiite them, who acquitted himfelf like a woithy fon of Madame Paradis, and fpared my brothei the tiouble of even copying them. But the moft whimfical confequence of this correfpondence was, my brother having become minifter, and the young lady a wife, fhe had occafion to write about fome affair to her old lover, and was much furprized at not finding, in his anfwers, either the ftyle of the letters fhe had prefeived, or even the fame handwriting : we may learn by this, that minifters, and thofe who arc deftined to become fo, do not always do that of themfelves, from which they gain the moft honour.

As

As I faid to Moncrif, there is nobody but is convinced of the neceffity of pleafing, and who has not, more or lefs, the defire of doing it ; but this is not all ; talents are moreover neceffary. Every actor upon a theatre carries with him the defire of being applauded ; yet there are many who come off with being hiffed and hooted. To fucceed, two kinds of talents are neceffary; thofe which nature gives, and cannot otherwife be acquired, ftature, figure, and an agreeable voice; natural, eafy, gay, and amiable wit ; thofe who poffefs not thefe advantages, fhould procure to themfelves a fictitious amiability ; though it is never worth that which is real, and what may properly be called innate : but ftill it is of fome value ; it is ftudied, but it muft appear natural ; is infenfibly gained by habitude ; and the occupation of improving acquired advantages becomes agreeable.

The defire of excelling cannot be too much concealed ; on the contrary, what ought to be moft remarked, or fuppofed in you, is the defire of making others appear to advantage. Affection, or at leaft the appearance

pearance of it; admiration, real or pretended; flattery, delicately managed, never fail
to fucceed. When you perceive that any
particular vice is difpleafing, affect the oppofite virtue. This contraft is the art of
pleafing in fociety, what the *claro obfcuro*
is in painting: the colouring muft be
heightened by contrafts; the colours muft
be laid on thick, and the pencils managed
with delicacy. Good-nature, fincerity, and
complaifance, muft be affected, yet tinc-
tured with a little criticifm.

A fatirical character is frightful and difpleafing in itfelf; but, as able phyficians
transform poifons into remedies, men of
great wit manage criticifm and irony fo as
to amufe fome perfons, and correct others,
without faying any thing offenfive; and
what elfe is fable and good comedy?

Let us acknowledge that we ftrive not to
pleafe others but from a motive of felf-love:
but it is neceffary to veil it fo as to prevent
its being even fufpected. Let us go ftill
further, and add, that we muft not be too
anxious about people whom we wifh to
pleafe:

pleafe: they are embarraffed by being fpoken well of in their prefence ; they would often prefer being criticifed, provided it did not exceed what they could defend with advantage.

Compliance is the laft fpring to put in motion, and which acts well in fecret only : fuch as are known to be of an accommodating character are fufpected ; we are inclined to look upon them as deceitful, and even treacherous.

We eafily perfuade thofe who are in affliction, that we ourfelves are affected by it, becaufe whoever partakes of trouble cannot be fufpected of interefted views ; but nothing is more difficult than to perfuade thofe who are happy, and arrive at great employs, that we rejoice fincerely at their good fortune : they think, and with reafon, that we fhould trouble ourfelves but little about it, if our perfonal intereft were not concerned therein. Men, in a fubordinate fituation, are not thanked for their complaifance ; it is looked upon as one of their obligations ; it is even, fometimes, by
this

this they get their bread; but it is very valuable in superiors, provided it be not suspected to take its source from weakness or simplicity.

Indulgence for faults, which is founded upon indifference only, humiliates him who experiences it, and renders odious the person by whom it is exercised.

A disdainful air, a contemptible tone, make great men hated; but a low and cringing manner, make them despised, which is still worse. A noble politeness is what they ought to be ambitious of, and which they often possess; but that which is equally rare and precious in all ranks is equability. Unhappily its opposite is not discovered till after a certain time of probation; we are frequently seduced into strong connexions, before we discover that those with whom we have formed them are unworthy of our esteem, because they have for sometime imposed upon themselves the necessity of pleasing; on the first neglect, their defects, and insupportable humour appear; the beginning of the acquaintance was serene and agreeable; the end of it becomes clouded, and

fometimes tempeftuous; but when an engagement is formed, life paffes in regretting
the firft moments ; they return but feldom,
and it is neceffåry to confole ourfelves for an
attachment to a perfon of a capricious and
unequal character, by recollecting the agreeable moments we have paffed together, and
by enjoying the hope of finding others like
them.

The reflection with which Moncrif finifhes his book, appears to me to be the moft
fenfible thing in it, and is as follows : " A
" man, on entering the world, fhould expect
" to find two judges of all his actions,—
" reafon and felf-love, or the intereft of
" others. The firft of thefe judges is always
" equitable and impartial ; the fecond fe-
" vere, and frequently unjuft ; it is the
" child of jealoufy ; let us ftrive not to
" allure it : this is the means of pleafing
" and fucceeding."

I have related in a few pages, all the
maxims worth quoting from Moncrif's
book ; *de la neceffité et des moyens, de plaire,*
in which there are three hundred.

U

ESSAY

ESSAY XXXVIII.

ON INDIFFERENCE EXEMPLIFIED IN THE
CHARACTER OF FONTENELLE, MON-
TESQUIEU, AND HENAULT.

I HAVE often heard this bad maxim.
advanced, "that he who is not a
great enemy, is not a good friend:" by
which is undoubtedly meant, that he who
is not capable of ftrong hatred and vengeance, cannot be warm in the fer* ce of his
friends. But let us make a diftinction between the exceffes into which our paffions
may lead us, and the confequences of a
wife and deliberate attachment; friendfhip
ought to be of the latter defcription only; if
it became a paffion, it would lofe its ref-
pectability; and be attended with all the
dangers of love, which is the caufe of as
many evils as hatred and vengeance. God
preferve us from too much love, as well as
from too much hatred; but we ought to
love to a certain degree: the heart of man
has need of this fentiment, and it is of ufe
to our minds, when it does not obfcure
them. But hatred and the love of vengeance

geance cannot do otherwife* than torment us : happy are they who feel not thefe paf-fions; cannot we on the principle of rational affection, ferve our friends with alertnefs and conftancy, and be even tenacious in affairs in which they are interefted? Is it neceffary to be cruel to one man, becaufe we are friendly to another? Does the malice of a perfecutor, and the unremitting affection of a friend, flow from the fame complexion of mind? By no means; for my part, I declare myfelf a weak enemy, not only in force but in intention, although I am a zealous and fteady friend.

If I have received fome reproaches upon my pretended indifference for people with whom I live habitually, three of them deferve many more, and I do not efteem them lefs on this account—their names are well known in the world, fince the firft is M. de Fontenelle, the fecond the Prefident de Montefquieu, and the third, the Prefident Henault. The firft is charged with and convicted of a kind of apathy, perhaps blameable with refpect to others, but excellent for his own prefervation; being taken up

with

with himfelf only, and amiable enough to make others concerned for his welfare, he has by managing his weak and delicate conftitution, always indulging his eafe, pufhed his carreer to eighty years of age, with the pleafing hope of feeing the whole revolution of the century. Each year gives him a new degree of merit, and adds to the intereft his friends have in his exiftence. They look upon him as one of thofe mafter-pieces of art, carefully and delicately wrought, and precioufly preferved, becaufe it is impoffible to make their equal. He makes us not only recollect the brilliant age of Lewis XIV. the end of which fome of us faw, but alfo the wit of Buiferade, Saint-Evrémont, Scudery, and the tone of the hotel de Rambouillet, the air of which we may believe he has breathed upon the fpot. He has this tone, but foftened, improved, and adapted to the prefent age, lefs obfcure and pedantic than that of the Beaux-Efprits, which founded the academy ; lefs finical than that of Julie d'Augennes, and his mother. His converfation is highly agreeable, mixed with fentiments lefs refined than ftriking, and with pleafing anecdotes, without being fatirical,

cal, becaufe they never relate but to literature or gallantry, and fociety. All his
tales are fhort, and for this reafon more
ftriking; they finifh by fomething witty,
which is a neceffary condition of fuch narratives. The eulogiums which he pronounces
at the Academy of Sciences, have in them
the fame fpirit as his converfation; they are
confequently delightful; but I do not know
if his manner of prefenting them be fuch a
one as he ought to make ufe of: he attaches
himfelf to the perfons of Academicians, ftrives
to characterife, to paint them; even enters
into details of their private life; and as he
is an agreeable painter, his portraits are admired: but might not fome of them be compared to fine engravings, found at the head
of the works of certain heroes? they prefent
us with their phyfiognomy, but leave us
with a wifh that they had done fomething
more.

It feems to me that the eulogium of an
Academician, fhould be the extract or crayon
only of his academical works. It may be
objected to this, that there are Academicians whofe works and talents furnifh not

U 3   matter

matter of great eulogium, but on one hand, even the barrennefs or refufal of eulogiums, is one means of preventing the Academy from admitting fubjects incapable of doing it much honour: on the other, the protection which thofe who are honorary Members only, have granted to the fciences, the favours they have procured for the learned, may be advantageoufly fpoken of in their behalf, and at leaft their zeal applauded.— It muft, however, be agreed, that Fontenelle in artfully paffing over the drynefs of matters to which thofe who were the fubjects of his encomium applied themfelves, fays generally what is neceffary. It is to be feared, his fucceffors and imitators will find it eafieft to fpeak but little upon the fubject, otherwife they will fail in it entirely.

To return to the perfonality of Fontenelle, we know he loves nothing to a great degree; but I pardon him his indifference, and love him better on account of it; we love him for himfelf only, without requiring a return or being flattered by it.—We may fay of him what Madame de Deffant faid of her cat—"I love her exceedingly, becaufe fhe
" is

" is the moſt amiable creature in the world;
" but I trouble myſelf little about the degree
" of affection ſhe has for me: I ſhould be
" very ſorry to loſe her, becauſe I feel that I
" manage and perpetuate my pleaſures, by
" employing my cares to prolong her exiſt-
" ence."

The Preſident de Monteſquieu is not ſo old
as Fontenelle, but has full as much wit, although of quite another kind—it ſeems as
if more ought to be expected in ſociety from
the Preſident, becauſe he is more lively,
even appears more active, more ſuſceptible
of enthuſiaſm. At bottom, theſe two minds
are tempered alike; Monteſquieu never makes
himſelf uneaſy for any body, he has no ambition on his own account; he reads, travels
and gathers knowledge; at length he writes,
and ſolely for his pleaſure. Being a man
of great ſenſe, he makes an agreeable uſe
of what he knows, but there is more wit
in his books than in his converſation, becauſe he is never anxious to ſhine in it. He
has preſerved the Gaſcon accent, which he
has from his country (Bourdeaux) and thinks
it in ſome meaſure beneath him to ſtrive to

U 4   get

get rid of it. He is carelefs in his ftyle, which is more ingenious and fometimes more nervous than pure; there is no order nor method in his works, which are for this reafon more brilliant than inftructive. He had an early tafte for a kind of bold philofophy, which he has combined with French gaiety and levity, and which has made his *Lettres Perfannes* truly a delightful work. But if on one hand, this book has been much admired, it has on the other, been juftly complained of; there are paffages which a man of wit may eafily conceive, but fuch as a prudent man ought never to let appear in print : thefe paffages, have, notwithftanding, eftablifhed the reputation of the book and the author. He would not have been of the Academy without this work, which ought to have excluded him from it. The Cardinal de Fleury, fo prudent in other refpects, fhewed on this occafion a pufillanimity which may be attended with great confequences. The Prefident refigned his employment, that his non-refidence at Paris might not be an objection to his being received a Member of the Academy. His pretext was, that he was going to apply him-

felf

felf to a great work upon the fpirit of laws.
The Prefident Henault, on quitting his employ, gave the fame reafon. Thefe gentlemen were rallied by their friends, who told
them, " They quitted their profeffions in
order to learn it."

The fact is, Montefquieu wifhed to travel,
to make philofophical remarks upon men and
nations, already known by his *Lettres Perfannes*: he was warmly received in Germany, England and Italy. We do not know
the whole extent of the obfervations and reflections he made in different countries.——
fince his return, he has publifhed but one
work, printed in 1734, intituled, *Confiderations fur les caufes de la grandeur et d. la deca-
dence des Romains*. In this work he appears
more fenfible, enlightened and referved than
in his *Lettres Perfannes*, the matter keeps
him from wandering. It is faid, he is preparing to publifh his great work upon the
fpirit of laws: I know already fome parts of
it, which fupported by the reputation of the
author, cannot but augment its credit ; but
I fear the whole will not have this effect,
and that there will be more agreeable chap-

ters

ters to read, more ingenious and feducing
ideas, than true and ufeful inftructions upon
the manner in which we ought to digeft
and underftand the laws. It is, however,
a book which has been, and ftill is greatly
wanted, although much has been written
upon the fubject.

We have good inftitutes of the Roman
civil laws; we have tolerabe ones in the
French laws; but we have none publifhed
of general, or univerfal ones. We have
no *Efprit des Loix*; and I doubt much of our
friend Montefquieu's giving us one which
will ferve as a guide and compafs to all the
Legiflators of the world. I know him to
have all poffible art; he has acquired vaft
knowledge in his travels, and in his retreats
to the country; but I predict once more, that
he will not give us the book we want, although there will be found, in what he
is compofing, many profound ideas, new
thoughts, ftriking images, fallies of wit and
genius, and an infinity of curious facts,
whofe application fuppofes ftill more tafte
than ftudy.

I now

I now return to the character he bears in society; great mildness and gaiety, a perfect equality, an air of simplicity and good nature, which, considering the reputation he has already acquired, is a peculiar merit. He is sometimes absent, and strokes of *naiveté* escape him, which make him appear more amiable, as they form a contrast with his acknowledged wit. I forgot to speak of his little poem in prose in the Grecian taste, intitled *Le Temple de Gnide*. I know not if the reputation of the President gained by his *Lettres Perfannes*, has not contributed to make this trifle esteemed above its merit: it contains much wit, sometimes grace and voluptuousness, whose touches in some places are rather strong, and there reigns a kind of philosophical observation, which characterises the author, but it is different from those of his other works.— Fontenelle certainly could not have written *les confiderations fur les Romains*; but *Le Temple de Gnide* would have been better constructed by him than by Montesquieu.

I will not oppose the gallantry of the President to that of Fontenelle, because Montesquieu

·tefquieu had none: he writes little or no
poetry, but he is found amiable in fociety,
independent of gallantry and poetry. Fontenelle has, on the contrary, need of thefe
refources ; the gracefulnefs and manner in
which he delivers that which from the
mouth of any other man would be infipid,
make his fcience and erudition appear to advantage, although they are perhaps not very
·profound.

The Prefident Henault, will not perhaps
hold fo diftinguifhed a place in the temple of
memory as the two others, but I find he
deferves to be preferred to them both in
fociety : he is younger than Fontenelle, and
lefs troublefome, becaufe he requires lefs
complaifance and attention; he is on the
contrary, very complaifant himfelf, in the
moft fimple, and at the fame time elegant
manner. This virtue feems to coft him
nothing ; for which reafon there are people
unjuft enough to believe him indifcriminate
and prodigal in the ufe of it ; but thofe who
know him well and are near to him per-
ceives that he knows how to diftinguifh ;
and that a found judgment and great knowledge

ledge preside at the diftribution. His character, efpecially when he was young, appeared formed to fucceed with women; he
had wit, grace, delicacy and refinement—
he cultivated fuccefsfully mufic, poetry,
and light literature; his mufic was not of a
profound compofition, but agreeable—his
poetry was not fublime; however, he undertook a tragedy; it is weak, but neither ridiculous nor tirefome. His other poetry is
like that of Fontenelle, harmonious and
witty: his profe, eafy and flowing; his eloquence is neither mafculine nor fublime,
although he gained premiums at the *Academie Francoife*, thirty years ago. It is
never ftrong or elevated, dull or infipid: he
was fometime father of the oratory, and has
contracted in that fociety a tafte for ftudy,
and acquired fome erudition; but this without the leaft pedantry. I have been affured,
that in a court of judicature, he was a good
judge, without having a perfect knowledge
of the laws, becaufe he has an upright mind
and a found judgment. He never had ma-
gifterial haughtinefs, nor the vulgarity of
the limbs of the law. He does not pride
himfelf upon his birth or illuftrious titles:
he

he is rich enough to be independent, and in
this happy fituation, ufing no pretenfions,
he wifely places himfelf below infolence, and
above meanness. There are women of fufficient confideration, who have overlooked his
want of birth, even of perfonal advantages,
and vigour. He has ever conducted himfelf
on thefe occafions with modefty, never car-
fying his pretenfions too far; nothing was
ever required of him which was improper
he fhould do,—at fifty years of age, he declared he would confine himfelf to a ftudious
and devout life; he made a general confeffion of all his fins, and it was on this occafion he permitted himfelf the following
pleafantry, "we are never fo rich as when
we remove." His devotion is as free from
fanaticifm, perfecution, fournefs and intrigue, as his ftudies are from pedantry.—
He applys himfelf to compofe an *Abrége
Chronologique* of our hiftory, which will
have the merit of an exact chronology,
well compofed tables, and a fummary of
facts methodically arranged, and yet without being dry, fterile, infipid, or tirefome.
We may not only feek and find therein
every thing neceffary to fix in our minds
the

the principal epochas of our hiftory; but we
fhall be able to read with pleafure this a-
bridgement, from beginning to end; the
author having prepared for the reader reft-
ing places, if I may be allowed the expreffion, in the long route he has to get through.
The moft interefting facts will be related
with clearnefs and precifion, and particular
remarks will determine at each-epocha, what
were then our manners and principles: finally, this book, excellent in itfelf, will ferve
as a model, according to which many other
good and ufeful books may be compofed.
There is reafon to believe, that all the different hiftories will foon be written in the
fame manner, and that this firft work will
be the bafis of a new and inftructive kind.
I agree, neverthelefs, that the literary reputation of the Prefident Henault, will never
equal that of Fontenelle or Montefquieu;
but I am of opinion, that his only work will
be more ufeful than all theirs; becaufe it
will open a new carreer to the progrefs of
fcience; whilft the others will only produce bad imitations, who will go aftray,
in endeavouring to tread in their fteps. But
to reduce to a few words the character of

2   the

the President Henault, he is accommodating without deceit; mild without infipidity; officious without intereft or ambition; com-plaifant without meanefs; a good friend, without enthufiafm or prejudice : in fhort, he is as perfect a model in fociety as his book is in its kind.

ESSAY

E S S A Y   XXXIX.

ON THE NATURAL TURN FOR SCANDAL
AND RAILLERY.

THE love of fcandal is fo founded upon
the malignity natural to moft men, and
efpecially to women, that this vice will
never be out of fafhion; the levity of our
nation makes fcandal more common in
France than any where elfe. But at leaft,
we abhor calumny, we look upon it as a
vice, the principles of which are the moft
culpable, and its confequences may be the
moft pernicious, We are as fearful of becoming calumniators as murderers, and this
with much reafon. As for fcandal, when
it is well retailed, is a means of pleafing in
fociety,—it animates converfation,—thofe
prefent are amufed by fpeaking ill of the
abfent: one company is made to laugh at
the follies of another. But this fportivenefs
muft be light, agreeable and fatirical: let
us leave to old and peevifh devotees, the bad

X   habit

habit of malignantly flandering their neighbours,—of reproaching young perfons with
defects, which they compenfate by fome
good qualities, or with faults againft which
the aged cry fo loudly, only becaufe they
can no longer commit them.

To rally agreeably, it is neceffary to have a
graceful delivery; and this is no common
talent. Light circumftances are fometimes
added to the ftory, to render it more poignant; but it muft not be lengthened by
them, nor the narration retarded. Mix
your recitals with but few obfervations,—
draw no conclufions fiom them, but leave
your auditors to make fuch malignant reflections as you will eafily fuggeft to them;
thefe will be fo much the more approved of,
as they will believe them to come from
themfelves. I knew in my younger days,
fome excellent ftoiy tellers; they feem to
be more rare at prefent; I think fo perhaps,
by anticipation, from the mania common to
old people, of believing that eveiy thing
degenerates; but, however, this may be, I
mean to form fome day a lift of the good
ftory-tellers of my time, and to characterife
each of them by fome one of theii beft ftories,

ries, which I shalleasily recollect. Madame Cornuel compared stories to those *matelotes*, (rich ragouts, like turtle) of which it is said, the " fish is eaten for the sake of the sauce ;" in like manner said she, the best stories are best related. We have a proof of this in the famous tales of the Abby de Boisrobert, at which the great Cardinal Richelieu laughed so much. Douville, brother to the Abby, has had them printed, and nothing is more insipid on being read ; but this is because we have no longer the story-teller to make us relish them, yet it was not he who wrote them.

The man whom in all France I have heard tell the best story is the Duke of Maine, legitimated son of the late King ; he was otherwise a weak Prince, and had but middling talents ; his wife who prides herself upon being superior to him, in point of understanding, does not tell a story so well as he does ; and their two sons, the Prince of Dombes, and the Compte d'Eu, who in in other respects do not pass for men of genius, possess their father's talent to a great degree.

X 2

The

The age is certainly become more moderate in many refpects; flander is not fpread
with malignity and ill humour; its confequences are more feared; men are become
circumfpect, left fimple difputes fhould become ferious affairs, which they wifh to
avoid.   Perhaps, (let us fecretly acknowledge it) we are become a little cowardly;
but when we are unfortunate enough to
be fo, the true means of concealing it is
to avoid difputes, and to this end it is
neceffary to take timely precautions.   After
all, I like the prefent age better than I fhould
have done the preceding one; men were
certainly brave and daring; but even the
moft prudent people were not in fafety, becaufe they were befet with thofe who were
quarrelfome.   Society is at prefent more
fafe; we have fcarcely any thing to fear but
trifling difputes or pleafantries eafy to be
born with when we know how to reply to
them.   Formerly men devoured each other
like lions and tygers; at prefent, we play
with each other like little dogs, which
gnaw, or young kittens, the ftrokes of
whofe claws are not mortal.

I like

I like the raillery of men of wit, even
though I fhould be the fubject of it, better
than the circumfpection of fools : nothing
can be more dull or ridiculous, than fome
of my acquaintance of this defcription ;
their infipidity makes one almoft fick ; from
infipidity comes *ennui* ; and *ennui* is the peft
of fociety.

ESSAY

ESSAY XL.

THE COUNTENANCE AN INDICATION
OF THE INTERIOR CHARACTER.

THE Countenance is a thing merely
exterior, but, from which, there are
certain confequences to be drawn, to know
the interior character and difpofitions of
perfons. A firm and fteady countenance
fuppofes that a man preferves a prefence and
a compofure of mind; on the contrary, an
embarraffed Countenance indicates confufion, and a difturbed mind. Therefore
thofe who are expert in gallantry, like
fkilful politicians, know how to take advantage of the appearance of the Countenance
to forward their defigns.

It would be equally impolite and awkward to difcompofe women in public;
there are private opportunities when we
ought to be lefs circumfpect. So the politician, in his private conferences, hazards
blunt

blunt and unexpected propofitions, obferves the effects they produce upon him who was not prepared to receive them, according to which he pufhes his point, or retreats. A certain and general rule in fociety is, that an amiable man never ftrives to embarrafs any body, and takes fuch meafures as not to be embarrafled himfelf; for nothing but embarraffment makes men of fenfe appear like fools.

As foon as a man is in place, or has acquired a fortune, he prefently acquires haughtinefs and airs of importance, which is eafily believed to be the diftinguifhing mark and proof of fuperiority. Neverthelefs the more we are elevated, the more affable we ought to be, except on certain occafions, wherein it is neceffary to fhew that we feel what we are, and to check thofe who would otherwife forget it, and fail in what is due to us.

I have fomewhere read, that we ought never to lay afide an air of authority, fo far as not to have it in our power to refume it

when

when neceffiry; becaufe appearance is often neceffary to evince reality.

Never make a great blow with a timid
air, the effect would be loft : but appear to
pity thofe whom you are obliged to punifh ;
feem forry to refufe thofe whofe demands
you cannot comply with, and to be happy
and fatisfied at having it in your power to
confer upon them fome favour. I fhall be
anfwered that all this is foon faid, but very
delicate and difficult of execution ; I acknowledge it ; but it is what a man in place
muft ftudy to acquire. *Hic meta laborum.*

Great bab'ers and tale-beaiers have feldom a firm Countenance, or, at leaft, eafily lofe it. Fools never have it ; but half
wits poffefs it fometimes, and then it is a
great merit in them, as it conceals a part of
their folly. As a giave Countenance is
generally accompanied with flownefs in
deliberation, this gives time to reflect upon
what is to be faid or done ; men of this defcription make fewer miftakes and foolifh
expreffions.

The

The Countenance of fuperiors is never embarraffing to people who have been well brought up: he has learned betimes the danger of being infolent; but meannefs is always contemptible. Moreover, as an honeft man has nothing to reproach himfelf with, he is never embarraffed in anfwering queftions which are put to him; and, if he has to afk in his turn, he gives his reafons with that confidence which virtue and juftice infpire. It is equally neceffary to be brief in the expofition of our reafons, in the narration of circumftances and ftories; in thefe we ought to prefs on to the point upon which they turn, abridge the preambles, and fay no more than is neceffary to lead to and difcover it. The fame in requifitions, no more fhould be faid than is abfolutely neceffary to make known the defired object, and the reafons which may be decifive and determinate, for the perfon to whom the requifition is made, divefting it alfo of every acceffory, and changing the prologue into an overture.

It is more difficult for fuperiors to conduct themfelves with their inferiors. To receive well a folicitation, they ought to know

know to whom they fpeak, and be acquainted with the matter in queftion, which
is not always the cafe on the firft approach :
whilft they are ignorant of the bufinefs,
they ought to watch and attend ; neither
to difcourage nor flatter with hopes, but to
hearken, and, if it be neceffary, to bring,
by degrees, the folicitor to the point, always
avoiding all appearance of unfavourable pre-
poffeffion : finally, to promife nothing but
what they are fure to perform, and to give
no hopes but fuch as are juft and reafonable.
Moreover they ought to blend their politenefs with that art which is not acquired
but by a great knowledge of the world, and
which cannot be learned in the duft of the
cabinet. Bufinefs is done by men, and with
men ; but, on the one hand, thofe who
have lived enough amongft them to acquire
the art of fatisfying a numerous audience,
have frequently led too diffipated lives to
have profoundly ftudied the bottom of
affairs with which they are charged ; on
the other, men who have grown pale over
papers, have not been fufficiently in the
world. In both thefe cafes there are rifks,
but rational people are well aware of them,
and take their meafures accordingly.

ESSAY

E S S A Y XLI.

THE CHARACTER AND SUMMARY OF THE CURIOUS MANUSCRIPTS OF THE ABBE DE CHOISY.

IT has been long fince obferved that men of high birth are lefs infolent than thofe who arrive at eminence without that advantage; but what has not been fo generally remarked is, that the greateft princes are naturally timid; accuftomed to think themfelves above all men, the leaft idea of fuperiority intimidates them; they feldom meet with men of higher rank than themfelves; but the reputation of wit, fcience, knowledge of every kind, and even perfonal advantages, are, for them, fo many objects of deference. They perceive themfelves inferior in certain refpects, to fome of their fubjects and courtiers. I know princes, who would be more embarraffed in converfing with an academician, than he would be in haranguing them publicly. The timidity

dity of our princes is manifefted by a filly look, by a ftammering, and an embarraffed countenance.   It would be as ufelefs as ill-timed, to give examples of them.

Converfation is the confolation and re-ward of ftudious and learned people ; it re-frefhes them after the bufinefs of the cabin-et, and, perhaps, by ufing alternately, thefe two means, one becomes as profitable as the other.   This is true with refpect to youth, who may improve as much from the converfation of people who have feen a good deal, as from old books, full of great doc-trine and variety of facts.   But converfation alone is not fufficient, becaufe it is gene-rally too detached ; as reading fatigues, becaufe books fix the attention too long on -the fame object.   I know a religious order, · (that of the Jefuits) whofe principles are fo many problems, cenfured by fome, ad-mired by others, but, from among whom, many good authors have affuredly been pro-duced.   This fociety admits, as far as it is poffible, none but fubjects of happy difpo-fitions ; and, during the courfe of their ftudies, the young fathers have a converfa-

tion

tion of four hours with the old ones, who
have acquired moft fcience, experience, and
knowledge of the world. Thus, with the
Jefuits, men become communicative, open
and amiable, whilft in the other orders, ori-
ginally founded upon a reclufe, heimitic
life, one part of the day paffes in chaunt-
ing the praifes of the Deity, and the other,
in folitary ftudy, meditating in retreat, and
filently liftening to mafteis.

When we have contracted an eaily tafte
for improvement from converfation, we are
happy to be near old people who are capable
of relating what they have feen and known
the moft inteiefting : there is a manner of
profiting by this, and of avoiding repeti-
tions, to which they are but too fubject.
They muft be examined upon things with
which they are likely to be acquainted, and
we may be affured they will relate them with
pleafure ; they may be led from epoch to
epoch, from object to object, on different
days, and under different pretexts, not to
fatigue them : we may be fure of reading
in their memory, as in a book, what it contains the moft interefting and curious. I

acted

acted in this manner with my relation, the
Abby de *Choify*, with whom I afterwards
lived during the laft years of his life. He
died in 1724, upwards of eighty years of
age. I muft agree, notwithftanding all the
friendfhip he had for me, that he was not a
man very eftimable ; his mind was weak,
and was more diftinguifhed for his focial
qualities than good conduct. He became a
member of the academy, and gained fome
degree of reputation there, becaufe he
wrote and fpoke well. Otherwife, he did
not appear worthy to become a bifhop, nor
to be employed in any important affair : he
always felt the effects of his effeminate education, and being no longer of an age to put
on a woman's drefs, he never was capable
of thinking like a man. Notwithftanding
all his defects, he was agreeable to liften to
in his old age ; his memory was ftored with
anecdotes of the court, which he had fre-
quented, although he was never of any confequence there ; and of the academy, in
the midft of which he had lived for a long
time. He had tafte enough to judge of a
fentiment or a witty expreffion ; therefore,
of the great number he had heard, fome of
the

the beft remained in his memory; thefe he
repeated frequently, and which I have retained: I found part of them written in the
papers the Abby left me; for he put all his
work into my hands a little before his
death. I have felected what appeared to
me the moft interefting, of which I have
formed three great volumes; but not being
able to refufe the communication of them
to a lady of the family, who was defirous of
reading them, fhe kept them a long time,
and gave them to the Abby D'Olivet, who
took from the manufcript a work in two
little volumes, which he got printed in
Holland, under the title of *Memoires pour
fervir à l'Hiftoire de Lewis XIV. par feu M.
l'Abbé de Choify, de l'Academie Françoife.*
Thefe two volumes certainly contain, if the
expreffion may be permitted, the flower of
my manufcript. However, there ftill remains fome thoughts which I can mix with
reflections upon the works of the author,
who, on giving them into my poffeffion informed me upon what occafion they were
written.

There is only an abridgement in his Memoirs of what he more than once related to

me

me in detail. His mother was a woman of wit, but, in my opinion, very intriguing : she was in the secret of the conspiracy of Cinqmars, which terminated so unhappily for that young nobleman, his friend, and M. de Thou ; that affair was founded on a real intrigue of ambitious and inconsiderate women. The Princess Marie of Gonzague, afterwards Queen of Poland, extravagantly in love with M. Cinqmars, who had already made a good fortune for a man of the family of a little Parisian bourgeois, took it into her head, that the grand cquerry, in connecting himself with the enemies of the state, might make the Cardinal de Richelieu, (already ill) tremble, and procure himself the constable's sword. Certainly nobody, of the present age, would think of making themselves useful by such means, but they were thought adviseable an hundred years ago. Madame de Choisy was in the secret of this imprudent intrigue, and the Princess Marie of Gonzague had assured her that she would make her husband keeper of the seals ; but the good man, M. de Choisy, father of the abby, did not suspect that his wife gave herself so much trouble about his fortune.

He

He was intendant in Languedoc, and ordered to arreſt M. de Cinqmars, at Mont-
pellier, and to ſeize all his papers. He
found him employed in burning a great
part of them, and, ſurely, thoſe which
would have ſerved to conviɛt him. M. de
Choiſy, from pure goodneſs of heart, let
him burn as many of them as he choſe." You
are right," ſaid the grand equerry to him,
" in treating me with ſo much complaiſance ; you would be very ſorry to find what
1 have juſt burned." In faɛt, they were
letteɪs from the Princeſs Maria, and, perhaps, fɪom Madame de Choiſy, her confidant ; the reſult of this was, that, although
ſufficɪent proofs were found to condemn
M. de Cɪnqmars, there were none which
diſcoveɪed the intɪigue of the women.

The abby had often repeated to me what
he ſlɪghtly mentions in his Memoirs ;
that it was an effeɛt of the policy of the
Cardinal Mazarine, that MONSIEUR, brother to Lewis XIV. was brought up in the
moſt effeminate manner, to render him pu-
ſillanimous and contemptɪble ; at preſent,
this would appear, to us, to the laſt degree
ſtrange and ridiculous. Madame de Choiſy
gave

gave into the extravagance, in confequence of her turn for intrigue, and fhe made her fon adopt the fame manner, to make her court to Monfieur. With refpect to what regards this prince, we can only fhrug up our fhoulders, on feeing Cardinal Maza- jine adopt fuch pitiful means ; they were, as ufelefs in effect, as injudicious in the con- trivance. Monfieur was not lefs brave in war, notwithftanding his bad education, and, if he always found himfelf inferior to Lewis XIV. it was becaufe nature had not given him fuch talents. On the contrary, every thing poffible had been done to ren- der Gafton, brother to Lewis XIII. formi- dable, but he was never otherwife than a contemptible prince. The Abby de Choify preferved, as long as he could, that imper- tinent habitude of dreffing like a woman, and the follies he was guilty of, under that adjuftment, are but too well known.

One of the Manufcripts which he left me, contains his hiftory, under the name of "The Countefs of Barres ," and, though not yet, I believe it will be printed ; as the fame perfon who has publifhed the Memoirs of the Abby de Choify, has given copies of

this

this trifle : it will be found not badly written, containing pleafurable details, not too
modeft, but very agreeable to read. The
hiftory will at the fame time be thought
improbable ; I can, however, certify it to
be a very true one. The old abby, a long
time aftei he had written the life of David
and Solomon, both edifying hiftories, and
the hiftoiy of the church, related to me
again his follies, with an unfpeakable pleafure, and I looked with aftonifhment at a
man, whofe life had been full of fuch ftrange
impropieties.

One of the longeft pieces of Manufcript
ftolen from me, is the Memoirs of the Life
of Caidinal de Bouillon, the abby's intimate
fiiend fiom their childhood to death : I will
not repeat here what has been printed ; but
may juftly conclude from it, that the Cardinal de Bouillon was a prelate of a middling capacity, who finifhed his career in
the moft defpicable manner. He was exiled,
and deprived of the revenues of his benefices,
for attempting to make head againft Lewis
XIV. and his minifters He recollected
that his anceftors fold themfelves dear ; but
they had fomething to difpofe of, the prin-

cipality and ſtrong place of Sedan; they
were well paid for theſe, in conſiderable
lands and court honours; but they fell from
independent princes, to rich, illuſtrious,
and important courtiers. They could do
nothing better than make their court to,
and pleaſe Lewis XIV. or render great
ſervices to the ſtate, like M. de Turenne,
whoſe perſonal conſideration ſupported the
Cardinal de Bouillon, as long as this uncle
lived. After the death of M. de Turenne,
the cardinal continued his improper conduct at court, and was, at length, a ſufferer
by it.

In the piece concerning the Cardinal Bouillon, there are two articles which are quite
foreign to it, but which characterize well
enough two miniſters of Lewis XIV. one
of whom is M. de Pomponne. The Abby
pretends that Madame de Choiſy contributed
to make him miniſter, becauſe ſhe found
means to ſhew the king the letters which
Monſ. de Pomponne wrote to her when he
was ambaſſador in Sweden; it is added that
the king admired them, and conceived a
great opinion of their author. It is aſtoniſh-
ing that Lewis XIV. was under the neceſſity
of

of having recourfe to an ambaffador's private letters to a woman, to judge of his capacity ; but, without doubt, the king looked upon them to be moie genuine, natural, and lefs ftudied, than the difpatches
the ambaffador addreffed to him, or to the
minifter of foreign affairs.   Madame de
Choify was an old friend of M. de Pomponne, and to whom he feemed to open his
heart, without difcovering to her the fecrets
of ftate : from thence Lewis XIV. concluded he would be a great minifter ; he
was, however, no moie than an honeft and
prudent man, of middling talents.   Chance
has put into my hands all his correfpondence, minifterial and private, during the
five years he was in Sweden, which I have
preferved in my library ; I do not think it
very brilliant, but fenfible.   He correfpond-
ed with M. de Lionne, who was far fuperior
to him in his manner of writing.   Nothing
can be more elegant than the anfwers of M.
de Lionne to the Compte d'Eftrades, ambaffador in Holland, which were printed
there, with the difpatches of that ambaffador.   Men, deftined to politics, ought to
read this book, to form themfelves for negociations and public affairs.   It difcovers

with what art M. d'Eſtrades conducted the Dutch to the point to which he was inſtructed to conduct them; it was not, perhaps, always conformable to their intereſts; but, in that caſe, he made them ſwallow the golden pill ſent them by M. de Lionne. The miniſter and ambaſſador did not always explain clearly, in their diſpatches, what their real deſigns were; but they underſtood each other (to make uſe of a proverbial expreſſion) *like two pick-pockets in a fair.*

Another anecdote regiſtered in the memoirs of the Abby de Choiſy, conceins M. de Croiſſi. It is ſaid this miniſter was unjuſtly accuſed of being incapable of writing good diſpatches. One of his fiiſt clerks, of the name of Bergeiet, took upon himſelf, with an affected modcſty, all the credit of them. The abby aſſures us that nothing was more falſe. This is neither the fiiſt nor the laſt time a like accident has happened to miniſters, whoſe modcſty and reſerve have given favouiable oppoitunities to their ſubalteins. Simple and natural prepoſſeſſion attributes every thing to ſupeiiors; cenſoiious and malignant minds, all to ſubalterns. Reaſon and juſtice divides

between

between them the merit of what is well done; feconds have advantages enough, as they are not refponfible for what is blameable and dangerous*.

The Abby de Choify had the Abbey of St. Seine, in Burgundy : it is not very confideiable, fince, at prefent, it does not exceed fix thoufand livres a year. But he had moreovei, the priory of St. Lo, in Normandy, which is a very beneficial one, and he was Dean of the cathedral of Bayeux, even before he was in orders. With all thefe he had an income of fourteen thoufand livres a year. He entered into holy orders on his voyage to Siam. It appears by the journal of this voyage that, on the 7th of December, 1685, he received the four leffer oiders; on the 8th he was fub-deacon, on the 9th deacon, and on the 10th a prieft,

Y 4   all

* Beigeret had the impudence to folicit the place in the Academy Francoife, vacant by the death of M. de Cordemoi he obtained it in 1675, and held it till the year 1684, when he died, without having ever compofed any woik, not even, as repoited, his difcourfe of admiffion, which, however, is, in general, but a middling performance. He was replaced by the Abby de St. Pierre.

all of which he received from the hands of the Bishop of Metellopolis, who made the voyage to Siam with him, on board the same vessel ; by means of which, he was, on leaving France, a tonsured clerk, and a priest when he arrived at Siam.

The second Manuscript I found in the papers of the Abby de Choify, is intituled, *Memoires de M de Cofnac, d'abord Evéque de Valence, puis Archevéque d'Aix.* He was a man of much wit, said many good things, and invented excellent stories. In his youth he busied himself a good deal in the intrigues of two courts, that of the Prince de Conti, brother to the great Conde, and that of Monsieu, brother to Lewis XIV. he quitted them succeffively, on account of some dispute, whose origin and motives are well related in the Manuscript which the Abby d'Olivet got almost reprinted, intituling it, *Livre feptieme des Memoires pour fervir à l'Hiftoire de Louis XIV.* The court of these two princes cannot be described with greater truth and naiveté than the Abby de Choify has done in this Manuscript ; wherein, occafionally, are found, interefting and agreeable anecdotes of the

I   court

court of Lewis XIV. : their authenticity
may be relied upon ; for, although I was
not fully aflured of this, they carry fuch
an air of franknefs and probability, as would
alone prevent the leaft doubt of it.

I have but two circumftances to add to
what has been printed by the care of the
Abby d'Olivet : one of them concerns the
fufpicions harboured upon the extraordinary
circumftances of the death of Madame Hen-
riette, firft wife of the Duke of Orleans.
It is known that this princefs was taken ill
one evening in fummer, at St. Cloud, after
having drank cold liquors, prefented to her
by an officer of her pantry, or her cup-
bearer. Her death caufed a general con-
fternation ; thofe moft affected by it, were
the officers of the houfehold ; they were
afraid, and not without reafon, of lofing
their offices, which, in the houfes of princeffes, depend upon two lives, that of the
princefs, and of thofe who hold them.
Monfieur removed their fears, by promifing
them, that when he fhould marry again,
they fhould hold the fame places with the
new Duchefs of Orleans, as they had with
the firft. The poor creatures, waiting for
this

this event, lived as well as they could without falary or maintenance from the Duke;
and few of them had laid up anything : one,
only, returned rich to Paris, where he
bought a houfe, eftablifhed himfelf, and
appeared contented with his fate. A few
years afterwards, Monfieur, having married the Princefs Palatine of Bavaria, fince
mother to the regent Duke of Orleans, who
died in his regency, kept his word with
all the dependents of the defunct, and prefented a lift of them to Madame, faying
that none of them were dead fince the de-
ceafe of their firft miftrefs, neverthelefs fhe
perceived but one place vacant ; the princefs afked the reafon—as for that man,
anfwered Monfieur, he is very well, but, I
believe he will never ferve you ; he was
the firft officer of the pantry, or the firft
cup-beaier. According to all appearance,
Madame daied not examine further what
this meant. I am fure of this anecdote ; I
know people who have feen the old officer;
they have told me his name ', which I have
forgot; he never fpoke firft of the court of
Monfieur noi of Madame ; and, although
he

* Morel. Vide Mff. de Colbert.

he lived at Paris, never went to the Palais Royal, to St. Cloud, or Verfailles; it is faid he was difconcerted even when interrogated about his old miftrefs. It was the Abby de Dofnac, who being very old and Archbifhop of Aix, having learned that Saint Francis of Salles had juft been canonifed, exclaimed, " What, *M. de Geneve*, *my* " *old friend?* I am delighted at his good for- " tune; he was a well-bred and agreeable, " and even an honeft man, although he " cheated at piquet, at which we have of- " ten played together."

It will eafily be believed the company laughed. " But, Monfeigneur," faid fomebody, to him, " is it poffible a faint fhould " cheat at play?" "Oh!" replied the archbifhop, " he defended himfelf by faying " that what he won was for the poor."

I found, moreover, in the papers of the Abby de Choify, two little romances, well written, and which have never been printed, but the ftories are not very interefting; one is of knight-errantry, the other in the Oriental manner; alfo the adventures of an Abby *de Saze*, who became converted by a miftake

miftake of the perfon; a director of the feminary, a man of great piety, wrote to an
Abby de Saze, formerly a libertine, but afterwards a conveit, that he would go and
pafs fhrove-tide with him, to employ in
pious meditations that time which men of
the world paffed in profane diverfions.
The fimilarity of names caufed a wrong-
headed valet to give the letter to the Abby
de Saze, whom he found providing for his
carnival, not only vile amufements, but
even real parties of debauchery. The abby
opened the letter, which was like a thun-
der-clap to him: in his firft movement he
became furious; in the fecond, agitated
and troubled; finally, in the laft, he took
a firm refolution to become a convert. He
went to confeffion, which he had not done
for many years before: the confeffor after
having reprimanded him, but giving him,
at the fame, time confolation, encouraged
him to fay mafs, which he had not done for
a long time, although he was a prieft, and in
poffeffion of great benefices: he faid it, and
with fo much compunction, that he expired at the end of the facrifice.

                                            The

The Abby de Choify has left a little
hiftory of Madame de Guercheville; moft
of the anecdotes it contains are known.
Every body knows this lady was very handfome; that Henry IV. was deeply in love
with her; that fhe refufed his addreffes;
and, that the king conceived fo high an efteem for her, that he named her maid of
honour to the queen, telling her, that if
he had known a more virtuous woman in
his kingdom he would have given her the
preference: but the abby related to me,
verbally, a circumftance of this lady, which
I do not remember to have met with any
where elfe. Henry IV. knowing that Madame de Guercheville was at la Roche Guy-
on, refolved to make her a vifit, and fent
a gentleman to inform her, that the chace
having led him into that part of the country, he begged a fupper and a bed in her
caftle. The lady anfwered refpectfully,
that fhe would do every thing in her power
to make the king's reception fuch as it
ought to be. The enchanted monarch arrived, and found, at the bottom of the ftairs,
Madame de Guercheville, full dreffed, and
preceded by all her fervants; fhe conducted
him modeftly to the moft elegant chamber.

He

He faw, on paffing by the kitchen-door, preparations for a great fupper, and the lady announced to him, that as foon as he fhould be repofed, it fhould be ferved up effectively. The fupper was ready as foon as he was prepared for it; but, upon the point of fitting down to table he learned that Madame de Guercheville had ordered her coach, and was gone from the caftle. Aftonifhed and mortified he fent to her to know the reafon of the ftep fhe had taken; her anfwer was, " A king ought to be the " mafter in every place he goes to, and I " am very glad to be free in thofe I in- " habit."

The anecdotes of the Marquis D'Arquien, father of the queen of Poland, wife of Jean Sobiefki, collected by the Abby D'Olivet, are inferted in the hiftorical Memoirs of Lewis XIV. and form the eighth book.

I found, afterwards, in the abby's papers, a fragment which has not been publifhed, undoubtedly becaufe thofe who copied the others thought this badly arranged: it is fo, in fact, but it does not, on that account, contain lefs interefting ideas, and curious remarks.

remarks. It appears that in 1692, a little academy was formed at the Luxembourgh, whofe object was to take up that which did not enter into the fyftem of the three royal academies · the Academy Francoife, that of Sciences, and the Academy of Belles Lettres, which were already eftablifhed; the fiift fifty years, and the two others twenty or thiity previous to it. Some people weie of opinion that the law of nations, policy, jurifprudence, theology, and even moral philofophy, were not within the juiifdiction of thefe academies. It feems that it was to treat on thefe matters, and examine books of the fame kind, that the new academy was eftablifhed. The affemblies were to be held at the Abby de Choify's at the Luxembourgh, once a week only, on the Tuefday, and was to be compofed of no more than thirteen academicians, the mafter of the houfe included, who was to act as prefident. Nine of thefe thirteen are known in the literary world; the Abbies *Dangeau, De Choify,* perpetual fecretary, *Teftu, Renaudot,* and *De Caumartin,* Meffieurs *D'Herbelot, Peirault, Fontenelle,* and the *Prefident Coufin.* The Abby de Choify, Fontenelle, Perrault, the Abby Teftu, and the

the Abby Renaudot, were already of the Academy Francoife, and the Prefident Coufin became a member of it afterwards; but D'Herbelot was of the Belles Lettres only. I have the journal of what paffed in this private academy for the year 1692 only; perhaps it was of no longer duration. The academicians were bound to fecrecy of what was faid among them, becaufe, as politics were to be difcuffed, reflections, improper to be divulged, might be made. The fame fecrecy was obferved with refpect to moral and philofophical obfervations. Thefe precautions were very wife; and, it is very probable, that this attempt was unfuccefsful, folely on account of their not being obferved.

Among the numerous obfervations contained in this journal, a few of them appeared to me worthy of attention. The Abby Renaudot maintained, at that time, that Varillas quoted in his manufcripts, in the king's library, what never exifted. Another academician faid, there were, in Clélie, and other modern romances, portraits which Varillas had wholly inferted in his hiftory;

hiftory, that Varillas had not blufhed at pil-
fering from Scudery.

Perrault read there his poem, on the Cre-
ation of the world; fome paffages were
highly approved of, but others feverely criticifed; the Abby faid there was too much
imagination in a poem founded upon Gene-
fis; that it was not permitted to make Mo-
fes a better natural philofopher than he
ought to appear according to his text, and
that, above all, care fhould have been taken
not to have made him a difciple of
Defcartes.

The Abby de Choify communicated to
the affembly, the tranflation of the Imitation of Jefus Chrift, which he had undertaken. He confulted the members upon
the title of this book, fo much refpected,
which, according to his opinion, was not a
proper one, for the book does not at all
treat of the imitation of Chrift, but of the
interior confolations which chriftians may
procure themfelves. Although it was agreed
that the Abby was right, they reprefented
to him the neceffity of leaving the title as
it had firft appeared. One of them recol-
Z   lected

lected, that in the sixteenth century a tranfl-
lation of the imitation was published with
the title of *L'Internelle Confolotion*, and that
it had no fuccefs, becaufe the book of imitation was not underflood by it.

The Abby was prevented for the fame
reafon from changing the titles of fome chap-
ters, whofe matter did not corefpond with
what they promifed. Finally, they told
him, that if he wifhed to alter the tranflations already known of the imitation, it was
neceffary to examine fcrupuloufly the Latin
text, compare the manufcripts one with the
other, eftablifh his authorities, &c. &c.
The Abby anfwered his fellow Members,
that all that would be *la mer a boire*—to
drink the fea dry : he took no farther notice
of . and arranged his tranflation according
to his fancy.

I cannot forbear relating a fingular anecdote upon this tranflation, by the Abby de
Choily. He dedicated it to Madame de
Maintenon, who was then a devotee, and
declared miftrefs to the King. To make his
court to this Lady, the Abby put at the
head of his book, an elegant engraving of
Madam

Madame de Maintenon, kneeling at the foot of a crucifix, and at the bottom, were the following words from David, *Audi, filia, concupiscet rex decorum tuum*—"Hearken, daughter, the King will defire thy comlinefs." Every body was fcandalized at this application : the Abby was foon obliged to take away the print from the remaining copies, having made prefents only of a few before hand. He would not even give me a copy with the print. The Bibliomanes bought it very dear.

In a differtation read by M. d'Herbelot, in the little Academy of the Luxembourg, upon the origin of the name of Pope, and the eftablifhed cuftom in the Latin Church, of giving it to the Bifhop of Rome exclufively, I find, independently of what is generally known, that it was a great queftion in 1630, under the Pontificate of Urban VIII. what title fhould be given to the Cardinals : they were upon the point of being called *Perfectiffimi* and *Your Perfection*; at length thefe paffed into *Eminentiffimi* and *Eminence*. It is remarkable, that Urban VIII. ordered them to be called fo, under pain of excommunication. M. Camus, at that time, Bifhop of Belley, wrote and

Z 2 preached

preached devout romances, and introduced into thefe works fome very fingular things. M M. les Cardineaus, had abandoned to the Bifhops, the title of *Illuftriffim* and *Reveren-diffimi*, as they give to their valets their old purple cloaths and dirty linen.

The Abby Renaudot, read a differtation upon giants, in which there are very curious things; but I think, I have read moft of them in fome other work. I will only remar', that this differtation was ocafioned by a letter the Prefident Coufin had inferted in the *Journal des Savans*, of which he was then the author; the letter was from a Vicar of Laffay, in the Diocefe of Angers, who faid, he had found in his garden a fepulchre, which contained a fkeleton of feventeen feet two inches long : he offered to fhew it to the curious.

It is known that the education of the great Conftable Montmorency, had been fo neglected as not be taught to read and write : yet he carried a book to mafs, but this was merely for the fake of appearance. He figned patents and pancartes * in a very fingular manner,

* Papers containing the duties on merchandizes.

manner, upon the word of his Secretary,
who laid them before him : he made twenty
great fcrawls one after another, after which,
his Secretary ftopped him, faying Monfeigneur there are enough. The company were
fhewn feveral fignatures of this kind. This
gave occafion to fome one prefent to relate
an anecdote of a Bifhop of Angers, whofe
name I think, was Arnaud.—Becoming
blind, he had an iron ftamp made, upon
which his name was engraved, (Nicolas); he
made ufe of this to fign difmiffions, letters,
and other papers, to which his fignature was
neceffary. It was alfo remarked, that this
cuftom was not rare among the Princes of
Italy, and that the iron was called in Italian
cachetto: it is known in Spain by the name
of *Stampilla* ; it ferves for royal difpatches ;
but it contains no proper name, for in Spain,
every thing is figned and expedited with
thefe words, *Yo el Rey—I the King* ; and this
formula always takes place, even when
the difpatches are for Italy or the Low
Countries. It was added, that the ufe of the
ftamp might be attended with the greateft
danger, were it only becaufe it rendered the
King's name lefs fure and refpectable; that
it is true, this fignature in France is moftly

Z 3   falfe

falfe; but at leaft, that of the Secretaries is not fo, that if the latter could ever be fuf-'pected, the unhappy fubjects would not know to whom to complain, when they received orders, upon whofe execution their foitunes, and even lives depended.

The Abby de Dangeau advanced in one of thefe academical conferences, that in truth, Popes were the firft and moft accommodating people in the world. Pius IV. by a bull in 1564, granted to the Bohemians the communion of two kinds : his fucceffors have, at different times, canonifed the ufurpations by fecular princes, the lands and poffeffions of ecclefiaftics; but at length, added he, they are afked for fo many, that it is impoffible for them to confent any longer. They have oppofed the marriage of Priefts and Bifhops; they could not do otherwife. If this were agiced to, every benefice with cure of fouls, and otheis, would become hereditary ; and tl c clergy with fmall ftipends, would bring difgrace upon ecclefiaftical dignities, and finally upon religion itfelf.

It appears that the academy at the Luxembourg finifhed, becaufe queftions too delicate

licate were propofed in it, and the academicians, being divided, difputed fo warmly
upon thefe objects, that they were exafper-
ated, and at laft feparated.

I forgot to mention a remark I made in
thefe memoirs, that the minifters of ftate,
even the firft of them, had not, by virtue
of this title, a feat in parliament, and that
they were never looked upon as great officers
of the crown.

Charles VI. and Charles VII. were declared
major in parliament without perfonally appearing there; the firft was declared fo by
the Duke of Anjou, his uncle, and the fecond by the fimple fact.

The Abby de Choify left me a collection
of *bosn mots*, in which there are many known
to all the world, but others more rare, fingular and agreeable : I will give a fpecimen
of them.

The Chevalier de la Ferti was young
and inconfiderate ; the king, who was kind
to his relations, granted him five hundred
crowns upon his caffette, faying to him,

Z 4 " Young

" Young man, I will encreafe this fum
" every year in proportion as you fhall be-
" come more prudent." "Ah, Sire," replied
the Chevalier, " your Majefty does not
" know to what you engage yourfelf, I fhall
" ruin you." Yet, notwithftanding this
gafconade, the chevalier continued his extravagance. The following is a ridiculous
one. He was at Lyons, in a merchant's
houfe, where they played at Pharo; the
bank was compofed of Louis d'ois and
crowns : he began to play upon his credit
and favourable appearance, and rifked immediately a thoufand Louis, which he won ;
he rifked double, and loft; he retired in-
ftantly, faying, " *Parblue, voila un coup im-*
" *payable* ;" which, in fact, he never
paid.

M. Morlau, firft phyfician to the Duchefs
of Burgundy, going one day, I know not
for what purpofe, to the prince's with a
fword, was jocofe upon his adjuftment, and
faid, " Monfeigneur, do not you think I
" refemble Captain *Spezz a ferro*, of the Ita-
" lian comedy ? It is impoffible to refemble
" him lefs," anfwered the prince, " *Spezz*
" *a ferro* never killed any body."

                                        The

The Marquis of Dangeau, well known to the Abby de Choify, and whom I have known myfelf, was at a famous courtier's, and one of the wits of the court of Lewis XIV. He was admitted into the *Academie Francoife* in 1668, and died in 1721. It was not till after the death of the king that he dared to acknowledge he was not only the confidant of that monarch, in his amours, during his youth, but that he affifted him with his pen to write letters of gallantry to Madame de la Valliere. This good lady took infinite pains in anfwering them, and was, at length, obliged to get her themes corrected by this fame Marquis of Dangeau. He took alfo upon himfelf to write poetry for the king; and, fearing left he fhould make it too good, he did little honour to the monarch, who at length renounced both genuine and adoptive poetry. It is faid, that Monfieur and Madame having one day difputed a queftion of gallantry, they both applied to the Marquis, who fecretly wrote for each of them, fome verfes upon the fubject, and that the king, to whom were they fhewn, judged thofe of Madame to be the beft.

Every

Every body has heard of the Memoirs of the Marquis of Dangeau; they are a manuſcript journal of the court, from the year 1686 to 1720; I have read them all: it is true they are charged with much minutiæ; but there are alſo many intereſting anecdotes: if he did not write them day by day, he has, at leaſt, reviſed them carefully, and he would not have ſuffered any thing abſolutely falſe to eſcape him. We may ſay, that if they be not a true hiſtory of the court of France, for thirty-five years, they are good materials of which it may be compoſed.

The Abby de Dangeau, brother to the Marquis, and, like him, of the *Academie Francoiſe*, was the intimate friend of the Abby de Choiſy. Dying a little before him, he left him three or four great collections of remarks of every kind, which came to my hands with the papers of the Abby de Choiſy; and, in which, there are, certainly, excellent things; but, as the writing is extremely bad, I am afraid I ſhall never have the ſatisfaction of extracting from them the precious matter they may contain.

3   The

The Abby d'Aumont had taken a box at the comedy, and was waiting in it for the ladies of his company, when the Marſhal d'Albret arrived. From a motive of reſpect to this nobleman he was ſhewn into the box wheie the abby was, who found himſelf obliged to give way to the marſhal. The abby withdrew much diſpleaſed, and ſaid, grumblingly, between his teeth, "Look " at the brave marſhal, he has never taken " any thing in his life but my box."

Cromwell ſent his Excellency Lockart to France, with the title of ambaſſador, where he was received with all the ho-nours due to his rank. One day the old Marſhal Villeroy, governor to Lewis XIV. aſking this Engliſhman why Cromwell, in-ſtead of taking the title of protector, had not got himſelf declared king. "Monſieur," replied Lockart, " we know the extent of " the prerogatives of a king, and limit " them accordingly, but we are ignorant " of thoſe of a protector." Lockart was right, new titles are neceſſary to new power.

At the time of the forced converfion of our fouthern provinces, which have been called *dragonnades*, the Marſhal de Teffé fent a detachment of dragoons into a village, to force the inhabitants to converfion. The people, alarmed, wrote immediately to the Marſhal, and, to avoid the pillage with which they were threatened, infoimed him, their intentions were to abjure their errors. M. de Teffè ordered the captain to return with his detachment; the latter, vexed to fee fo great a booty efcape him, faid, on his arrival, to the general, "Monfeigneur, "thofe rafcals laugh at you; they have "not given us the time even to inſtruct "them."

Gregory XIII. owed his elevation to the pontifical throne, principally, to the Car-dinal Borromée, who had given him his vote, and procured him thofe of his friends, becaufe he thought him a difinterefted man. But, as foon as the pope was inſtalled, he began to enrich his family at the expence of St. Peter, which obliged the Cardinal Bor-romée to fay to him, "Holy father, had "I known that, on being created pope, you "would have held fuch a conduct, you
"fhould

" fhould neither have had my voice,. nor
" thofe of my friends.—Good," faid the
pope, " did not the Holy Ghoft know
" it ?"

The Abby de Boifrobert being one morning with the Caıdinal de Richelieu, faid
feveral difagreeable things of a magiftrate of
the firft order, and attributed to him much
ridicule ; a little valet de chambre took it
into his head to fay to him, " Monfieur
" l'Abby, take care of what you fay ; I give
" you notice that I will inform M. * * *
" of it, to whom I am greatly attached,
" becaufe he is my relation.—Friend," replied the Abby, " tell M. * * * whatever
" you pleafe ; on my part, I will inform
" him of your pretenfions to be his relation,
" and he will be more vexed with you than
" with me."

The Queen, Chriftina, paffing by, I know
not what city in France, was harangued by
a conful, who was a Calvinift ; he was elo-
quent, and fhe hearkened to him with attention and pleafure : "But, Sir," faid fhe,
to the conful, " you have neither fpoken
" of my abdication nor of my converfion
" to

" to the catholic faith.—Madame," replied he, " I undertook to pronounce your eu-
" logium, and not to give your hiftory."

Philip IV. having loft the kingdom of Portugal, Catalonia, and fome other provinces, took it into his head to take the furname of Great ; the Duke of Medina-
Celi faid, " our mafter is like a hole, which
" grows the bigger the more matter it
" lofes."

Madame B———. of a very diftinguifhed family in the magiftracy, was witty, and perfectly underftood the the art of pleafantry ; being in a very numerous company, fomebody had the courage to fay to her that her hufband appeared to be of a weak conftitution ; " Really," faid fhe, " I have
" heard my mother-in-law fay, that M. M.
" B———. have, for more than two hundred
" years that they were known in the world,
" been impotent from father to fon : this
" lady has, however, brought forth a fon,
" which is, at prefent, the laft of the fa-
" mily."

Monfieur

Monfieur le Prince, ready to give battle, at Nerwinde, to the Imperialifts, commanded by the General de Mercy, an excellent officer, perceived, after a rude cannonade, that the enemy made a falfe manœuvre : ·· Ah !'' cried he, '' *Mercy* is cer-'' tainly killed.'' He fell upon the Germans and gained the victory. What he conjectured was true. It was upon the tomb of this general that the following honourable epitaph was engraved: *Sifte, viator, heroem calcas: Stop, traveller, thou treadeft upon a hero.*

Monfieur le Prince was one day in his coach with a very tirefome fellow, who teazed him with ftupifying ftories—'' Sir,'' faid he to him, '' either do not put me to '' fleep, or let me fleep on quietly.''

The fame Monfieur le Prince went frequently to the houfes of the minifters of ftate, and feemed to pay his court to them : '' What do you want with thofe people,'' faid the Count de Grammont to him ; '' do '' you wifh to become a prince of the '' blood ?''

M. de

M. de Turenne being prepared for a battle, charged the young Duke de Choiseul,
son of the Marechal Dupleſſis Praſlin, to
take poſſeſſion of a poſt which he pointed
out to him ; but the young officer neglected
to make ſure of it, thinking he had no oppoſition to fear : " Sir, Sir," ſaid the general to him, " I beg of you to follow my
" directions ; it was for want of ſuch a pre-
" caution that I was beat at Rhetel by the
" Marſhal your fathei."

The Abby de Choiſy pretended to the
peſſeſſion of an anecdote upon the manner
in which Meſſieurs de Cruſſel, d'Uzez, were
made dukes and peers in 15'2, the year of
the affair of St. Bartholomew. Catherine
of Medicis, wiſhed to gain over, or rather
deceive the Admiral de Coligni ; ſhe offered
him the dignity of duke and peer : he re-
fuſed it, that he might not render himſelf
ſuſpected by the Huguenot party. But, as
he was greatly in love with the Counteſs
d'Uzez, he aſked the dukedom for her huſ-
band, and obtained it. The new Duke
d'Uzez was promoted and received, and a
ſhort time afterwards the Admiral was maſ-
ſacred.

The

The fecond volume left me by the Abby de Choify, contains the fix firft books of the work printed under the titleof *Memoires pcur fervir a l'Hiftoire de Louis XIV*. but I have found at the end of the volume, a converfation between the abby and the Marquis de Canillac, upon the ftate of the court in 1720, which the Abby d'Olivet dared not publifh. The marquis was a man of great wit, favoured by the regent, who had made him a member of the council of the regency, and of that of foreign affairs: there are fome good anecdotes in this converfation, a few of which I fhall relate.

The Marquis de Canillac pretended that the regent was not naturally of a bad difpofition, but loved what was fingular and extraordinary; that he was fyftematical, which made him adopt the fyftem of M. Law.

It is generally agreed, that if this fyftem had been well underftood, and confined within proper bounds, it would have faved the kingdom: but it was carried much too far; M. Law himfelf had not underftanding enough; he was, like the regent, fingular

A a   and

and fyftematical, but did not know how far
to carry his ideas : when he was controller
general he committed one fault upon another. He thought himfelf an adept, and,
in fact, I have been affured by people of reputation, who knew him at Venice, that
he poffeffed the never-failing means of win-
ning at play whatever fums of money he
pleafed. But it requires more art to enrich
a flate than an individual. The regent faid
one day to the Marquis de Canillac, that the
bank, being in difcredit, a new one was
neceffary, " You are miftaken, Monfeig-
" neur," anfwered the marquis ; " you
" once had one, but you have let it efcape ;
" and never will be able to find it again."

I will add, that when the regent died,
the people appeared fo furious and defperate,
at the injury which the great number of
illufive bank-notes had done to many fortunes, that it was neceffary to double the
guard to conduct his body to Saint Denis ;
but when the Parifians had felt a little the
adminiftration of Monfieur le Duc, and
the brothers, at Paris, they agreed that the
regent was to be regretted.

The

The third volume of manufcripts of the Abby de Choify, contains the hiftory of the pretended Countefs of Barres. This fcandalous book has not been entirely printed there are five books in my manufcripf, three of which only have been given to the public ; but I will enter into no detail upon this work, which does no honour to my relation and old friend.

It will eafily be fuppofed I have all the works the abby ever wrote, and that he made me a prefent of them upon a fine paper and on a good letter. I will give my fentiments in a few words upon each, for they are very numerous.

The Abby de Choify did not begin to write till he had entirely quitted the ridiculous and fingular life he had led; not even until fome time afterwards. He returned to Paris, and, wearing the drefs of his profeffion, was like women who have been gallant and coquettifh, and are become old ; they have the choice of play, intrigue, wit and devotion. The Abby de Choify took up all of thefe, one after another. At firft he played, and loft the greateft part of his

fortune

fortune ; his benefices were all he had left.
He poffeffed, among others, the abbey of
Saint Seine, to which he retired, and became acquainted there with the famous Buffy
Rabutin, exiled to his eftate in Burgundy, who
advifed him to leave off play and become
an author. Buffy perceived the abby had
information and ftyle fufficient to compofe
books of devotion, written in an agreeable
manner, which would be read by men of
the world, to whom thefe kind of books
aie commonly tirefome. The abby benefited by this advice, but not until fome
years afterwards. In the mean time he
came to Paris, and became very intimate
with the Cardinal de Bouillon, who, in the
moment of departure for Rome, where he
was going to affift at the Conclave of 1676,
propofed to the abby to accompany him in
quality of conclavift, to which he confented. He has frequently related to me very
interefting details of this Conclave, and
which prove that the Italian cardinals are
gieat adepts in petty intrigues. The abby
affured me that a fevere illnefs which he
had in 1683, made him refolve to change his
conduct, and that fince that time his devotion had been fincere. It was foon after

this

this illnefs that he compofed, in concert
with his friend, the Abby de Dangeau, his
firft woik, which was printed in 1685. It
confifts of four dialogues, upon the Immortality of the Soul; the Exiftence of God;
upon Providence; and, laftly, upon Religion. I will fay nothing about this book,
which treats of fuch ferious matters: I
avow, without referve, that it fatigued me,
although well written. The year following, 1686, he was guilty of what may be
called his laft extravagance, his voyage to
Siam. All the world know the journal he
printed of it: fome paffages are dry, and
others enlivened by ftrokes of wit and agreeable details. In general, the epocha of
the arrival of the Siamefe in France, and
that of the French ambaffadors at Siam, are
capable of furnifhing many philofophical
reflections; it was a political comedy, fuch
as there were many in the reign of Lewis
XIV. they appear ridiculous at prefent, but
they contributed to the glory of the monarch, and that of the nation, infeparable
fiom each other. The Abby de Choify
amufed himfelf, for fome time after his
return, and entertained the court and city,
with the recital of his great voyage: his

printed

printed relation made the author fully
known, and opened to him, in 1697, the
doors of *l'Academie Francoife*. I have remarked, in the difcourfe pronounced at his
reception, two thoughts, the firft of which
appears to me ridiculous, and the fecond
a very fine and juft one. He fays that the
new academicians ought to act like the
cardinals, who remain fome time with their
mouths fhut, till, in a confiftory, the Pope
opens them with ceremony, that is to fay,
permits them to fpeak. This is a proof
that members were not then received into
the academy as foon as they were elected.
The other paffage in the Abby's difcourfe
is, that there was, between Lewis XIV.
and the academy, an intercourfe, which naturally led both to immortality. Lewis
XIV. granted it his protection, and the academy augmented his glory.

To fpeak fucceffively on what occafions
the Abby de Choify diftinguifhed himfelf as
an academician, I muft begin by obferving
that in 1704, *l'Academie Francoife*, wifhing
to confer an honour upon M. Boffuet,
which few others have received; the fame
day that the Abby, fince Cardinal, de Polignac
was

was received at the academy, in the place
of the illuftrious M. Boffuet, Bifhop of
Meaux, independently of the eulogium which
his fucceffor, and the director made of him,
the Abby de Choify was defired to compofe
one of fingular merit : this eulogium took
up the remainder of the fitting.   The fubject was fine, but I found nothing worthy
of it in the Abby's difcourfe.

The laft year of his life, the Abby received the Abby d'Olivet; his difcourfe was
fhort and fimple ; the good man was worn
down, but he impofed upon himfelf this
tafk, becaufe the Abby d'Olivet was his
friend.   I know not if it be on this account
he took from me his memoirs, and had them
printed in Holland.

The following year, 1724, the Abby de
Choify died ; his fucceffor, M. Portal, firft
prefident, and M. de Valincourt, director,
defcribed him fuch as he was in the latter
part of his life, amiable in fociety, eafy in
intercourfe, gentle in manners, poffeffed of
natural grace, and an infinuating lively
turn, officious, a faithful friend, brilliant,
and full of fallies in converfation, although

A a 4   he

he was modeſt, and appeared to forget him-
elf in favour of others : his gaiety was mild
and tranquil, of which he bore the character in his features.   With refpect to his
merit, as his writings are of feveral kinds,
he has been moſt approved of as an hiſtorian, and it is, in fact, in what he appears to
the greateſt advantage.   He publiſhed, in
1668, an interpretation of the Pſalms,
wherein were pointed out the remarkable
differences between the Hebrew text and
the Vulgate ; it was preceded by the life of
David, in which he compared this monarch
to Lewis XIV.   The book had no fuccefs ;
but the Life of David pleafed, not only on
account of its being well written, but,
becaufe it was the faſhion of the times to
praiſe Lewis XIV. it was therefore re-
printed fingly, and foon followed by the
life of Solomon, written in the fame ſtile of
flattery, and, which was ſtill more admired,
efpecially the paſſage wherein he reprefents
Solomon giving audience to the ambaſſadors
of the Indian king.

Des penſées Chrétiennes, which he publiſhed
in 1690, had little fuccefs ; it did not, how
ever, prevent his giving, in 1692, a tranſ-
lation

lation of the Imitation of Jefus Chrift, of which I have already fpoken. Difcouraged by the criticifms on this work, he confined himfelf to writing hiftory, in which, in my opinion, he fucceeded perfectly ; for, if his ftyle does not always appear noble enough for the fubject of which he treats, it is, at leaft agreeable and pure, and is read with fatisfaction. The books of the Abby de Choify, which I advife my friends to read, and efpecially the ladies with whom I am acquainted, are, two or three volumes *D'Hiftoires de Piété et de Morale*, which he acknowledges to have written in oppofition to the *Petits Contes de Fées,* greatly in vogue towards the end of the laft century. Great courage is neceffary thus to oppofe hiftory to fable, fo delightful to the imagination of women, and, perhaps of men alfo. Yet it muft be acknowledged, that the Abby did his beft, and transferred the ftyles of Madame de la Fayette, and Madame d'Aunoy, into moral and edifying ftoies. There are twenty-one in number, and, if they be not all really excellent, they are delightful to read, and not difficult to procure.

Their

Their fuccefs encouraged the Abby to give, in 1695, *Les Vies de Philippe de Valois, du Roi Jean, de Charles V. de Charles VI.* and, finally, that of Saint Lewis. They were much approved of at Court, and put into the hands of the royal children, as infinitely proper to give them inftruction. Effectively, nothing is more inftructive than hiftory, written with ufeful views, with good fenfe, and mixed with moral reflections, given in a few words, and rifing naturally from facts.

The Abby is not curious in inveftigating fingular and extraordinary difcoveries, as producing no utility, nor even exciting admiration ; they are fcarce known at prefent, perhaps, becaufe they were neglected ; and from which no rules of conduct can be prefcribed, no conclufions drawn, to know the human heart, nor even the manners of the early ages ; becaufe they are, for the moft part, extraordinary and ifolated circumftances ; and, that the knowledge of the manners of a nation can only refult from an union of a great number of facts.

At

At length the Abby undertook his hiftory of the Church, although thofe of M. de Tillemont, and the Abby de Fleury, were already begun; but thefe three authors could fcarcely agree. M. de Tillemont overcharged this work with an erudition which, on one hand made it valuable, but on the other, not proper for the common clafs of readers; moreover he has treated of the fix firft ages of the church. That of the Abby de Fleury began to appear in 1691, but it was eafy to difcover that, although excellent, and a work of a moft fenfible and methodical author, it took fuch a turn as to prevent its being finifhed in a reafonable time. That of the Abby de Choify was, on the contrary, fo abridged, as to give hopes of its being foon terminated; and, in effect, although he was fixty when the firft volume appeared, in 1703, the laft volume was publifhed in 1723, and the hiftory brought down to 1715. This work is by no means overcharged with erudition: on the contrary the author has been too deficient in that refpect, accufed of quoting no authorities, and of having, under pretence of giving the hiftory of the Church, written

that

that of the Chriftian world, from the birth
of Jefus Chrift.

But he wifhed his hiftory to be within
the capacity of every body, and he has certainly fulfilled his object ; he has drawn all
his information from the beft fources, becaufe the facts he has given are generally
known.   It was not poffible for him to inform his readers of the progrefs of religion,
and of the contefts it was the caufe of, without giving the hiftory of the whole Chriftian world.   He has not entered into a detail
of controverfies, becaufe this would certainly have been fatiguing ; but he has never
failed to explain, very clearly, in what here-
fies confifted ; from whence they fprung ;
what great events they have produced, and
when they were terminated.   The Abby
had very delicate points to treat of ; fuch as
the crufades, the councils of Conftance and
Bale, and the religious wars in France ;
all which he got over with much wifdom and
addrefs.   All his idle obfervations are confined to the laft volume : but, on the other
hand, he has ufed much art in fpeaking of
Janfenifm.   This volume contains his voyage to Siam.   In fact, the Hiftory of the
Church,

Church, by the Abby de Choify, is fufficiently good, very agreeable, and, perhaps,
the beft for women to read.   I have recom-
mended the perufal of it to moft of the ladies of my acquaintance, for which they
have thanked me, as well as for that of the
Lives of the Five Kings of France of which
I have fpoken.   The Abby wrote alfo, in
1706, the Life of Madame de Miramion :
this lady was his coufin-german, which
was a good reafon for his writing her life,
but not equally fo for its being read by the
public.

ESSAY

ESSAY XLIV.

ON THE ERUDITION, FINE TASTE, AND ELEGANCE OF CARDINAL POLIGNAC

I SEE, fometimes the Cardinal de Polignac, and he always infpires me with the
fame fentiments of admiration and refpect.
He appears to me to be the laft gicat prelate of the Gallic church, who profeffes eloquence in the Latin as well the French
language, and whofe erudition is very extenfive. He, alone, among the honorary
membeis of the Academy of Belles Lettres,
underftands and fpeaks the language of the
learned of which this academy is compofed;
he expreffes himfelf upon matters of erudition, with a grace and dignity proper and
peculiar to himfelf. It may be remembered
that M. Boffuet, whom the Cardinal, at that
time Abby de Polignac, replaced in 1704,
at the Academy Francoife, was the laft prelate who had a diftinguifhed rank among the
theologians and polemical writeis : The converfation of the Cardinal is equally brilliant

3   and

and inftructive : he knows fomething of every
fubject, and relates with grace and perfpicu-
ity every thing he knows : he fpeaks upon the
fciences, and upon matters of erudition, as
Fontenelle wrote his worlds, in reducing
the moft abftracted matters to the capacity
of the vulgar ; and renders them in terms
which men of education and refinement ufe
in treating familiar fubjects of ordinary
converfation.

Nobody relates more elegantly than the
Cardinal, and without entreaty ; but, in
the moft fimple narratives, wherein erudition would be infipid from the mouth of
another, it finds graces in his, from the
aid of his perfon and elegant pronunciation.
Age has deprived him of fome of thefe advantages, but he preferves ftill, enough of
them, efpecially when we call to mind the
many great occafions in which his graces
and natural talents have fhone.   My uncle,
the Bifhop of Blois, who was nearly his
cotemporary, has frequently fpoken to me
of his younger days.   Never was a courfe of
ftudy made with more reputation than his :
not only his themes and compofitions were
excellent, but he had time and facility to
affift

affift his fellow-ftudents, or, rather, to do
their duty for them ; fo much fo, that the
four pieces which gained the two premiums
and the *acceffits*, in the college of Harcourt,
where he ftudied, were all compofed by
him. When he was engaged in philofophy,
at the fame college, he would maintain, in
his public thefes, the fyftem of Defcartes,
which it was then found difficult to eftablifh : he acquitted himfelf with great reputation, and confounded all the partifans
of old opinions. Neverthelefs, the ancient
doctors of the univerfity having taken it ill
that he fhould have combated Ariftotle, and
not having been willing to give a degree to
the enemy of the preceptor of Alexander,
he confented to maintain another thefis, in
which be read his recantation, and made
Ariftotle triumph over the Cartefians themfelves.

No fooner was he received doctor in theology, than the Cardinal de Bouillon took
him to Rome, to the conclave of 1689,
wherein the Pope, Alexander VIII. was
elected. As foon as the Abby *de Polignac* was
known in this capital of the Chriftian world,
which was then the centre of the moft profound

found erudition and refined policy, he was generally loved and efteemed. The French cardinals and ambaffador judged him the moft proper perfon to make the Pope hearken to reafon upon the articles of the famous affembly of the clergy of France in 1682. It was difficult to perfuade the court of Rome to fwallow this pill; yet the wit and eloquence of the Abby *de Polignac* brought it about: he was charged to carry the news of it to France, and had, on this occafion, a private audience of Lewis XIV. who faid of him, in French, what the Pope, Alexander VIII. had faid in Italian : *This young man has the art of perfuading you to believe every thing he pleafes ; whilft he appears at firft to be of your opinion he is artfully maintaining a contrary one, but he gains his end with fo much addrefs, that he finifhes always by convincing you he is right.* He had not yet put the finifhing ftroke to this great affair before the Pope recalled him to Rome. He affifted again at the conclave wherein Innocent XII. was elected, and he returned to France the following year, 1692.

About two years afterwards the king named him ambaffador to Poland, a very

delicate

delicate appointment, from the particular circumftances at that period. John Sobiefki was in a very declining ftate of health; Lewis XIV. wifhed not only to preferve fome credit in Poland, but to give, for a fucceffor to the declining king, a prince devoted to France. The Prince of Conti had offered himfelf, and Lewis XIV. charged fecretly the Abby *de Polignac* to endeavour to get him elected, notwithftanding the op- pofition to the Queen Dowager, who was a French woman, but who, with much rea- fon, favoured her children, in fpite of all contrary cabals. The Abby, keeping his inftructions very fecret, arrived at the court of Sobiefki a year before his death; he de- lighted all the Polanders by the facility with which he fpoke Latin; he might have been taken for an envoy from the court of Auguf- tus, if he had not been heard to fpeak French to the Queen, who was feduced by his wit and appearance; but fhe could not abandon, on his account, the intereft of her family. Sobiefki died, and the general diet affembled to chufe a fucceffor. The eloquence of the Abby *de Polignac,* the promifes and hopes with which he allured the Polanders were, at firft, attended with fo much fuccefs, that

a great

a great part of the nation, headed by the primate, proclaimed the Prince of Conti; but in the fame moment, the fums which the Elector of Saxony had diftributed, caufed a double election, in which this German prince was chofen. Both pretending to the crown, they both arrived to fupport their party, and continued to employ the means which had, at firft, been fuccefsful; but thofe of the Elector were more effectual and folid. He had money and even troops; the Prince of Conti, on the contrary, after having received kingly honours at the court of France, went on board a French veffel at Dantzick, where he ftayed fix weeks, but without any other means of proving the legality of his election, than the good face and eloquence of the Abby *de Polignac*. Thefe refources were foon exhaufted; the Prince of Conti, and even the Abby, were obliged to return to France.

Although the court of France was too juft and well informed not to perceive that it was not the fault of the ambaffador if his miffion was not crowned with a more brilliant fuccefs, he was, notwithftanding, exiled from Verfailles for four years. He em-

ployed

ployed this time ufefully, to encreafe his
mafs of knowledge, which was already
very great. Finally, in 1702, he was fent
to Rome in quality of Auditor of the Rota*.
He now found new opportunities of diftinguifhing himfelf, and gaining admiration,
for which he was recompenfed by a nomi-
nation to the Cardinalfhip, by James, King
of England.

He was upon the point of enjoying the
honours of his new rank, when he was recalled to France on account of fome very
critical circumftances. He was obliged, in
1710, to go with the Marfhal d'Huxelles to
Gertrudenberg, charged by Lewis XIV. to
propofe to the enemies of this monarch, his
                              fubmiffion

---

* The name of an ecclefiaftical court at Rome, compofed of twelve prelates, one of whom muft be a German, another a Frenchman, and two of them Spaniards, the other eight are Italians, three of whom muft
be Romans, and the remaining five, a Bolognefe, a
Ferraran, a Milanefe, a Venetian, and a Tufcan.

This is one of the moft auguft tribunals in Rome,
and takes cognizance, by appeal, of all fuits in the ter-
ritory of the church, as alfo, of all matters beneficiary
and patrimonial.

TRANSLATOR.

fubmiffion to the moft humiliating conditions, in order to terminate the war. Unhappily all the wit and eloquence of the future cardinal was there ineffectual. At
length, after two years were elapfed, he
was named plenipotentiary to the famous
congrefs of Utrecht ; it muft be remarked
that he was at that time named, at Rome,
cardinal *in petto*, and, though all the people
knew who he was, he did not appear as an
ecclefiaftic, either in drefs or title : his drefs
was fecular, and he was called the *Compte de
Polignac*. It was in this fituation of an *incog-
nito*, that he was prefent at all the negoti-
ations of Utrecht, to the moment of figning
the treaty ; he then declared it was not poffible for him to fign the exclufion of a monarch from his throne, to whom he was in-
debted for the cardinal's hat ; he withdrew,
and came to enjoy, at the court of France,
the honours of the cardinalfhip.

The new political fyftem which was
adopted, after the death of Lewis XIV. exiled him to his Abby of Anchin, in Flanders.
Thefe good Flemifh monks trembled to fee
him arrive in their monaftery ; but they were
afflicted even to defpair when he left them,

B b 3   after

after the death of the Cardinal Dubois and
of the Regent. They were not capable of
appreciating his wit, nor of underftanding
his erudition ; but they had found him
mild and amiable, and fo far from plunder-
ing them, he embellifhed their church, and
re-eftablifhed their houfe.

He was obliged to return to Rome at the
death of Clement XI. and he affifted at the
conclaves wherein Innocent XIII. Benoit
XIII. and Clement XII. were elected. During the two firft pontificates he was charged
with the affairs of France at that court.
This city was ever the fineft theatre of his
glory : one would have thought its ancient
grandeur entered with him into the capital.
On his part, when he returned, he appeared
charged with the fpoils of Rome, fubdued
by his wit and eloquence ; and it may li-
terally be faid, that, in his laft journey, he
tranfported a part of ancient Rome to Paris,
by placing in his hotel a collection of antique
ftatues and monuments taken from the pa-
laces of the firft emperors.

I cannot fee the Cardinal de *Polignac* without recollecting all he has done and learned

for

for fixty years paft; I remain, as it were, in ecftafy, when near him, and in the greateft admiration of every thing he fays. It is obferved that his manner is become old as well as his perfon; it is true that his tone has outlived the mode. But is it not becaufe we have abfolutely loft the habitude of hearing the language of fcience and erudition, that the Cardinal begins to be tirefome to us? for, otherwife, nobody treats thefe matters with lefs pedantry than he does: if he quotes, it is always *a-propos*, becaufe, having a prodigious memory, it furnifhes him with what is neceffary to fupport converfation in every point, let the fubject be what it may. For my part, who have finifhed my ftudies, but who have yet a great deal to learn, I declare I never received more agreeable leffons than thofe he gives in converfation.

Being a good deal taken up about the Cardinal, I have juft read his difcourfe of admiffion at the *Academy Francoife*, in 1704. Nothing can be more elegant and noble; and this immenfe collection, begun almoft an hundred years ago, contains no difcourfe equal to his: it is the moft perfect model

for

for thofe who have a like tafk to fulfil, obferving always that the academician, whom
they fucceed, and the circumftances in
which this kingdom is, at the time they
fpeak, may infinitely increafe the difficulties of it. The Abby de *Polignac* had difficulties to encounter, but he got over them
in fuch a manner as gained him univerfal
applaufe ; and, had it been cuftomary at
that time, the academy would have rung
with their plaudits.

The Cardinal has a pupil and friend,
thirty years younger than himfelf, who,
confequently, cannot be reproached with
having manners different from the fafhion :
this is the Abby de Rothelin. He has a good
deal of wit, a ftrong memory, and much
knowledge, but not fo extenfive as that of
the Cardinal ; he fpent with him feveral
years at Rome, and has been twice his conclavift. There he faw what honour erudition conferred on the Cardinal ; he endeavoured to tread in his fteps, and is become, like him, a member of the *Academy
Francoife*, and honorary of that, *des Infcrip-
tions* and *des Belles Lettres*. But his eloquence is neither fo natural or noble, as that
of

of his mafter. He has more vivacity in converfation, which fparkles with more ftrokes
of wit; he has, perhaps, received more
fiom nature than the Cardinal, but he does
not know how to employ fo well what was
acquired fiom others, nor to reap the fruit
of his ftudies.

The Cardinal has undertaken a Latin poem, which he intitules *Anti-Lucretius*, and
is a refutation of the fyftem of material-
ifts. He recites paffages from it to perfons
whom he thinks capable of judging of their
merit ; and his Eminence has done me the
honour to repeat feveral of them.

They are admirable paintings and defcriptions. If one knows the Latin ever fo little,
and remembers the authors of the Auguftan
age, he would imagine that he read them
over again by hearing thefe paffages. But
a poem againft Lucretius, of equal length
with the original, and divided into nine
books, requires the life of a man to carry it
to perfection. The Cardinal began too late,
and cannot flatter himfelf with the hope of
living to finifh it. It is faid he means to
charge the Abby de Rothelin with this tafk,
who

who, from vanity, will not refufe it, and
will think it an honour to put the woik of
his refpectable friend in a ftate to appear before the public.   But, to this end, the aid
of fome able piofeffor of the univeifity will
be neceffary ; the Abby will never accomplifh it of himfelf.   Moreover, when the
Anti-Lucretius appears, it will undoubtedly do honour to the Cardinal's abilities, as
well as the Abby's, and even thofe perfons
who fhall have affifted him in finifhing it.
But who, at prefent, will read a latin poem,
entirely philofophical, of five or fix thoufand lines ? Scarcely would a tianflation of
it, in profe or veife, be turned over.
Gieek is entirely foigotten ; it is to be feared the Latin will foon be fo, and that the
Cardinal de *Polignac*, the Abby de Rothelin, and a certain M. le Beau, coming up in
the univerfity, will be called *the laft of the
Romans.*   Even the Jefuits begin to neglect
Latin ; they find it more eafy to wiite in
French ; this gains them more honour and
profit.

The figure of the Cardinal and that of
the Abby are ftill more different than their
turn of mind.   That of the firft is elegant
                                        and

and noble, and announces what he is, and has been. If we were to paint from idea a great prelate, a learned cardinal, a wife and worthy ambaſſador, a famous Roman orator, we ſhould ſeize the features of the Cardinal de *Polignac*. The Abby de Rothelin has, on the contrary, a fine and ſenſible countenance, but appears to have delicate lungs; his figure is agreeable, but quite modern; that of the Cardinal is, at preſent, a beautiful and precious antique.

ESSAY

ESSAY XLIII.

ON ABBY ROTHELIN's EXTRAVAGANT
TASTE FOR MEDALS AND BOOKS.

THE Abby *de Rothelin*'s curiofity is of
two kinds, which belong equally to
erudition, medals and books He has, of
the firft, a confiderable collection of all
forts and forms.   His filver medals are, as I
have been told, eight thoufand in number,
to which muft be added, three hundred me-
dallions of emperors, and four hundred of
Grecian cities. His feries of laige and fmall-
er medals, in bronze, are upwards of nine
thoufand.   He began this collection at
Rome, under the infpection of the Cardinal
de Polignac.   His eminence having, on his
part, collected fome, the Abby hopes he
will leave them to him, and that, by this
means, his cabinet will become the fineft
and moft precious ever in the poffeffion of an
individual in France. The Abby will not
be at all infenfible of the poffeffion of fo
iich a literary domain; for, although a man
of

of quality, fufficiently wealthy, amiable, and a good companion, he is accufed of loving medals to fuch a degree, that when he finds one carelefsly laid, and is unobferved by the proprietor, he does not hefitate to put it in his pocket, and, afterwards place it in his cabinet : except in this he is by no means knavifh.   He is rather too poignant and in-difcriminate in raillery : the cardinal's dif-pofition was equally remote from fatire or fcandal.

The Abby *de Rothelin*'s other tafte, is in books. His literary collection begins to be very confiderable; he fhews it willingly, and with oftentation, and makes curious re-marks on fome printed works which he alone poffeffes : he explains in what their merit confifts ; the rarity and fingularity by which they are diftinguifhed.   As he com-monly fpeaks to people lefs learned than himfelf, they believe all he fays, and·con-gratulate him upon the poffeffion of fuch a precious treafure, which will be fold for a great price after his death.   Senfible people think there is a little quackery in this, and I am of the fame opinion.

In

In a taste for books we must distinguish
master-pieces in composition, the most splen-
did editions, and elegance of types. Their
merit is visible, and we cannot refuse them
a place in a rich library, especially when
we are assured that the editions are as correct as they are handsome.

It may therefore be conceived that the
first books printed in any language are
sought after like so many historical monuments of the arts and printing; but it
seems to me that otherwise the value of a
library should consist in the intrinsic merit
of the books, and in the utility they may
be of to those who possess them. People
who are, or wish to become well-informed,
ought to have a great number of books of
every kind; those of less pretensions, ought
to confine themselves to books proper to
their situation, and such as are useful to
their daily amusement and instruction. To
wish to go further is folly and abuse; yet I
think this folly seems pretty general. The
Abby *de Rothelin* inspired with it the Compte
de Hoym, minister of the king of Poland,
Elector of Saxony, at the court of France,
and who has been persuaded that, although

2   unlearned,

unlearned, he ought to have the fcarceft
books of every kind, and to get them mag-
nificently bound. M. de Boze, perpetual fecretary to the Academy *des Belles Lettres*, has
alfo begun to colleſt books of erudition ; he
has had, and will continue to have, the power
of perfuading the illiterate rich to make the
fame acquifition, without their knowing the
reafons that induce them. The Abby *de
Rothelin* and M. de Boze can, at leaft, tell
the kind of merit for which they fought after fuch or fuch a book. The reafons are,
fometimes, frivolous enough ; but, however, they know them ; inftead of which,
thofe into whofe hands thefe books may
hereafter fall, will buy them dear, for the
fole reafon that their firft poffeffor efteemed
them highly.

It is diverting to imagine that there will
come a time when people, who know not a
word of Latin, will give an exoibitant price
for books written in that language ; that
they will even give an hundred piftoles for a
book, becaufe it is honoured in the catalogue
with the epithets fcarce and .fingular, and,
that a great price has been offered for it in
a preceding fale.

I met

I met one day with one of thefe *bibliomanes*, who had juft paid a great price for a fcarce book : " Apparently, Sir," faid I to him, " it is your intention to get this book re- " printed." " By no means," anfwered he, " it would then be no longer fcarce, " and thereby lofe its value ; moreover, I " know not if it be worth while." " Ah, " Sir," replied I, " If it deferves not to be " re-printed, how can it be worth the price " you have given ?"

In fpeaking of the Abby *de Rothelin*, I find myfelf infenfibly engaged in treating of the *mania* of books. I know not if what I have juft remarked may, in time, be of ufe to fome of my friends, or to people for whom I ought to be moft interefted ; be this as it may, I have given my opinion freely, let thofe who pleafe benefit by it.

ESSAY

ESSAY XLIV.

ON THE SINGULAR MEMORY AND ERU-
DITION OF ABBY LONGUERUE, AND
OTHER LITERARY ANECDOTES.

I WAS, for feveral years, acquainted with
a man, much lefs amiable than the Cardinal de Polignac, but famous for his immenfe erudition, founded upon his memory,
which was, in truth, aftonifhing; this was
the Abby *de Longuerue :* he died in 1732, upwards of eighty years of age. In his childhood he appeared a prodigy. Lewis XIV.
paffing by Charleville, the Abby's country,
wifhed to fee and hear him. He feemed to
know every thing at an age when other
children know fcarcely any thing. He
maintained his reputation to the end of his
life. Coming early to Paris, he was confulted as an oracle on matters of every kind.
Although efteemed a man of much fenfe,
he was never of any academy, but received
many compliments upon his memory. I

afked

afked him how he managed to arrange, and retain in his head, every thing that entered it, and to recollect every thing when wanted. " Sir," anfwered he, " the elements " of every fcience muft be learned whilft " we are young; the firft principles of " every language, the *a b c*, as I may fay, " of every kind of knowledge : this is not " difficult in youth, fo much the lefs fo, as " it is not neceffary to penetrate far, and " that fimple notions are fufficient : when " once they are acquired every thing we " read places itfelf where it ought to be: " the fum of acquired knowledge infen- " fibly becomes accumulated and perfectly " diftributed. Therefore," added the Abby, " I have ftudied nothing, methodically, " almoft thefe fifty years ; but I read fome- " times one book, fometimes another, and " thofe in preference which may teach me " fomething new, or recall to my mind " that which cannot be too much incul- " cated. It is in this manner I am become " poffeffed of the nomenclature of all my " books. my local memory indicates to " me the place in my cabinet, or apartment, " where they are; I am therefore fure, in " cafe of need, to give clear directions to " thofe

" thofe I fend to feek them; they bring
" them to me, and, in this, I find always
" the proof of what I have advanced of my
" memory."

The Abby *de Longuerue* has, however,
found that the memory muft not be too
much relied upon : he wifhed to make an
exertion of it, in which he did not quite
fucceed. In 1718, it was argued with him
that nothing was more difficult than to give
an hiftorical defcription of France, and which
fhould be neither long nor uninterefting : he
pretended to be capable of doing it from memory, without confulting any book, but
entirely by the aid of fome charts, which
he was to have before his eyes ; and, that he
would call to mind the origin and hiftory
of each province, city, and principal place,
and the diftinguifhed houfes of the kingdom. He began to dictate this defcription to
the Abby Alary, who was then a little boy,
the fon of an apothecary, and thought himfelf very happy to write under his direction :
the work appeared in 1719, a volume *in folio*.
He read fragments of it in manufcript and
printed detached fheets, to feveral people,
who could not ceafe admiring how fuch pro-

found refearches could have come, as from
their fource, without the leaft difficulty to
him. But as foon as a few whole copies
were publifhed, it appeared that correct
works were not to be compofed in this
manner; many notable errors were found
in his hiftory, befides bold and hazarded
opinions, not fufficiently eftablifhed. The
Abby was obliged to take out many leaves,
which were faulty, and put in others more
perfect; this greatly encreafed the expences
of his edition. I muft remark, that copies,
wherein thefe corrections have not been made,
are now fought after, and God knows why;
for the only difference is, that fome are
faulty, and others corrected. Nowithftand-
ing all this, the Defcription of France, by
the Abby *de Longuerue*, is a good and ufeful
book; it is an hiftory of France by provinces, and, confequently, written upon an
entire new plan. The manner in which all
the great fiefs of the crown were formed
is related therein, when, and how they became fubject to the king's authority, and
finally united to his domain.

The Abby *de Longuerue* wrote two hiftories, one of the Cardinal de Richelieu, the
other

other of the Cardinal Mazarine, with two
defcriptions of their adminiftration.   Thefe
two fragments remain in manufcript ; what
they contain moft curious are fome anecdotes, which the Abby learned from people
who had lived, and been employed under
thefe minifters.   The Abby frequently repeated them to me, feveral of which I wrote
down.   I have alfo made other notes from
what he communicated ; for, in returning
from my vifits to him, I always found
fomething worth remembering and committing to paper.   Some of my notes are as
follow :

The Abby pretended that our language
had made no real progrefs but for fifty years
of the feventeenth century, from the year
1630 to 1680.   It was, however, in this
interval that *L'Academie Francoife* was eftablifhed, the members of which applied
themfelves, at firft, very ufefully, to purify
the language.   What old expreffions it has
loft, faid the Abby, ought not to be regretted, although fome of them were defcrip-
tive and natural, but harfh and ill-found-
ing ; thofe fubftituted for them, are more
foft, and render equally well the thought.

But,

But, since the year 1680, which may be looked upon as the most biilliant epocha of the age of Lewis XIV. what words have we added to the dictionary, except a few, borrowed from the arts, and which are frequently ill applied, and taken in a bad sense? The Abby thought the style had gained no more, since that epocha, than words ; but, in this, I do not think he judged right.

The History of Don Carlos, so well written, by the Abby de St. Real, is certainly romantic. The Abby *de Longuerue* knew a Spanish book, which demonstrated that it was quite the work of fancy ; this opinion is, however, founded upon a passage of the history of M. de Thou : but this historian is as ignorant of what passed out of the kingdom, even in his own time, as he is worthy of belief upon all that happened in France, during the sixteenth century, because he was himself a witness to part of it, and that his father had a great share in the affairs immediately preceding.   There were then no Gazettes, and few ambassadors residing in the different courts, who kept up a regular correspondence.   M. de Thou was not in a situation to discover the truth

truth of reports which were fpread in the kingdom, particularly thofe relative to the Spaniards, which always appeared to us fuf-picious, as propagated by our natural enemies.

Meffieurs de Bouillons had got their genealogy drawn up and printed, with great pomp and magnificence; they had already diftributed feveral copies of it at court: when it was fpoken of at the king's fupper, " Sire," faid the Prince de Condé, " if we " believe this genealogy, Meffieurs de Bou-" illon are more noble than we are; for " they make themfelves defcended from " the firft Dukes of Aquitaine, who were " fovereigns, whilft the grandfather of " Hugh Capet was but a fimple individual ; " but, after all," added the Prince de Con-dé, " it is not for us to tell them what we " think of it; I am but a younger brother : " it is your duty, Sire, who are the elder." This reflection did not fall to the ground. The next day, the king informing himfelf of this genealogy, fuppreffed it, and forbad the fale, which greatly mortified Meffieurs de Bouillon.

The

The Abby *de Longuerue* though*t* he was certain that the Dutch offered, in 1632, to Lewis XIV. in order to appeafe him, the cefffion of every thing on this fide the Rhine, and which is called Dutch Flanders and Dutch Brabant, and to preferve nothing more than their feven provinces. It was M. de Louvois, and a vain idea of glory, which difpofed Lewis XIV. not to be contented with the offer. He was very wrong, and reduced, injudicioufly, to the eve of ruin, the unhappy republic of Holland, which it was his intereft to preferve. By fecuring to himfelf the propofed barrier, the king would have taken the ten remaining provinces; and joined them to France, which would have been, to make ufe of a popular expreffion, giving the fineft poffible form to his meadow. Upon this the Abby faid that France had three acquifitions only to make; all belonging to her ancient poffeffions, and wifhing to do more was a folly. Thefe acquifitions were, firft the Low Countries, which we ought always to flatter ourfelves the Houfe of Auftria will fome day cede to us *to round her own meadow* on the oppofite fide. Secondly, Savoy, which we may alfo hope to obtain, in an agreeable manner,

manner, by encreafing the poffeffions of the Duke, on the fide of Italy, where we rifk nothing in procuring them for him, and putting it out of his power to penetrate into the kingdom. Thirdly, Lorraine, which the Abby was perfuaded we might have whenever we pleafed. He did not count *Avignon* among the acquifitions to be made ; for, faid he, the Pope is no more mafter there than the Bifhop of Strafburg is in Alface. However, the Abby judged more according to his own opinion, than that of wife politicians, that diftant acquifitions and poffeffions were improper for us. He told me he had known a man who demonftrated to Colbert, that it was a folly for France to have great poffeffions in Ame-rica, and particularly in the Eaft-Indies ; that it was neceffary to leave the Englifh, who have, as we may fay, but a foot of land in Europe, to make eftablifhments in the new world ; and to the Dutch, who are nearly in the fame fituation, to make conquefts in Afia : that, after all, if we had, at fecond-hand only, what is brought from thofe countries, we fhould not be the poorer, becaufe France would find within herfelf, not only every thing of the firft ne-ceffity,

ceffity, but ftill the means of employing
all the arts which fupport Epicureanifm
and luxury, and bring fo much money into
the kingdom M. de Colbert, faid the Abby,
fell into a great paffion with the man who
had fpoken to him fo freely, and would
never fee him again ; but, becoming angry is
not giving an anfwer.

' The Cardinal de Richelieu was not a
learned man,' but he knew well how to do
without being fo : it is fufficient for a minifter to encourage and protect the fciences
he is not obliged to poffefs, nor even cultivate any of them; but what is extraordinary, the Cardinal thought no more of
fcience than of the learned. He had ftudied theology a little in his youth, becaufe,
being deftined to the church, it was neceffary
to him ; and, to gain ecclefiaftical prefer-
ment, it was neceffary to be able to maintain a thefis againft the Calvinifts ; the Cardinal had therefore compofed, or, at leaft,
had affifted in the compofition of fome works
of this kind, which he got printed with
much pomp and magnificence, at the Royal
printing-office. He was at the expence of
cafting Hebrew, Chaldean, Syrian and

3   Arabick

Arabick characters, to make a Polyglot
Bible, in the manner of that which did fo
much honour to the Cardinal Ximenes ; but
he underftood no language but the French
and the Latin ; fcarcely had he read our profane authors . he was ignorant of hiftory,
had no knowledge of antiquity, and knew
nothing at all of natural philofophy nor ma-
thematics ; on which account he never recompenfed thofe who applied themfelves to
the ftudy of thefe fciences.   He let André
Duchene, who was ceitainly the beft com.
piler of hiftory, and who lived during the
adminiftration, or, rather the reign, of
the Cardinal, die for want.   Neither the
accuiate fciences, nor thofe of nature made
any progrefs during his time.   He encouraged the arts, but it was to make them
ferve his luxury.   He eftablifhed an academy of grammar, eloquence, and poetry, in
which he has perhaps done a greater fervice
to the nation than he thought at firft ; he
did this becaufe he loved poetry, and pretended to write it.   Neither ftudy nor
knowledge is neceffary for this ; genius
alone is fufficient ; it muft be acknowledged the Cardinal de Richelieu was not
wanting in it, and it was eafy for him to
                                        fupply

fupply the want of habitude in this kind of compofition, becaufe he had poets at the court, who wifhed for nothing better than to put rhime and meafure to his thoughts.

M. Colbert thought very differently : he certainly was not more inftructed, perhaps even lefs than the Cardinal; but he had zeal enough to encourage all the arts, fciences, and every kind of talent; he looked upon them as a fource of honour for his king, and even of profit to France. Fortunately Lewis XIV. was of the fame opinion ; and, although more ignorant than his minifter, he had more tafte, and was more difficult to deceive, than Colbert. When people's reputation could reach his ears, he never failed to recompenfe them, according to their merit. M. Colbert, incapable of judging for himfelf, in an infinity of circumftances, chofe guides upon whofe advice he formed his opinions ; but his oracles were not always fure and impartial : in matters of erudition the Abby Gallois Chapelain was his guide in poetry, and Perrault for all that came within the arts and fciences. Chapelain, who died before Colbeit,

bert, was replaced by the Abby Talle-
mant.

I once faw the Abby *de Longuerue* in a
great paffion, about the abridgments which
remain to us of the ancient hiftorians. I
cannot forgive Juftin for depriving us of the
great hiftory of Pompey. Paul Diane has
taken from us that of Feftus ; Florus was
near lofing us that of Livy, and Cornelius
Nepos the lives of illuftrious men in Plutarch. I do not remember who it was of
the company who anfwered, very fenfibly,
it was not to be wondered that abridgments
only remained to us, and great books were
loft. Before the invention of printing thefe
were fo dear to purchafe, or get copied, that
all a man of moderate fortune could do, was
to procure abridgments of them; even at
prefent, now books are not fo dear, the fortune of the generality of people, and the di-
menfions of their apartments, do not permit them to have voluminous works. But,
moreover, is it not doing a fervice to moft
readers, to put into their hands clear abridgments, methodically, and well compiled,
which contain the moft interefting facts.
It is neceffary the abbreviator fhould quote
his

his authorities; they may then be confulted in great libraries, wherein all the voluminous works are depofited. But, if the abridgment be acknowledged an exact one, it ought to be fufficient for common readers ; and great books fhould be referved for thofe whofe intereft it may be to decide upon fome particular queftions, which cannot well be thoroughly examined without recurring to the fource.

The Abby was a good deal acquainted with the illuftrious Fenelon, Archbifhop of Cambray. He has always infifted that he had more wit than fcience, and that he was a weak theologian. In attempting to introduce wit and and fubtlety into his fyftem of devotion, he wandered from his fubject, and fuffered fome errors to creep into his work, intituled *Les Maximes des Saints.* M. Boffuet, his fecret rival at court, was more learned, a greater theologian, and a more able difputant. He took advantage of M. Fenelon's *faux-pas* to ruin him ; the good Archbifhop, unprepared for the blow, refolved to fubmit to it with a good grace; he was deprived of the cardinal's hat, which had been promifed him, and to which, it is
                                            faid,

faid, he was even named, *in petto*. In general M. de Fenelon was more mild and amiable in fociety, and M. Boffuet more learned, able, and even more dexterous in intrigues.

The Abby had alfo feen the Cardinal de Vendome, who was legate in France, the moft incapable and richeft of all the legates and cardinals : he became an ecclefiaftic late in life, and, being a widower, fome one faid, on hearing of his admiffion into the facred college, that it was the firft college he had ever entered. When he was legate, it was even neceffary to explain to him what the woid legate meant, and what were his powers and functions ; but he learned no more of thefe than thofe to whom he addieffed himfelf for information were willing he fhould know. He got his letters regiftered in the parliament, the Attorney General joined all the reftrictions he thought proper ; it was inferted he fhould do nothing but according to the king's good pleafure, and that his legation fhould continue no longer than his Majefty found it agreeable. Thefe were reftrictions made for all future legates, who are, and will for ever

be

be obliged to fubmit to the fame claufes and conditions. Therefore it was a ftroke of policy in Lewis XIV. to decorate with the title of legate this good Cardinal, who did not hold that office at the expence of the clergy : being rich, he had no need of great abbies, nor epifcopal or archiepifcopal fees, which he was incapable of governing. He did not underftand the Latin of the parchment and papers laid before him to fign, and fpoke French like his mother, and M. de Beaufort his brother, that is to fay, like the language of the illiterate vulgar : he faid *j'allions*, *je venions*, and could never harangue the king, either when he received the cardinal's cap, or when he had an audience as legate.

The Compte de R * * * was famous at court for his ftupidity. The Abby *de Longuerue*, who knew him well, has told me many things of him, independently of thofe known to all the world ; fuch as that of his never being able to tell which was the capital of the State of Venice ; and of his having faid he was aftonifhed the king expended fo much money in getting antiques from abroad, whilft there were fo many
able

able men in France who would make them
for him if he pleafed. The following appears fo *narve*, frank, and good-natured,
that I cannot but relate it. The day M.
R*** married Mademoifelle de *** who
was very ugly, but had a deal of wit, " Ma-
" dame," faid he to her, " you are not
" pretty, and they fay I am a fool ; let us
" mutually overlook our defeéts, and we fhall
" make the happieft man and wife in the
" world." She confented to the propofition, and they lived affeétionately together.
He was tall, handfome, and well made ;
their offspring became numerous, and now
figures at the court among thofe of the firft
rank.

The father of the Abby *de Longuerue* ferved under his friend, the Marfhal Fabert,
whom the Abby, when young, had fometimes feen as commander upon the frontiers
of Champagne, the Abby's country. Fabert was afthmatic, and died of a final ftop-
page of refpiration in the night. The people of Sedan and its environs were perfuaded
that the devil had ftrangled him. However ridiculous and abfurd this opinion may
be, it was founded upon the aftonifhing for-

D d   tune

tune the Marſhal had made, and upon what he ſaid himſelf, not quite publicly, but to his friends and confidents, who repeated it to others : He believed firmly in judicial aſtrology, and aſſerted he had been previouſly informed of whatever had befallen him. He was the ſon of a bookſeller at Metz, who, however, had arrived at the dignity of maitre echevin, or mayor of the city. The Marſhal was, at firſt, a private ſoldier, and diſtinguiſhed himſelf on ſo many perilous occaſions that he acquired, among his comrades, the reputation of a ſorcerer, who charmed cannon and muſket-balls, and prevented them from touching him. Every action, from which he retired with fortune and honour, procured him additional rank ; ſo that at the age of rather more than forty years, he was captain of the guards, and a general officer. He never loſt his firmneſs in whatever ſituation the army or troop he commanded, or his own perſon might be, he had always the *coup d'œil*, juſt and unerring, to judge of the ſtep it was neceſſary he ſhould take, and of the remedy to be applied to any difficulty : in other reſpects he was incapable of forming a regular plan of campaign, as his views were not extenſive ;

but

but he accomplished every commission with which he was charged. There was, probably, some policy in his manner of declaring he knew by magic or astrology all that was to happen, and, that he was sure never to fall in battle, or during the war; in fact he lived for some years after the peace of the Pyrenees.

The soldiers had a convincing proof of his not being invulnerable, for he had a thigh broken at the siege of Turin : all the surgeons were for cutting it off: M. de Turenne, under whom he served, exhorted him to suffer this operation : he answered that he would not die by piece-meal, and that death should have him altogether or not at all : he smiled at the same time, and said he knew he should get well of his wound ; he was fortunate enough to do so. He never won a pitched battle, but he saved, several times, the king's army, which had been drawn into difficult situations : he took Stenay in the presence of Lewis XIV. who thus made under him his first campaign. Another conquest, not less important was that of the Chateau of Clermont, in Argonne, capital of the little country of the

Cler-

Clermontois; it was looked upon as impregnable, and the reducing of it is still esteemed a prodigy. As soon as he had taken possession of it he ordered it to be rased, in which he acted judiciously, because it was an advanced post, which gave entry to the enemy into Champagne. Fabert was generally thought to be one of the most honest men in the world; his disinterestedness and modesty, on several occasions, were worthy of ancient Rome. He was not unlearned; he knew, at least, the ancient Greek and Latin historians, and might have observed therein, that the great generals of antiquity had sometimes made the soldiers believe they had to do with gods and dæmons

The Abby *de Longuerue* knew another marshal, much less estimable than Fabert; this was the Marshal d'Albret de Mioffens. It was only by making his court to Queen Anne of Austria and Cardinal Mazarine, that he had arrived at that dignity, without having ever distinguished himself in war. He was no more than a spurious relation of the House of Albret: but finding himself crowned with riches and honours, he had set up a false pretension to a legitimate descent fcent. He got a certain abby to compofe him a genealogy, whofe falfhood was fo eafily difcovered that it was generally laughed at. The Marfhal was a very idle talker ; fome years before his death he took it into his head to be in love with Madame de Cornuel, who lived to a very great age, and to whom many witticifms are attributed. He courted her for a long time, but, at length, perceiving his affiduity was in vain, he ceafed vifiting her. The lady, who cared little about him, faid jocofely ; " In truth " I am forry he has left me, for I began to " hearken to him."

I know but few more noble expreffions, and worthy the age of Lewis XIV. when every body prided themfelves upon being courtiers, than thofe of M. de Chamillart to M. de Beauvilliers, who was charged from the king to tell him to retire to his eftate of Etang. The Duke having put on a melancholy countenance, began by affuring him that he was extremely forry to be the bearer of a very difagreeable piece of news : " What, Sir," anfwered M. de Chamillart, " is the king ill ? Has any thing difagree- " able happened to the royal family ?"

" No,

" No, Sir," faid the Duke; " That be-
" ing the cafe," replied he, " My feais
" are removed." M. de Beauvilliers then
executed his commifiion, and M. Chamillart retired quietly to Etang, between St.
Cloud and Verfailles : he furvived Lewis
XIV. fix years, and died in 1721.

The Father Bouhours was amiable in fociety, fpoke and wrote with purity, for
which reafon the beft things he has written
are his Remarks upon the French Language ;
his ftyle was otherways languid, by paying
too much attention to it : his erudition was
not great, and his grand defect was want of
tafte ; but his rage was to write upon that
fubject ; fuch are his *Manière de Juger les
Ouvrages d'Efprit*, and his *Penfées Ingenieufes*.
He was miftaken in many articles in the
firft of thefe works, and has introduced
feveral falfe and bad thoughts into the fecond ; but thefe books would be ufeful, and
worth reading, if they had produced nothing but the excellent criticifm intituled,
Sentiments de Cleante, by Barbier d'Aucour.
It is not the firft time that criticifms of certain books have been found more ufeful
than the work itfelf, becaufe they prefcribe
rules

rules for tafte. Therefore a journal judici-
oufly compofed, would be of the greateft
utility, becaufe it would not only point out
to us good books, and thofe we ought to
read entirely, but the defects of others, and
in what they confift.

The Abby *de Longuerue* has left a difciple
whom I fee frequently, and who is, moreover, one of my intimate friends ; this is
the Abby Alaiy : as he will never read what
I am going to write, I will give my fentiments of him without referve. He made
his way into the world, under the protection and merit of the Abby *de Longuerue*,
with whom he paffed his youth, and wifhes to make people believe, that, like another
Elifha, that modern Elijah left him his
mantle, his wit, and his memory. He does
not, however, poffefs near fo much knowledge as his mafter. He was received into
the *Academie Francoife* in 1723, an honour
which the Abby *de Longuerue* had difdained.
In the early infancy of Monfieur le Dauphin,
the Abby Alary was appointed pieceptor to
this prince, that is he was charged with
teaching him to read, whilft the royal in-
fant was yet in the hands of women. How-

D d 4 ever,

ever, when the Dauphin was put under the care of men, the Abby Alary had no part in the learned education of the heir to the crown. I believe fome fufpicions of ambition and intrigue in his character, were prejudicial to him.

The Abby had formed a little eftablifhment, the particulars of which being already unknown to many people, will foon be forgotten by all the world; they are, however, woithy of being preferved. His eftablifhment was a kind of club, like thofe in England, or a political fociety, perfectly free, compofed of perfons who liked to reafon upon what paffed, and could jointly give their opinions without fear of interruption, or any bad confequences, becaufe they knew each other well, and the perfons admitted to an audience. This fociety was called the *Entre-fol*, becaufe the place in which the members affembled was an *entre-fol**, in which the Abby lodged. It was furnifhed with every thing neceffary; good chairs, a good fire in the winter, and, in fummer, the

* A floor between the ground and firft floor, almoft feven feet high.

the windows opened upon a pretty garden.
They neither dined nor fupped there, but
drank tea in winter, and lemonade, and re-
frefhing liquors in fummer : the Gazettes
of France, Holland, and even the Englifh
papers were always upon the table. In a
word, it was a genteel coffee-houfe. I went
there regularly, and frequently found perfons of diftinction, who had held fome of
the firft employs, both at home and abroad.
Even M. de Torcy went there fometimes.
This *coterie*, fo refpectable in appearance,
finifhed in an unexpected manner. Some
differences arofe between the courts of London and Madrid : Lord Chefterfield, the
Englifh ambaffador, finding Cardinal Fleury
refractory to the reafons of his court,
thought the nation might be made to underftand what the minifter could not be made
to comprehend. Having learned that a political club exifted in the neighbourhood of
the Luxembourg, in the apartments of the
Abby Alary, he demanded an audience in the
Entre-fol, went there, and pleaded the caufe of
the Englifh againft the Spaniards, before the
members who affifted, who, as it may be
fuppofed, applauded his eloquence, but decided upon nothing. The Cardinal, informed

ed of this adventure, forbad, in the king's name, the club to affemble, and, from that time, the Abby Alary never appeared at court. He lived at home, in tranquillity, and was very affiduous in the meetings of the academy, however, without compofing any work. He had the priory of Gournay-fur-Marne, a few leagues from Paris : this benefice is pretty good, and the priory-houfe ftands in a delightful fituation. The Abby leads there an happy, and even delici-ous life ; with all proper decency, he re-ceives amiable women, to whom he is com-plaifant, and who, when he becomes old, will willingly be the fame to him. In my opinion his manner of living is to be envied.

ESSAY

ESSAY XLV.

ON ABSENCE OF MIND.

HABITUAL Abfence of Mind is a real proof of folly, or, at leaft, of great inattention. How happens it therefore, that there are people who pride themfelves upon this abfence, and think to affume an air of importance and capacity. Inftead of paying attention to what is faid to them, they wifh to appear taken up with quite another thing : this is, in truth, contemptible. The only pretence fuch perfons can have is, that their pretended Abfence prevents them from giving immediate anfwers to embarraffing queftions ; but this is at the expence of their reputation. I like thofe better who hearken attentively, and reply flowly. This was the ancient method of perfons who difcuffed important affairs; but it is now no longer in fafhion. French *naiveté* cannot accommodate itfelf to it, and the multiplicity of affairs with which our minifters are taken up, do not give them fufficient time It is in Spain, only, where the national gravity permits people to fpeak and write with circumfpection,

cumfpection, and where men can confider at leifure what they have to fay, or commit to paper. I knew a Spanifh ambaffador, in France, who, impoituned by queftions inceffantly put to him, to which he was required to anfwer immediately, and, finding that even our young nobility fometimes let flip unreafonable expreffions, which he would have thought himfelf obliged to animadvert upon, if he had appeared to hear them, took the refolution of declaring himfelf deaf, and paffed four or five years at Paris and Verfailles, telling every body he was extremely hard of hearing. By this method he frequently diffimulated, and made people repeat their queftions two or three times, which gave him time to prepare his anfwer. Finally, when he had his audience of leave, it was remarked that his ear was very fine, and his artifice was difcovered when he had no longer occafion to make ufe of it.

I knew a woman of a certain age, whofe flow, but dignified manner of fpeaking, even in ordinary converfation, gave her the reputation of a woman of great fenfe. Every thing fhe faid was looked upon as fo many fentences and apophthegms.

ESSAY

ESSAY XLVI.

ON DOMESTIC ECONOMY.

IT is at prefent required of mafters and mif-tieffes of families, not to appear too much taken up with the care of doing the honours of their tables, &c. Nothing appears more ridiculous than to fee the lady of the houfe torment heifelf, give her keys to fervants to fetch diffeient things fhe has in her own particular keeping, which fhe diftributes, with circumfpection, on great occafions ; afterwards preffing people to eat of what fhe thinks good, as if they had it not in their power to have as good things fet before them every day. Thefe manners are fo impolite, provincial, and iuftical, that they aie even banifhed from the genteel citizen's houfes of Paris, from the provinces and chateaux. A houfe fhould be fo well regulated, that by a fign, or a word, from the mafter or miftrefs, every thing fhould be in its place, and the company well ferved. But if, in the courfe of the day, they fhould be difengaged from company, the

the miftrefs fhould referve to herfelf moments of recollection, in private, with her
fervants, when fhe fhould reckon the expences of the preceding day, and give her
orders for the prefent and fucceeding ones ;
fhould know what every thing cofts, and
what becomes of it. In houfes where mafters and miftreffes are too elevated to de-
fcend to thefe minutiæ, a trufty and faithful fteward ought to be charged with it ;
but, as in a well-managed theatre, the ma-
chinery and decorations fhould be fo well
prepared as to make every thing appear at
the moment of reprefentation, to be the effect of the ftroke of a magic wand.

I know a good citizen's houfe, the mafter of which is rich and eafy, wherein the
common order of things is reverfed. The
lady commonly charges herfelf with the
daily expences ; there the contrary is the
cafe ; the miftrefs of the houfe prides herfelf upon her wit ; and one great means fhe
employs to gain a brilliant reputation is, to
give regularly, on certain days, a dinner,
on others a fupper, to thofe who are reputed to have moft wit and information. The
fortune of her hufband is equal to thefe expences ;

pences; he kindly gives into them with a good grace, and is as well pleafed as the company with the elegance of her tafte. But, although he feems not to be interefted in the differtations at which he is prefent, afks no queftions, and never fays a word, I know, from good authority, that he amufes himfelf with them. How do we know that he does not liften as a critic; it is certain, that this man, who fays not a word, except in helping his friends at table, in the moft polite manner, who feems, in the houfe, as an humble friend to the lady, and to give orders about any thing, fpends all his mornings in regulating the family expences, and writing out the bill of fare for dinner: he fcolds his fervants when they fail in the leaft pait of their duty, and prefcribes them precife and exact laws for the future; his people tremble before him; he takes the liberty to reprimand his wife, when, by her fault, the expences are too great, or the dinner is not good enough.

There is nothing which a philofophical obferver may not turn to advantage; and this gentleman might find in the ftudy of thefe little domeftic affairs, an intereft of confiderable magnitude.

ESSAY

ESSAY XLVII.

THE EFFECTS OF AMOROUS CONNEC-
TION ON CHARACTER.

AFTER treating in this volume of fo
many different matters and objects, I
am now going to fpeak of love and women :
but I will not dwell long upon either of
them ; for I think, like Madame Cornuel,
who faid, we cannot be long in love, without doing foolifh things, nor fpeak much of
it, without faying filly ones.

It is difficult, in every peiiod of life, to
infpire a real paffion : but it is eafy to
make moft women conceive a momentary
one; many things contribute to this ; a fine
figure, the appearance of ftrength and vigour, the graces, wit, or the reputation of
it, complaifance, and, often, a decided
tone, and light manners, ambitious ideas,
and, finally, interefted views ; with fo
many refources, it is almoft impoffible that
every one fhould not find means to gratify

3   his

his inclinations during his youth ; but, in a riper age, it is neceffary to fix the affections. If we will not renounce every fpecies of gallantry, it is neceffary to accuftom ourfelves early to the fweet habitude of living with one whom we love and efteem; without which, we fall into the moft gloomy apathy, or infupportable agitation. The habitude of which I fpeak, is more agreeable and folid, when founded upon the permanent affections of the mind ; but this is not fo abfolutely neceffary as not to be difpenfed with. It is certain that the cares of a woman are always more agreeable to an old man than thofe of a relation or friend of his own fex; it feems to be the wifh and intention of nature that the two fexes fhould live and die together.

We become infenfible of a fettled habitude, and, as we do not perceive that a miftrefs grows old, and becomes lefs handfome, we do not obferve that her way of thinking becomes our own, and our reafon fubjected to hers, though fometimes lefs enlightened. We infenfibly facrifice our fortune to her ; and this is a neceffary confe-

quence

quence of the refignation we have made of our reafon.

Men fometimes pafs over the infidelities of women, becaufe they are not perfectly convinced of them, and that a blind confidence is a neceffary confequence of their feduction : but if, unfortunately, they come to the knowledge of them, it is impoffible for a man, fincerely attached to a woman, not to be fufceptible of jealoufy. This jealoufy takes a tinge of the character of the perfon who is affected with it. The mild man becomes afflicted, falls ill, and dies; if a repentance, which he is always difpofed to believe fincere, does not confole him : the choleric man breaks out into rage; and, in the firft moments, it is not known how far this may carry him ; but men of this difpofition are fooreft appeafed, and moft frequently to be deceived.

Pecuniary intereft fhould never be the bafis of an amorous connection · it renders it fhameful, or at leaft fufpicious: money, fays Montaigne, being the fource of concubinage. But when a tender union is well formed, intereft, like fentiment, becomes

3   common ;

common; every thing is mutual; and there is but one fortune for two sincere lovers. If they be equally honeft, and incapable of making a bad ufe of it, this is juft and natural; but frequently the complaifance of one, makes him or her partake too much of the misfortunes and errors of the other.

Love fhould never have any thing to do with affairs: it ought to live on pleafures only: but how is it poffible to refift the folicitations of a beloved object, who, though fhe ought not to participate in affairs which fhe has not prudence or courage enough to manage, yet having always, for a pretext, her intereft in your reputation, welfare and happinefs, how is it poffible to refift an amiable woman, who attacks with fuch weapons?

Some ladies have a real, others a borrowed reputation; that of the firft is pure and unfpotted, founded on the principles of religion, confequently the only genuine one; it belongs to women really attached to their duty, and who have never failed in the leaft point of it, whether they have had the good fortune to love their hufbands, who

have

have returned their affection; or whether, by an effort of virtue, they have been faithful to a man whom they have not loved nor were beloved by. There is another reputation, unknown to religion, which delicate morality, although purely human, does not admit, but which the world, more indulgent, will fometimes accept as good; that founded upon the good choice of lovers, or rather, of a lover, for multiplicity is always indecent. We are fo difpofed to think that each loves his likenefs, that we judge of the character of men and women by thofe of their own fex with whom they have formed an intimacy; but infinitely more by the perfons for whom they conceive a ferious attachment. Many a man of wit has eftablifhed the reputation of his miftrefs, without compofing madrigals for her, but by making known the paffion with which fhe had infpired him; many a woman of merit has created or eftablifhed the reputation of him whom fhe has adopted her chevalier. After all, it is more dangerous to folicit than to decline this kind of reputation: it happens more frequently that a man lofes himfelf by making a bad choice,

than

than he adds to his fame by making a good one.

If the public are indulgent to the attachments of fimple individuals, they are much more fo to thofe of kings and people in place, when they think them real, and do not fufpect in them either ambition, intrigue, or motives of intereft. All France approved of the love of Charles VII. for Agnes Sorel, becaufe fhe had the courage to fay to this Prince that, unlefs he recovered his kingdom, he was not worthy of her affection. The Parifians applauded the love of Henry IV. for *La Belle Gabrielle*, and fung with pleafure the fongs this monarch made for her; becaufe, knowing her to be handfome, and of a good difpofition, they imagined fhe would infpire the king with fentiments of benevolence.

Never did a woman love a man more fincerely than Madame de la Valliere loved Lewis XIV. She never quitted him but for God alone; and, fwelled with vanity as that monarch was, he could not complain of this rivality; fo much the lefs, as the Supreme Being had but the remains of

E e 3   the

the heart of his miftrefs, and, perhaps never poffeffed it entirely.

I have heard an anecdote of Madame de Valliere, which 1 do not remember to have feen in print   This lady was fo modeft, and had fo little ambition, that fhe had never told the king fhe had a brother, much lefs had fhe ever afk.d any favour for him. He was ftill young, and had made his firft campaign among the cadets of the king's houfehold. Lewis XIV reviewing his troops, faw his miftrefs fmile in a friendly manner at a young man, who, on his part, bowed to her, with an air of familiarity. In the evening the King afked, in a fevere and irritated tone of voice, who this young man was. Madame de la Valliere was at firft confufed, but afterwards told his Majefty it was her brother. The King, having affured himfelf of it, conferred diftinguifhed favours upon the young gentleman, who was father of the firft Duke de la Valliere, whofe widow and children are ftill alive.

The King's intrigue with Madame de Montefpan, was not of a nature to be approved

proved of so much as that he had with Madame de la Valliere ; yet the nation did not complain, because it was thought the love of this lady procured the public magnificent feasts and elegant amusements. The following verses were a good deal sung at that time.

Ah ! quelle est charmante
  Notre aimable cour ;
Sous le même tente
  On voit tour a tour.

La gloire et l'amour,
  Conquete brillante
  Et fête gallante
Marquent chaque jour.

On the contrary, the public were a good deal disgusted with the amours of the King and Madame de Maintenon, although more decent, and that a secret marriage had rendered them legitimate. It was observed that a love, conceived when both parties were in years, afforded a ridiculous spectacle : Moreover, Madame de Maintenon meddled with the affairs of government ; and it was when she most interfered with them, that things fell into decline, and that Lewis XIV. began to experience misfortunes, which were all laid to her charge.

E e 4   When

When the late Duke of Orleans, who was Regent, fell in love with Mademoiselle de Sery, he was not censured on account of it. The Duchess of Orleans, natural daughter to the King, was rather beautiful, but she was not amiable ; Mademoiselle de Sery on the contrary, was very much so. She had a son, and it was predicted of him that he would one day become Duke of Dunois. We see him at present, in Paris, under the title of Chevalier d'Orleans, Grand Prior of France. He has not fulfilled what was expected of him ; yet he has wit, and is, in many respects, amiable.

In process of time the Regent fell into such an irregularity of conduct, that the public were shocked at it. It was necessary for him to have many other brilliant and estimable qualities to be pardoned so great a defect ; but people were so much disposed to indulgence for him, that his affection for Madame de Parabere was approved of, because it was supposed she really loved him, and that he loved her, although he was frequently unfaithful to her.

Exterior

Exterior decency is generally admired, and princes and men of diſtinction ought to do nothing to diſguſt the publiç ; but, right or wrong, it is but too true, that in the end, this public aſſumes the authority of cenſuring, without delicacy, every fault : woe to them who are the firſt objects of groſs ſcandal ; they become the victims to its rage : the public judges and puniſhes them for it ; or, at leaſt , hoots at, hiſſes, and deſpiſes them ; but, when the number of the guilty increaſe to a certain degree, it is found, that although hiſſes aie ſuffi-cient to condemn bad pieces, they are not rods enough for thoſe men who deſerve to be laſhed : they then become tolerated, no-thing more is ſaid, and, what is worſe than all, a reſolution is ſometimes taken to imitate them. It muſt be acknowledged that the temptation to ſin is very great, when we arc ſure to do it with impunity ; and that people are made eaſy upon this head, when they are ſheltered from reproach and ridi-cule.

ESSAY

ESSAY XLVIII.

ON THE METHOD OF STUDYING, READ-
ING, AND SELECTING FROM AUTHORS.

I Return with pleafure to the favourite fubject of my reflections, becaufe it is that
of my tafte and amufement ; namely,
reading and ftudy. There are two forts of
them in the cabinet ; the one belongs to our
profeffions and functions : therefore the magiftrate ought to ftudy the general principles of jurifprudence, and give the greateft
attention to affairs fubmitted to his decifion. The minifter, of whatever kind his
adminiftration may be, ought to ftudy the
principles of the object committed to his
care, and apply them as occafions require.
The father of a family is obliged to think of
what may fecure or encreafe his fortune, to take care of his property, and keep
an account with himfelf as well as with
others. Thefe are neceffary ftudies and occupations, and muft not be neglected.
But there is another kind of ftudy, merely

ly pleafurable, free in its object, and which may ferve as a relaxation from ferious and neceffary ones. There are people happy enough not to be obliged to employ themfelves but in ftudies of that nature. Women, efpecially, if they be fortunate enough to amufe themfelves with reading, cannot read too much ; by a little method, and a proper choice of books, they will find infinite remedies againft laffitude, and abundant fources of inftruction.

Life, for a perfon who wifhes to be virtuous and amiable, is a continual ftudy. We improve in fociety by living and converfing with thofe whofe converfations and examples are worth hearing and imitating : we learn to difcover and avoid the ridicule of certain perfons, whom we but too frequently meet with, but with whom we ought to form no connection. However this ftudy of fociety cannot fill up all the moments of life ; it often experiences forced interruptions, longer than we would wifh for. It is then we ought to apply ourfelves to ftudy in folitude ; that is to fay, to reading : but we muft know how to read to advantage ; for doing it without method, choice or tafte,

is

is a real lofs to the cultivation of the mind ; it ferves, at moft, to fill up fome idle moments ; and, when we read in this manner, although we may have a good memory, we neither learn nor retain any thing.

For my part, my method of reading with advantage, books of all kinds, foreign to my profeffion, is as follows. In the firft place, I recollect the firft principles of all the fciences I learned in my youth ; afterwards I confider in which of thefe fciences I wifh to gain a more extenfive knowledge ; I do not feek it in didactic books, in treatifes made precifely to inftruct; fuch kind of reading would form too profound a ftudy, and require too much application, in which people who quitted other ferious ftudies for it, would find no relaxation : I feek for books which contain the hiftory of each fcience, the progrefs it has made in different ages, and the rational deductions of authors and artifts, to whom it owes its progrefs. I am perfuaded, that by this hiftorical ftudy alone of the arts and fciences, a man of the world may learn as much as he wifhes to know of them, and that a good Encyclopedia might be made by uniting the
hiftory

hiftory of each fcience and art, and fhewing how one derives from the other, and the relations that are between them.

My cuftom is, with books whofe fubjects appear interefting, to read them over, and then form a general judgment of the work : afterwards, if I think it woith while, I read them a fecond time, make extracts of the beft part of their contents, and what appears to me moft novel, and criticife the principal errors into which the author may have fallen. Such is my method with books of fcience and hiftory ; with refpect to thofe of fimple literature, poems, romances, &c. performances of which we muft not abfolutely deprive ourfelves, becaufe they are a dernier refort againft the fatigue and uniformity of more ferious books, I make no extracts from them, but content myfelf after reading them over, with writing, in a few words, my opinion upon each, to prevent thofe who may be tempted to read them after me, the trouble of beginning an author, by whom they would neither be amufed nor entertained.

There

There are books of a frivolous kind, in which I fometimes find fentiments worthy of being felected ; this is what I do : although the harveft be not abundant, it is, at leaft, precious. Nothing is, in my opinion, more infupportable, than the continued reading of a collection of poems ; they cannot be read but at intervals ; yet in taking them up frequently, till they are all read, very good things are fometimes found in them.

I know no other manner of judging theatrical pieces, than by the impreffion they have made upon me, and I am very careful to avoid examining whether they be according to the rules of the drama : in my opinion, there is but one thing to confider, whether there be a kind of probability in the intrigue and characters ; if the firft be interefting and the laft pleafing, I think the piece a good one. If it be well written, in verfe or profe, that is another advantage : but the real merit of the work does not confift therein.

The remarks I have made in reading, compofe, already, feveral great volumes :
they

they will not be quite ufelefs to my fon, if ever he forms a rational catalogue of his library.

A man, who has not, nor ever will read, muft, certainly, from his ignorance, be liable to fpeak abfurdly, for which he will be expofed to ridicule ; knowledge of the world, and the converfation of men of fenfe, will never fhelter fuch a man from raillery : but, on the other hand, a man who has done nothing but read and ftudied, has no knowledge of the world, and who has never mixed with good company, becomes a ftupid and unpolite pedant, and fpeaks abfurdly in another manner ; for, as men learn not every thing from books, fo books cannot fupply the knowledge of the world. The Abby de Longuerue, whofe memory and erudition I have fpoken fo favourably of, was himfelf an unpolite pedant ; we are aflured that Hugo Giotius, one of the moft learned men at the beginning of the laft century, and who was ambaflador in France, about an hundred years ago, was the worft ambaflador in the world. As he was ignorant of cuftoms, he underftood nothing of what paffed at court ; he kept
company

company with nobody but pedants of the univerfity, who taught him nothing ufeful, and from whom he could not learn the manner in which he ought to conduct himfelf with kings, queens, princes, and minifters. He went to the worft of all fources to feek information ; but what he gathered, he wrote to the States General in fine Latin, for he could not write either in French or Dutch : both himfelf and his wife weie objects of ridicule at the court of France, and nobody read his work, which has fince been fo much admired, becaufe it contains excellent maxims of natural and public right : yet it will never be learned from this great work, how we ought to act in negociations : on the contrary, the letters of the Prefident Jeannin, who was a mild and infinuating man ; thofe of the Cardinal d'Offat, a prudent man, who always made reafon triumphant, without offending anybody; finally, thofe of the Compte d'Eftrades, whofe difpatches are fo fine and fenfible, as well as elegantly written, are real models to be adopted : but none ought to be fervilely imitated : a public man fhould form a ftyle peculiar to himfelf, conformable to the character with which he is
                                    invefted,

invefted, to the manners of the court from which he is fent, and to that where he refides. Nothing fhould be more avoided in difpatches than an affectation of wit, but the greateft attention fhould be given to expofe facts in the cleareft manner to his court. With refpect to memoirs addreffed to the court with which he has to treat, there are fometimes reafons for thefe being more obfcure and perplexed.

I have always obferved that men of the robe, employed in foreign affairs, became more amiable and polifhed; and that, on the contrary, in intendancies, or provincial adminiftrations, they contracted a ftupid and impolite manner; the reafon is not difficult to be conceived; an ambaffador ftrives to make himfelf beloved, and the intendant pretends to make himfelf feared: one muft be a courtier, and has two courts to pleafe; the other exercifes the defpotifm of a fingle court upon its fubjects.

But I am wandering too far from my propofed object: I meant to fay, that to write books, equally ufeful and agreeable, a knowledge of the world was preferable to

F f   ftudy.

It is thus, Saint Evremond and Fontenelle have fucceeded. The latter acknowledged to me one day, that he had left off reading : " I have ftored my magazine," faid he, " a long time ago; at prefent I fell my " merchandize." But, to arrive at this point, three things are neceffary ; to read and ftudy methodically, to have a good memory, and, finally, a good ftock of wit, and a knowledge of the world. Yet we are told Bayle was wanting in the laft ; but he had fo much wit and information, that, on reading his works, no appearance is feen of what he was deficient in. How much muft this man have have amufed himfelf in compofing his Dictionary, and his *Nouvelles de la Republique des Lettres !* He went from object to object, and judged of every thing with liberty, fuperiority and eafe. His Journal is the beft that has been, or, perhaps, ever will be compofed. Every book is there felected, thoroughly examined, and judged of in a mafterly manner. If we may expect fuch another Journal, it muft be the work of a well-compofed fociety, directed by an enlightened prefident : whoever fhould eftablifh fuch a one, would render a great fervice to fciences and letters ; he would prevent

2   authors

authors from wandering, teach them how
to treat their fubjects, which, for the moft
part, they are ignorant of, and fhew them
the defects of their compofitions, as well as
thofe of their ftyle. Our academies would
not do too much by taking this upon themfelves, each according to its province; one
company alone would not be fufficient : and
it would ftill be neceffary to leave to the
Mercure, and the little hebdomadal 'criticifms, poetry, light literature, and romances.
Perhaps there will be, fome day, found,
among my papers, a rational plan of this
reformation of the Journals, and reflections
upon the extreme utility they might be of,
in compofing an hiftory of the progrefs of
our knowledge ; the moft interefting of all
hiftories that can be written.

I have a library, rather confiderable, but it
is compofed of books, all chofen for my
own ufe : it is a mifplaced and blameable
luxury to have more books than you can
read and confult ; yet it is the fineft, moft
noble, and, confequently, the moft excufe-
able of all luxuries ; I confefs, if I could enjoy one, it fhould be this. But it is neceffary, at leaft, to know, of what ufe books,

F f 2   which

which we read not ourfelves, may be to
others : it is both abfurd and ridiculous to
have fuch, whofe only merit confifts in being
fcarce. With refpect to books which have
no other recommendation than the goodnefs
of their edition, and the elegance of binding,
they are ftill a luxury ; but this is pardon-
able in thofe who are rich enough not to
mifs acquiring a good book, in the hope of
having a handfome one, otherways it would
be imitating the man, who, having ruined
himfelf in the purchafe of picture-frames,
was too poor to buy paintings.

When a library is limited, its compofition fhould befpeak the profeffion of its proprietor : it would be ridiculous to find nothing but poems and romances in that of a
magiftrate, and not to find in that of a military man either Polybius, or Cæfar's Com-
mentaries.

Serious ftudies require, in thofe who purfue them, an abfolute exemption from all
domeftic concerns. It is on this account
that a monaftic life is the moft proper for
ftudy, becaufe thofe who confecrate themfelves to it are always fure of wanting for
nothing

nothing, either for the moment, or when they fhall become incapable of labour. From hence it may be concluded, that if ever the Monks be deftroyed, erudition and inftruction will fuffer confiderably. To this it will be anfwered, that there are many orders of Monks who neither ftudy, nor apply to any thing; to which may be replied, that government fhould rather ftrive to make them ufeful than deftroy them.

It is a great fatisfaction to a man who reads and ftudies, to have a perfon with whom he may reafon upon what he has read : *fcire tuum nihil eft, nifi te fcire hoc fciat alta,* fays a Latin poet ; but it is neceffary to chufe thofe with whom you wifh to reafon upon what you know and have juft read; for if, unfortunately, you fall into the hands of talkative cenfors, thofe eternal difputers, it would be better never to have begun a communication of ideas in your life, than to have addreffed yourfelf to fuch people. If you apply to a fool, the fatisfaction is ftill as little. In fuch unfortunate circumftances, the beft way is to keep to yourfelf what you know.

Forced

Forced ftudies are tirefome and fatiguing; on the contrary, thofe which are voluntary, flow almoft infenfibly. I know a woman, who, having been a long time intimately acquainted with a man, wrote to him almoft every day, even when they were in the fame town, giving him an account how fhe fpent her time; what fhe had read, and communicating to him her moft fecret thoughts. The gentleman died, and his heirs were polite enough to return to the lady all her letters. Being one of my particular friends, fhe had confidence enough in me to let me read them, and even gave them into my poffeffion: I perufed them with all imaginable pleafure; they were full of wit, of thoughts and reflections, equally fenfible and juft; and were arranged in progreffive order. I put them together, and they made four volumes in quarto; after this I paid her a vifit, and made her repeat what fhe had many times faid to me, that fhe could not conceive how it was poffible to have patience enough to write a book. "Well, Madam," faid I, "know " that you have written a confiderable one, " better than moft of thofe we efteem, " which I have brought for your infpection."

I put

I put immediately into her hand her four volumes in quarto. " There," faid I, " is " fomething more valuable than the letters " of Madame de Sevigny, and, perhaps, " than the Effays of Montagne." She received my compliment modeftly, and was obliged to acknowledge that it is poffible to write a book, almoft without knowing it. I gave her back her four volumes; but, as I am a great tranfcriber of notes and extracts, I copied from different parts of the work, about one volume, which I preferve as being precious.

Montagne learned Latin without a mafter, at leaft without rudiments, by habitude and rote. I knew the time when the fcholars of the Jefuits college were obliged to fpeak Latin to the fervants about them, when they afked for the moft common neceffaries. The Latin, fpoken on thofe occafions, was certainly bad ; it was called *kitchen Latin :* but, fuch as it was, it created an habitude of fpeaking that language. This cuftom has fince been left off; it was pretended that it ferved only to accuftom the children to make folecifms. I have, however, found it ufeful to thofe who, travelling in Ger-

many,

many, Hungary, Bohemia, and Poland, ſtood in need of Latin to make themſelves underſtood. The habitude they had con- tracted when young, helped them over many difficulties, whilſt thoſe who go from college at preſent, are puzzled with them, although they have made Latin verſions, themes and poetry, and have even gained premiums. As for Greek, it is uſeleſs to think of ſpeaking, or underſtanding it with accuracy. You may know their ſentiments without tranſlating books from this dead language, becauſe it is already done. But it is neceſſary, at leaſt, to know how to read Greek, to poſſeſs the firſt elements of the grammar, and eſpecially the Greek roots, upon which Meſſieurs de Port Royal have written an excellent work. It is incredible how uſeful the knowledge of the Greek roots is in learning the etymology of moſt terms of arts and ſcience. If our language, in its firſt barbarous ſimplicity, be not de- rived from the Greek, it muſt, at leaſt, be acknowledged that two thirds of the words we make uſe of at preſent, come therefrom, either directly or indirectly.

There

There are didactic books fo tirefome and difagreeable, although very exact, that they may juftly be called determents from ftudy, as we fay old and ugly women are antidotes to love. Young people fhould be fpared the fatigue of fuch books, by fubftituting others, which infpire curiofity and defire. To intereft the reader is the great art every author of a book fhould ftudy. It ought to be the end and object of him who writes upon fcience, of the hiftorian, the inventor of romances, and the writer of comedies. But this is not all, it muft be kept up to the end of the work : *hoc opus, hic labor eft.*

People to whom I have communicated my extracts, and fome of my remarks upon different objects, have reproached me with not having a *ftyle of my own* ; to which I anfwer, what fignifies it, if I have the ftyle of the fubject to which my attention is directed ? it is principally to this ftyle one ought to be attached. In writing upon every kind of fubject, it is neceffary to obferve what an author of a comedy is particularly attentive to, giving each perfonage the language proper to him ; and the moft effential of all is clearnefs of expreffion, and juftnefs of thought.

It

It muſt not be believed that imagination ex-
tends the ideas, it is the judgment; becauſe
this either elevates itſelf, or deſcends, in a
right line, from conſequence to conſequence;
whereas the imagination moves by fits and
ſtarts, and wanders, for want of attaching
itſelf to a fixed object.

There are two manners of cultivating the
memory; one is by learning by heart, long
paſſages from poems, entire harangues, and
pages of cyphers: with this kind of memory wonderful exertions are made, but
very uſeleſs ones: I call the other kind of
memory, *by judgment.* By this ſort of memory we retain the ſenſe and order of things;
if this be not a real memory, it is ſurely a
good one; and by which we are beſt inſtructed. It applies to what we have ſeen
and read, and fatigues leſs than the firſt,
for we retain every thing without perceiving it, and, as it were, without wiſhing
to do it.

Men of great genius have no need of reading to conceive grand and fine ideas, and to
form projects and plans not only brilliant,
but ſometimes very good and uſeful. Yet
reading

reading is ftill of great fervice to them, to rectify their thoughts, and fhew them, by the example of thofe who have had fome of the fame kind, to what inconveniencies they would be expofed by purfuing them with too much ardour and precipitation. It has long fince been faid, that hiftory has anticipated experience; that experience is neceffary to thofe who might conceive projects too vaft, and be carried too far by their ideas.

The epiftolary ftyle is that moft neceffary for women. Thofe who are difpofed to write well in this way, have no need of taking pains to fucceed. They muft even take care not to lofe that eafy, natural, and rather foft turn, fometimes witty, fometimes voluptuous, which is truly the ftyle of women. As a lady muft have neither an appearance or a manner too mafculine, a look too bold, or her head too elevated, fo her ideas and expreffions muft not be too afpiring, nor her ftyle what is called lofty; it muft always appear as if fhe wrote rapidly, and her phrafes fhould not be overcharged. I do not believe there are any women who, after having written a work

or

feries of letters, ever gave them to be corrected by fome confidential male or female
friend, whom they thought capable of writing better than themfelves. It is either neceffary to entruft to a fecretary the compofition of a whole work, or that the author,
himfelf, fhould revife what he has done,
and, after having corrected the firft rough
draught, look it over again, rectify, and
give it the laft touches; otherwife he will
run the rifk of giving the woik to the public in a patched ftyle, which will evidently
appear to be by two different hands.

The ftyle of Voiture, which was formerly in great reputation, is now juftly decri-
ed. He is a buffoon, who has fome wit,
but without elevation or juftnefs. Balfac,
on the contiary, whofe ftyle is equally an-
tiquated, had an elevation of idea and expreffion. People who know how to make the
moft of every thing, might ftill piofit from
Balfac, by fome thoughts and turns of
phrafes. But, I muft again repeat, that the
beft rule for ftyle is to adapt it to the fubject
upon which we have to treat. I read with
pleafure the letters of a celebrated Intendant
of the late reign; his name was Bagnols;
they

they were juftly looked upon as true models for correfpondence in public affairs. They were fhort, without the leaft drynefs, and were clear and nervous. A ftupid fubaltern could not miftake the orders the Intendant gave, nor refufe to conform to them ; and, a better proof is, a man of fenfe could not fail to admire them, and be convinced by the reafons they contained; for he never gave an order without affigning a reafon.

I now return to memory, to fpeak of thofe who have none at all. There are people who, to aid the little they are poffeffed of, are obliged to make an *agenda* of every thing they have to carry into execution. A certain Intendant of Tours, who lived at the beginning of the prefent century, was famous for this. His *agenda* was frequently ftolen from him, and read, and laughed at in his prefence. There was found written in one of them : " I have taken a refolution " to fhave myfelf in future, becaufe my " fervants are butchers, who flay me." And, a little lower down, " I will fay " God's death no more, this is an improper " expreffion for a magiftrate and an intend- " ant; it is better to fay dog's death."

M. * * *

M. * * * was not, however, quite fo fingular in his memorandums of this kind, as a man, who went frequently from Paris to Lyons, and who wrote in his *agenda*, " to remem-" ber to be married in paffing by Nevers."

Notwithftanding all I have juft faid againft *agenda*, I make ufe of them fometimes to advantage; it is not that I want memory, but I have not one exact enough to remember, at the appointed times, all I have to do in the day. This kind of memory is very rare; *agenda* fupplies the want of it; but I never think of committing to paper my refolutions and rules of conduct. I know a very learned man, and of great application, who makes very ufeful refearches, and reduces them wonderfully to order, with the pen in his hand; but the poor man has neither wit nor memory. I have learned from this oddity a very fingular circumftance: A man of quality wifhed to have his genealogy; he applied to the perfon of whom I have juft fpoken, knowing him to be learned, exact, and fond of employing himfelf in that way. M. B*** did him this fervice with the greateft pleafure; he turned over hiftorians and genealogifts,

made

made extracts from some old titles, and took copies of them; finally, after six weeks' labour, he gave every eclaircissement required. Two years afterwards, a man of the same family, but of another branch of it, not far removed from the former, not knowing who had drawn up the genealogy of his cousin, begged M. B*** to make him one also. The good man set to work immediately; and found the same proofs, but without recollecting any thing more than to have had occasion to read the same papers, but when, and for why, he had forgot. The two cousins having communicated to each other their genealogies, found them alike, mentioned respectively the author, and found him to be the same man.

I have read, in an eulogium of the Abby de Louvois, that he was brought up, according to the wishes of his father, who was then high in power, and neglected nothing to make his son an able man. The most learned people devised methods on purpose to teach him every thing in a short space of time. "He was fed," says his panegyrist, " with the elixir and quintes-
" sence of every kind of science, as the
" richest

" richeſt and moſt delicate are with ſtrong
" broths, juices of meat, and eſſences of
" the beſt fruits." The compariſon is a
good one ; but, as good ſtomachs are neceſſary to thoſe who are fond of ſuch rich
cookery, to digeſt all the aliments, reduced
to ſmall quantities, ſo it requires a well or-
ganiſed head to retain the principles of all
the ſciences, reduced to abridgment. But
the perſon in whom this firſt education has
ſucceeded, need give himſelf no more trouble for the reſt of his life, to become the moſt
learned man in the world: every thing con-
veys to him inſtruction, encreaſes the maſs
of his knowledge, and fixes itſelf upon a ba-
ſis already eſtabliſhed in his head; he cannot hold a new converſation, nor open a
book, without finding a new ſource of information. It is, perhaps, in this manner,
that people at court, appear to know, and
really do know *every thing*, without, ſeem-
ingly, *ever having learned any thing.*

The Engliſh have very little ſtyle, and
ſtill ieſs method ; but they have ſtrong and
elevated thoughts: accuſtomed to overlook
prejudices in matters of policy and government, their daring genius is the ſame in
every

every refpect. Their pleafantries are neither mild nor cautious; their fatire is violent, but fometimes very delightful. We are already acquainted with Dean Swift, one of their moft ingenious and fatirical authors. His work is well enough tranflated into French. It is generally more eafy to render Englifh pleafantries into other languages, than to tranflate, for inftance, Italian ones into French, and ours into any language whatfoever, becaufe Englifh fatire falls upon things, and the perfons are well defcribed, and in very ftriking colours; whereas the Italians play upon words, and the French flutter round the object at which they laugh; they joke and play with it as a cat does with a moufe; confequently thefe pleafantries are very difficult to underftand and render. Nothing can be better written, or more agreeable to read, than the papers of the Spectator. If the Englifh had many like this, we could not be too anxious to become acquainted with them : but I forefee that we fhall have many bad tranflations of this firft and excellent Englifh author; that from hence a new tafte of literature will be eftablifhed among us; that the French, who never know how to check their enthu-

G g   fiafm,

fiafm, will *Anglify* themfelves, and that we fhall lofe many of our graces in acquiring fome of their fpirit, ideas, and libeity of thinking and writing. Voltaire has already faid, that when men think forcibly, they exprefs themfelves forcibly alfo; this is true; but ftrength of thought may be carried too far, and become equally rude and difgufting in ideas and ftyle.

ESSAY XLIX.

ON THE LITERARY CHARACTER OF
VOLTAIRE.

VOLTAIRE, with whom I have always
associated, since we were together at
college; whom I love personally, and esteem in many respects, is not only a great
and harmonious versifier, but, what every
body does not know as well as I do, a
great thinker. His abode in England elevated his soul, and strengthened his ideas : he
is capable of publishing them courageously,
having the same strength of mind which
some authors have had, who dared to pub-
lish what nobody before dared to write
moreover he has a gracefulness of style,
sufficient to express and make pleasing certain ideas, which would disgust, were they
rendered by any other person. The heroic
trumpet, which he put to his mouth in the
Henriade, became an agreeable pipe in some
of his fugitive pieces. It is not uniform,

G g 2   but

but he knew how to vary its tone ; perhaps
all he wants as a poet, is imagination ;
but this is, at prefent, very difficult to
have, there have been fo many people full
of it, that whofoever would produce any
thing quite new, would create ridiculous
and frightful monfteis. There are two
paits in tragedy, intrigue, and that of detail and veifification. Voltaire does not tii-
umph in the fiift, but he is fuperior in the
fecond; and a proof that this is the principal one is, the difference between the fuccefs of his theatiical pieces, and thofe of
othei authois, fuch as la Grange Chancel,
who excels in all the fable of his tragedies, but which are pitifully written. *Voltaire*, in details, is neither fo great as Corneille, or fo tender and amiable as Racine ;
perhaps he is not even equal to Ciebillon ;
but ftrokes of wit, and delightful poetry,
are fo frequent in his pieces, that the fpec-
tator or reader has not time to examine
whethei any thing better might be produced.
The profe of *Voltaire* is fully equal to his
verfes, and he fpeaks as well as he writes.
Nothing can be more clear than his phrafes,
they are contracted without ftiffnefs ; no
unnatural period, nor rhetorical figure ; all
his

his adjectives agree with their fubftantives : finally, his profe is a model which his co-temporaries ftrive always to imitate, without wifhing to acknowledge it. His Hiftory of Charles XII. may have fome defects, con-fidered as an hiftory ; his *Lettres Philofo-phiques*, contain bold thoughts and criticifms, which certainly are not always juft ; but his ftyle is admirable. *Voltaire* is only forty years of age ; if he lives to be old, he will write a great deal more, and be the author of works upon which much will be to be faid both for and againft. Heaven grant that the magic of his ftyle may not give credit to falfe opinions and dangerous ideas ; that he may not difhonour this charming ftyle, in profe and in verfe, by applying it to works whofe fubjects may be unworthy of the painter and the colouring ; that this great writer may not produce a multi-tude of bad copyifts ; and that he may not become the chief of a fect, to which it will happen, as to many others, that the difci-ples will miftake the intention of their patri-arch.

ESSAY

ESSAY L.

THE DECLAMATION OF THE ACTORS OF THE THEATRE FRANCOIS DEFENDED.

I HAVE frequently heard the Actors of the Theatre Francois reproached with their finging manner of fpeaking; this reproach is, in my opinion, ill founded. What is declamation, efpecially in verfe, if it be not finging? There is no harm in finging poetry, or animated profe, which is cadenced, and ought to be harmonious; but the finging muft be juft, and conformable to the true fenfe of the words: I do not fpeak of little comedies in profe; they ought to begin in the tone of converfation. But as kings, princeffes, generals of armies, or men of the world, fpeak not in verfe, efpecially in rhime, tragic verfe muft be declaimed with animation and cadence. The Roman orators pronounced their difcourfes in the forum, with a flute accompanyment,

3   nyment,

nyment, which regulated and modulated
their tones; fo mufical fcenes ought to be
nothing more than a fine noted declamation,
and better fupported by an accompanyment,
well adapted to the fenfe of the words and
fituation of the actors. Even the fympho-
nies, executed in the orcheftra, ought to
have a fubject, which is, I believe, called
a motive, to fignify and indicate fomething. It is alfo neceffary that the mufic
of a fcene in French fhould be compofed for
words written in that language, without
which it varies from the fenfe and object.
Lulli, although a foreigner, was careful
to confult on this head, all the authors of
the words of his operas ; and it is perhaps
owing to this, that fome fcenes of their
dramas, being well rendered and fung, intereft us fo much. Deftouches and Cam-
pra were equally attentive in this particular ;
it appears that Rameau, a new compofer,
very eftimable, learned and agreeable, in
other refpects, neglects it, in which he
does very wrong ; he fpoils the reprefentation, and makes it unnatural. Our mufic
ftill retains fomething of the age of Lewis
XIV. it is noble and expreffive ; let us not
render it unnatural, or — upon reflection,

do

do — Gentlemen, do with it as you pleafe. After all, it is well worth while to difpute about, to difcufs a thing, upon which every perfon ought to decide according to its effect, and the fenfation it gives him ; in this cafe it may well be faid, that we muft not difpute upon tafte. I have juft declared mine in mufic, and efpecially in lyric fcenes ; but let every one judge of it in his own way, and feel fuch fenfations as are moft agreeable to himfelf. It is, at moft, for men of the art to difcufs the principles from whence thefe fenfations refult : it is fufficient for the generality of mankind to feel them.

F I N I S.

Lightning Source UK Ltd.
Milton Keynes UK
UKHW010656061118
331792UK00013B/2482/P